EROS IDEOLOGIES

Laura E. Pérez

EROS

IDEOLOGIES

Writings on Art, Spirituality,

and the Decolonial

Duke University Press   Durham and London   2019

© 2019 Duke University Press

All rights reserved

Printed in the United States of America on acid-free paper ∞

Designed by Mindy Hill

Typeset in Garamond Premier Pro by Westchester Publishing Services

Library of Congress Cataloging-in-Publication Data

Names: Pérez, Laura Elisa, author.

Title: Eros ideologies : writings on art, spirituality, and the decolonial /
    Laura E. Pérez.

Description: Durham : Duke University Press, 2019. | Includes bibliographical
    references and index.

Identifiers: LCCN 2018008238 (print)

LCCN 2018009627 (ebook)

ISBN 9780822372370 (ebook)

ISBN 9780822369219 (hardcover : alk. paper)

ISBN 9780822369387 (pbk. : alk. paper)

Subjects: LCSH: Art. | Spirituality. | Feminism. | Love. | Decolonization.

Classification: LCC N7445.2 (ebook) | LCC N7445.2 .P469 2018 (print) | DDC 700.2 — dc23

LC record available at https://lccn.loc.gov/2018008238

Cover art and frontispiece: Mariana Ortega, *Cómeme el corazón* (2007), detail.

Duke University Press gratefully acknowledges the support
of the Abigail Reynolds Hodgen Publication Fund in the
Social Sciences, at the University of California, Berkeley,
which provided funds toward the publication of this book.

MAY THIS WORK BE

for the Greater Good.

If you live according to an
example, you live the life of that
example, but who should live
your own life if not yourself?
So live yourselves. . . .

The knowledge of the heart
is in no book and is not to be
found in the mouth of any
teacher, but grows out of you
like the green seed from the dark
earth. Scholarliness belongs to
the spirit of this time, but this
spirit in no way grasps the dream,
since the soul is everywhere that
scholarly knowledge is not.

—CARL G. JUNG,
The Red Book: Liber Novus

To love is first of all to
accept yourself as you actually
are. "Know thyself" is the
first practice of love.

—THICH NHAT HANH,
Teachings on Love

Each of us needs to undergo
a tremendous philosophical
and spiritual transformation . . .
awakened to a personal
compassionate recognition of
the inseparable interconnection
between our minds, hearts,
and bodies.

—GRACE LEE BOGGS,
The Next American Revolution

The act of writing is the act of
making soul, alchemy. It is the
quest for the self, for the center
of self. . . . We start writing to
reconcile this other within us.

—GLORIA E. ANZALDÚA,
"SPEAKING IN TONGUES: A LETTER
TO THIRD WORLD WOMEN WRITERS"

CONTENTS

ILLUSTRATIONS

Eros Ideologies is a collection of writings that explores the possibilities for individual and social shifts that move us beyond either/or binaries, beyond us-versus-them mentalities that dehumanize us all. In the end, I am not so much interested in who is to blame for racism, sexism, homophobia, abuse, and violence against women and our planet, and so on, but in what continues to drive such mistaken orderings so that we might think and act beyond them. The arts are among the most valuable laboratories for creating relevant new forms of thought often signaled by aesthetic innovation in their own nonverbal form. Experimentation in an artwork's form allows us to not only imagine things differently but also experience from a new perspective — to see that it is possible. Ideas about how things should be are received from the cradle as cultural assumptions. The work of reflecting on these, and when necessary rethinking these into new, personally and socially healthier directions, is a socially significant act of exercising personal power, and a gift, because social change begins with innovation and transformation in our thinking.

That creativity is a vein of gold in all walks of life and not only in that of the artist is suggested by common enough ideas like "life is an art," "artfulness," and so on. It is claimed as the secret of highly successful entrepreneurs in best-selling book after book. From spiritual and psychological perspectives, creativity is an enriching path toward greater personal authenticity, a way of discovering — beyond socially received conventions — what feels most

PREFACE.1   Mariana Ortega, *Cómeme el corazón* (2007).

appropriate in the continually shifting landscape of our lives. More collectively, through creativity we help envision and produce the neighborhoods,
cities, countries, and planet we can enjoy in good conscience because they are
more just and not the product of the suffering of others.

Learning to listen to our inner promptings, to trust our proverbial gut,
to be — that is, to feel, think, and act — as feels right for us is a practice that
integrates and synchronizes body, mind, and "spirit," by whatever name we
call the incommensurable, the enigmatic, and the unknowable in the natural world of which we form part. *Eros Ideologies* joins company with those
writing and visually thinking about mind-body-spirit integration. This integration, I want to argue, is vital to decolonization. To the writings of spiritual teachers and healing professionals who follow spiritual practices from
African diasporic, Buddhist, Hindu, Native American, and Western traditions, I add further reflections toward better understanding the decolonial
as intensely embodied, personal, psychological, and spiritual practice, alongside cultural, economic, and geopolitical work. Sigmund Freud's (1856–1939)
concept of the superego, the normative authority-figure complex internal-

ized through the parents and other authority figures, made clear already to the generation following him, that of another great psychiatrist, Carl G. Jung (1875–1961) — and certainly by the generation of Frantz Fanon (1925–61), Michel Foucault (1926–84), and Gilles Deleuze (1925–95) and Félix Guattari (1930–2004), in their respective books, *Black Skin, White Masks* (1952), *Discipline and Punish* (1975), and *Anti-Oedipus: Capitalism and Schizophrenia* (1972) — that the psyche is the prime field on which ideologies of domination rationalized as "natural" or "normal" first take root.[1] The psyche was therefore key to these thinkers to gaining greater freedom, personal well-being, and self-realization, and was intimately related to external struggles for social justice and world peace. Decolonial thought and practice seeks to understand, move beyond, in a word, to heal, the wounding caused by the dehumanizing, fragmenting effects of the racism, sexism, homophobia, classism, patriarchy, and human centrism that we inherit through the histories of colonization of the Americas, as elsewhere in the "Third World." But while many seeking human and social well-being observed the crucial place of psychology in social action theories, even the psychiatrist and anti-colonial guerrilla fighter Fanon was still immersed in European philosophy and knowledges, unable, under the reign of materialist science, to make use of other planetary philosophies and their differing worldviews of the nature and purpose of being. We are still immersed in literature, art, philosophy, science, popular culture, and "common sense" that still transmit pernicious views of human beings based on the color of their skin, ancestral cultures, gender, sexuality, class, legal ("citizenship") status, religion, and so on.

In these writings, often in dialogue, even when indirectly so, with the images of artworks that accompany them, I depart from a decolonizing, cross-cultural philosophical-spiritual thought of the indigenous Americas (Martínez Parédez 1960, 1973; Macias 2017; Cajete 2000; Marcos 2006; Cordova 2007; Maffie 2014), the African diaspora (González-Wippler 1999; Vega 2000; De la Torre 2004), Buddhism (Trungpa [1984] 2009; Hanh [1987] 1998, [1987] 2005, 2006, 2007), and Hinduisim (Nagler 2001; Gandhi 2004) that instead explore unity and difference as potentially simultaneous and harmonious realities: the human person as changing continuously and productively through respectful contact with people from all cultures and walks of life. In such thought, neither body nor sexuality in its multiple possible expressions, including the queer, is demonized, nor is intellect supervalorized in hierarchical difference to the emotional or physical bodies. I join company in such a project with U.S. women of color thinkers and artists who have insisted on the reality and political and social importance of spirituality, in dialogue with non-Western or hybrid (Western and non-Western) thought regarding the nature and purpose of being. Women of color intellectuals — such as Gloria Anzaldúa, who developed the phrase *spiritual activism* (2009, 292); Paula Gunn Allen (1992); Chela Sandoval (2000); Linda Tuhiwai Smith (2002); Leela Fernandes (2003); Lata Mani (2009); and M. Jacqui Alexander (2006) — are some of the decolonial thinkers who have labored to shift our understanding of being, freedom, justice, and power, in deep dialogue with non-Western spiritual philosophies of the interdependence of all life-forms.

I also aim beyond badly outdated and imbalanced ideologies centered in materialist philosophies, knowledge, and politics of Left and Right. What is necessary is the surviving, living wisdom of culturally diverse people from every corner of our country and the globe. In these diverse, culturally specific, and yet tellingly resonant ancient bodies of knowledge that have survived millennia of human destruction into the present, we find what I can only describe as a different reason based in deeper understandings of human and planetary realities. I strive to reimagine a sense of communal relationship and care for self, other, and the planet — an eros and an ideology centered in it — attentive to what our indigenous, African, Asian, and ancient European ancestors taught as common wisdom, and that elders from those cultures have been given for human and planetary safekeeping. Transmitted through millennia, we have with us highly intelligent, reality-based, deeply compassionate bodies of thought for the creation and maintenance of lives aimed at genuinely free, realized, peaceful, creative, and meaningful existence.

Guided by such thought, and mostly following the spirit of Audre Lorde (1984a, 1984b) and Chela Sandoval (2000), I write of the erotic, understood in its broadest sense, and not simply sexually, as respectful relationship and care for self and others, that is, as a socially and politically significant practice of love that is creative of authentic self and, in so doing, simultaneously world-making. Such practice of the erotic is politically ideological in its aim of individual and social transformation toward greater democratic freedom and well-being. Unlike materialist political ideologies of historically recent vintage of the Left and Right, still laboring under mechanistic and materialist notions of human, social, and planetary bodies, eros ideologies define being through the body, feeling, and culturally multiple forms of reason that are nondualistic. The eros ideological is premised on the interdependent, multiple, and changing nature of identities and being, in a unified field of existence that is characterized by the plurality of created forms or life. The effectiveness and longevity of a social and political practice is more firmly rooted in self-awareness and self-love — that is, respect and care of our own being as a constantly changing, shifting, transforming, self-revealing, increasingly self-aware amalgam of "body," "mind," and "spirit," which is unavoidably a work in progress.[2]

Studying literary, visual, and performance arts for nearly four decades, and spirituality for two, in *Eros Ideologies: Writings on Art, Spirituality, and the Decolonial*, I write from a mind tutored by something more than an intellect corralled by the tautologies of materialist empiricism. I write in an embodied practice and not solely a mental one. I research, reflect, think, feel, and write seeking truth, greater understanding of reality, and well-being beyond the intellectual, culturally limited, and indeed (neo)colonizing, Eurocentric, patriarchal, and heteronormative strictures that still dominate much of academic and mainstream intellectual cultures. I feel as I think and I write from yearning, from the unnamable, the barely known that I brush against when I take intuition, insight, dreams, and hope seriously.

To put it in the terms of psychiatrist Claudio Naranjo (b. 1932), in *Healing Civilization* (2010), I strive to write beyond patriarchy's "patristic" shadow side, its hierarchical, emotionless performance of anonymous objectivity, and instead to think and feel from its positive manifestation, as *philia*, the love of and respect for things and people, and for wisdom, and not just data and fact. In his three-part model of the healthy human psyche, Naranjo identifies the caring and compassionate function of the psyche as the matristic second form of love known in ancient Greek literature and in traditional religious writings of the West as *agape*. He identifies the undomesticated elements in instinct, desire, the natural promptings of the body, and the playful, creative spirit with the childlike *eros*. Naranjo's model of well-being is psychological, spiritual, and social and rooted in the capacity to express three of love's functions: to respect, to care, to be happy — *philia, agape, eros*. The healthy human psyche and, by extension, the healthy human society are characterized by a harmonious balancing of these three types of expressions of being human. Essentially, healthy humanness is characterized by Naranjo as the integration of different ways of loving, or caring that begins with the self, within one's own psyche and body, and therefore it can genuinely extend to others.

In my work, eros ideologies do not just describe the instinctual, the creative, the playful, the still unfully domesticated or socialized, aspects specifically identified with the function of eros by Naranjo and described by Freud as the libidinal and the special object of social and psychological repression (the Id), but they are central to art, as they are to the possibilities of personal self-realization and political transformation. As suggested by the subtitle of this book, *Writings on Art, Spirituality, and the Decolonial*, erotic energy and power, in the intention and capacity to relate deeply and respectfully across differences, and receptivity to the unknown or different are at the heart of the potentially positive, transformative work that art, spirituality, and the decolonial can do. The great nonviolent anticolonial activist Mohandas K. Gandhi (1869–1948) repeatedly described "God as Truth and Love."[3] Mesoamerican indigenous sages added creativity to that troika: the creative *is* the Creative and characterizes life (Martínez Parédez 1960, 1973; Cajete 2000; Maffie 2014). I do not fully understand the relationship between art, creativity, love, and the well-lived personal and social life, nor do I think it possible to do so. However, I do feel, perceive, think, and know that they are intimately connected.

This collection of writings is unified across a plurality of writing styles and voices, from the literary, journalistic, heavily annotated academic text to the curatorial essay to more hybrid poetic theorizations and philosophical poems, from critical reflection to emotional gesture and autobiographical meditation. There are twenty-one chapters, some quite short and evocative, some thicker and denser; together they are meandering paths in what I lovingly offer as a garden of fruitful heart-thought. *Eros Ideologies* may be entered anywhere. Nevertheless, arranged as is, the chapters flow one to the other, together and cumulatively deepening and returning to the core themes announced in the title and sketched here. The table of contents therefore is also composed of thumbnail images that point toward the heart of each chapter. My aim through such a structure is to practice writing and reflection as a plentiful garden: a coexistence of different forms of knowing and expressing, a welcoming and integrating into the processes of thought and analyses, feelings, intuitions, hope, and faith in the verdant power of creativity and eros to make ourselves a way forward toward greater flowering of individual, collective, and planetary well-being.

ACKNOWLEDGMENTS

To give thanks, according to Mayan spiritual elder don Pascual Yaxon, is the minimum duty we pay for the blessing of our life. Life is given us, not to be taken for granted, unfolding when in balance, according to *el plan invisible* for the greater good. A life and its fruits are made with and through others. My father, to whom this book is jointly dedicated, now with my ancestors, taught me that counting our blessings is a way to maintain a balanced view. Accordingly, I give thanks to the Creator for my life and its many blessings and the life on this precious planet that nourishes, inspirits, and sustains existence.

The many people that surround us with their care, affection, attention, and support help weave a basket of strength that helps us live well. My life and this book were nourished by countless acts of goodwill and camaraderie.

First I would like to thank my elders, beginning with my father, David Pérez Ordaz, with me now in spirit, and my mother, María Elisa Pérez Tinajero, who made brains, heart, natural creativity, and *convivencia entre familia y amistades* our daily bread. I also want to thank the spiritual elders who have helped guide or heal my path, in order of appearance: Gloria Anzaldúa, Valerie Maynard, Celia Herrera Rodríguez, don Miguel Chiquín, Estela Román, don Pascual Yaxon, Marcial Castillo, Claudio Naranjo, and don José Vela.

I thank my siblings, friends now, for whom I continue to grow in appreciation: my brothers, Jaime, *quien lloró en el vientre*, and Hugo, the sanest person I know; their families, my sisters-in-law, Trish, Karla, and Laurie; and my incomparably wise and generous Jaguar Prince sister, Silvia, and her court jester consort, Louis. I send love through ink and pixels to my nephews and nieces, whose greatest inheritance is the good hearts of their grandparents and parents: Kerrigan, Alex, Louis Jr., Samantha, David, Nathan, Allison, Jeff, David, James, and Rachel.

For our joyful antics and loyalty to each other though we rove in different jungles and forests, I thank my bosom buddies, monkey queens each and every one of them, in alphabetical order to prevent a scuffle: Zelda Artsen-Crichlow, Monique Barwicki, Graciela Lechón, my sister, Silvia, Berni Smith, and Brian Wieder. The bonds of loving friendship are as thick as blood and indestructible.

If brilliance means you have brains like dreadlocks and glow with for-reals knowing, then the word is well used to describe the ones I jump double-dutch with in visible and invisible corridors. They are the ones for whom the endnote hides a secret doorway to the real school of how to live what we claim to believe and strive to illuminate. The feminist and queer Chican@ and Latin@ Powers who live a graphic superheroine *novela* and who forever inspire me to practice flying with my *sabana* cape are, by order of appearance in my life: Tomás Ybarra-Frausto, *maestro*, whose traces I see in every new place I tread; Chela Sandoval, indescribably dazzling in soul and mind; the unfailingly noble and generous Yvonne Yarbro-Bejarano; the two Normas, one of fire, one of water, Alarcón and Cantú; three incomparable women warrior artists, Yreina D. Cervántez, Consuelo Jimenez Underwood, and Diane Gamboa. I also thank the gang I hang with in the visible and invisible corridors of *la otra,* truly universal university we labor to make, those who wear their hearts on their sleeves in high style: Luis León, Lara Medina, Mariana Ortega, Pedro Javier DiPietro, Miguel De la Torre, Jorge Aquino, Lois Lorentzen, Santiago Slabodsky, Marcia Ochoa, Cindy Cruz, Karen Mary Davalos, Guisela Latorre, the amazing Aldama brothers, Arturo and Frederick, and artist and art historian Ann Marie Leimer.

In a special place of respect I hold those whom I have had the pleasure and honor of teaching, whose lives are *veladoras* to all who know them, whose intellectual labor is ethical being, walking what they talk, by chronological order across two and a half decades: Marcia Ochoa, Irene Lara, Karina Céspedes, Angelina Villafañe, Daphne Taylor-Zúñiga, Agustín Palacios, Marcelle Maese-Cohen, Favianna Rodriguez, Angelina Villafañe, Alejandro

Wolbert Pérez, Edgar Mójica, Sara Ramírez, Wanda Alarcón, Ariko Shari Ikehara, Marcelo Felipe Garzo Montalvo, Vreni Michellini-Castillo, Marco Antonio Flores, David Preciado, and the many, many ethnic studies and other University of California, Berkeley, graduate students I have been lucky to know. At UC Berkeley, where I now feel like a growing vine, a flowering one, I hope, I thank my colleagues in the Chicana/o Latina/o Studies Program and the Department of Ethnic Studies who struggle to shift our humanly produced world beyond present exclusions, marginalizations, silences, and indeed the blindness of the neoliberal, patriarchal, heteronormative, and Eurocentric university and cultures.

For the research, editing, and other assistance that made preparation of this book easier and that was vital, thank you, Wanda Alarcón, Marco Antonio Flores, Paula Graciela Kahn, Julie Lee, Verenice Ramirez, and Josephine Shetty.

Finally, I want to thank the warp and weft of my daily life that allows its stretch and bounce and repairs all ensuing tears: John Philip Strohmeier, wordsmith, book crafter, seeker, weaver, and fellow troublemaker; and Maya Elisa Pérez Strohmeier, Grrl Power, Chicana Power to the Second Power, Reborn Amazon, Sparkle in the Eye of the Gods. For you, Maya, capitalization, epithets, and exclamations were made to flourish!

And to the publisher, politeness cannot demand that one feel the wonder of being published by the academic press I most love. For your courage, vision, and commitment to a more just planet through your publishing program and for your generosity in publishing my first and now this book, thank you, Ken Wissoker, the kindest, smartest editor a soul could wish for, and warm thanks as well to Jade Brooks and Olivia Polk, and the rest of the Duke University Press ensemble: you are an elegantly humane assembly.

To all of you I have had the wits to thank, and all of you the sieve of my brain has failed to name, I offer heartfelt thanks for your blessing in my life and, in return, wish you the selfsame abundance of goodness you have brought to my life.

You should know I have been conducting a scientific experiment with all those mentioned, and am now in a position to verify that we are each, in a literal, creative, affective, spiritual, and material way, each other's other self: *In Lak'ech.*

1

THE SOCIAL BODY OF LOVE

Crafting Decolonial Methodologies

FIGURE 1.1 Celia Herrera Rodríguez,
Flowers Fall along the Road (1997–2001).

THE ARTS ARE AN important part of constructing the social imaginary — the space from which we imagine, and then become; a space we inherit, reproduce, and inflect with the difference of our beings. Suffused with the poetic, the arts can be revolutionary language or vital energy, midwifing mental and shared social spaces beyond colonizations of unjust power.

The poetic, like desire, is not a language of certainty. It is the self-conscious refusal to define what is either beyond our comprehension or changing or changeable. It refuses the bluff or delusion of certainty behind denotation, opting instead for the greater truthfulness of connotation, of suggestion, of comparison — in short, of the act itself of striving for meaning, understanding, and expression.

My work has long and increasingly been concerned with crossing scholarship, the poetic, and theoretical reflection with each other as a performance of a more integrated form of knowing, speaking, being, over and against the dictate that art and scholarship, creativity and the critical mind are at odds with each other. Rather, I see them as being two routes that can and do cross and, in so doing, hybridize and enrich each other continuously.

As someone who studies the arts and writes, form is not mere surface to me. Neither is it a modernist obsession, nor an outdated literary or art criticism Formalist school concern. Form is a language in and of itself. It is the walk of the talk.

Perhaps this is why it has always struck me as contradictory to read or hear so-called revolutionary or radical thinking about how to change society expressed in an authoritarian, dry, pretentious, arrogant, or boring style that betrays an anxiety to be approved by the same ruling cultures that have produced the inequities being denounced, in performances that reveal having been mastered by the master culture.

A brief anecdote: I once wrote a paper in Spanish that I read to my mother. I spoke of patriarchy, globalization, neocolonization, and transnationalism in telling the story of a new friend and her community's plight as traditional

Aymara-Quechua people in racist La Paz, Bolivia. I was fired up and glad to be able to share my work in Spanish with my mother. But as I glanced up after my introductory paragraphs, she exclaimed: "*Ay Dios, hija, ¡como que estás masticando piedras!*" ("Dear Lord, my girl, it's as if you are chewing rocks!") I do not think, nor did I then, that all writing is for everyone, of course, but I did begin to deeply reflect on how scholarly and theoretical discourse and the proper disciplinary form that we are rewarded and punished for are practices that shape and misshape us.

Why is it that graduate school and the world of higher education can feel and indeed be so dehumanizing to those of us who are supposedly its adepts? And isn't it true that building love, joy, and creativity into our lives, here as anywhere else, is a profoundly liberating and decolonizing practice?[1]

As a thinker I want to think through various media, including art. As a writer, I want to create through various forms of thought — especially those from which I have been warned off — as part of the search for reintegration, as part of my own being true to my inner compass. But I also want to consciously dis-obey, to dis-order, to refuse the dictums that reserve creativity exclusively to the realm of the arts rather than to thought proper. I do not want to reproduce the kinds of knowledges and paths that are part and parcel of the mechanisms of silencing, marginalizing, misrepresenting, and rationalizing social, economic, gender, sexual, racialized, and other inequities — and that begin such work within me in a personal way.

Cross-dressing, performativity, and disidentification are three useful concepts based on "doing" being differently. Marjorie Garber (1997) points out that class-, racial-, and gender-based cross-dressing are alarming to some and liberating to others because they induce a crisis in our social categories: they scramble up assumptions around what is normal or desirable. Philosopher Judith Butler (1990, 1993) argues that gender is a learned social performance normalized through repetition. More broadly, the concept of performativity allows us to think about all behavior as learned and, therefore, as potentially unlearnable. Disidentification is a concept borrowed through various routes from psychology, and retheorized in the work of José Esteban Muñoz (1999) to describe queer performance artists of color, including drag queens who perform social identity differently, injecting undomesticated gender performances and desires into the social landscape against the pulls to reproduce heteronormative, "racial," or cultural homogenization.

How might such reflections benefit us in an effort to decolonize the production of knowledge as we know it, as it is represented to us from the halls of academia and its disciplines that are deeply embedded within the colonial adventures, and so complicit with the subjugation of negatively racialized peoples and their cultures, of women, of queer genders and sexualities, of the differently abled, of the poor? If postindustrialism and economic neoliberalism have shown the limits of enfranchisement of even college-educated Euro-American men in a period of heightened corporate greed with few nationalist loyalties, such a stripping away of external power also shows the spuriousness of the privileges of gender, sexuality, so-called race, and shared ethnic culture of the colonizer. It shows, as Chela Sandoval (2000) argues in conversation with Fredric Jameson's pessimistic analysis of the seeming impossibilities of the Left under postmodernist social and economic conditions, that we can form coalitions across historically deep and policed differences on the basis of common interests against a neoliberal capitalist globalizing politics. This is so because we are all increasingly experiencing dehumanization and social disempowerment. It feels like the possibilities of real social and personal change are rapidly shrinking for too many.

Born in 1915, one hundred years old at the time of her passing, and trained as a Hegelian philosopher (PhD 1940), Black Power movement activist, and social and economic theorist, Grace Lee Boggs argues in *The Next American Revolution: Sustainable Activism for the Twenty-First Century* (2011) that power is not something that is given to us. It is something we become aware of, claim, protect, enact — that is, power begins with us. We are literally the change for which we have been waiting. As the feminists of the 1960s and 1970s theorized, the personal is political, through and through. And the path of self-awareness, self-knowledge, and attunement of one's inner being with one's outer social practice are no longer matters to be pursued esoterically by lonely aspirants but rather a human necessity at large, for our human collectivity is as vastly in crisis as the environment. Therefore, the decolonial cannot only attend to outer social, cultural, economic, and political measures, laws, and policies. Practices that intend decolonial effects, I propose, must attend to the fertile ground of our psyches and our bodies, where the historic ideologies of colonization reseed and reproduce themselves hauntingly within us. If by the colonial and neocolonial at the level of the psyche we mean to indicate some sort of origin of the hierarchy of -isms that plague us as individuals and as a society, as Frantz Fanon indicated long ago regarding the internalization of racism among the colonized in *Black Skin, White Masks* (2008; *Peau noire, masques blancs*, 1952), then decolonizing practice must in some way be eros ideological, increasingly self-conscious, boundary-crossing performances, and disidentificatory acts of being rooted in a politics of respect for self and other, as modes of both immediate and lasting change.

The psyche, as Carl Jung called the soul (following the ancient Greeks), the mind, and the body, are key sites of different kinds of colonization, I want to argue. One of the key alienating features of the present is the assertion that the mind, body, and spirit (by whatever name we refer to the last) are split by nature rather than as a consequence of historically specific and nonuniversal human ideologies. This fracturing of what is ultimately the enigma of self and therefore of a more complex way of knowing beyond obvious deduction and rationalism is disempowering of the self as individual and social being (Jung [1933] 1965, [1945] 1953, [1961] 1989, 1990).

In Lak'ech is a Mayan concept that translates on one level as "you are my other me": *tú eres mi otro yo* (Martínez Parédez 1960, 1973; Macias 2017). It is not a metaphor but a seemingly paradoxical concept that expresses as statement of fact the interconnection of all being, and thus a deep, essential identity as living beings on this planet. For myself, it has become a window into another politics of performing individual and social being: an invitation to know yourself through me, the seemingly irreducibly other with respect to you, and vice versa. Rather than me as not-you, me as your other-you. The you, that like the many me's inside of me, I do not yet fully understand or even begin to *vislumbrar*, or perceive.

What does it look like to give up performances of having the upper hand when the day is done, or performance of resentful negations of inferiority, as Mariana Ortega (2006, 2016), María Lugones (2003), Chela Sandoval (2000), Trinh T. Minh-ha ([1989] 2009), and Gloria E. Anzaldúa (1987), alongside other U.S. women of color before (e.g., *This Bridge Called My Back: Writings by Radical Women of Color* [Moraga and Anzaldúa 1981]), have asked? What does it look like to get off the seesaw of the expectation of binary truths that ultimately rest on the false assumption of essential differences from each other and from the rest of the natural world?

What about difference and unity, difference and identity as paradoxical, coexisting truths? And I do mean truths plural, without ironic quotation marks. What about our joint humanity and the basic script of living our differences and cultural specificities as unique and constantly varying manifestations?[2] Why "must" we think in either/or? Why not be-ing as ellipses, as points of suspension, as markers of the unfinished or inarticulate ending of the plot in the making that is our individual lives and our social lives together as national and global communities?

Tú eres mi otro yo. But coalition across differences cannot mean I write for the dominant, that is, the dominating cultural other, to understand me by translating my different points of view into preexisting terms that would erase the initially "foreign" parts. And when I speak of cultural differences I am not only referring to the differences that we inherit from our different ethnic forebears; I mean as well the different family cultures that constitute our ways of understanding, and expressions of affection, remorse, disappointment, and so on, that we so often misrecognize because we read from our own horizon of emotional registers. This means we are first and foremost our own project — a project of immediate social and political consequences — and one that depends on our own mental health and well-being as the most solid basis of social and political action.

Decolonization is a concept and a practice that refers to analyzing the histories of domination of one nation or state over another and the myths that were necessary to rationalizing political, economic, and social subjugations by claiming that the cultures and humanity of the colonized were inferior. But colonization and newer forms of colonization are always a dehumanization of the dominators as well, who project onto others the parts of which they were taught in family and they, from the larger culture(s), to be ashamed, to repress, to uproot, to deny, to destroy. Although we may have learned to be cynical about it, the golden rule of countless religions and spiritual worldviews is to treat others as you wish to be treated. But a precondition of being able to do so sustainably, over time, and in the face of lack of reciprocity is self-love — not egocentric self-aggrandizement but affection, care, and compassion for the self. Because, alas, the footprints leading to and from fear, dislike, and hatred of difference and otherness circle the humble hut of our own being. The good news is that care of the self is an ancient, cross-cultural, truly universal human guide to living, a *How to Live for Dummies*. From a holistic perspective of mind, body, and spirit, we have a natural need to unfold, to become, to be tended, to be supported, parenting or gardening ourselves into greater and deepening integrity, self-realization, wholeness. Self-care is thus a prerequisite of a caring society and its government.

Decolonization is a process of attempting *to be*, from a place where we strive to be aware of and to rethink into new directions the historically received social constructions of identity, such as those of gender, "race," class, ability, and sexuality that we have incorrectly been schooled to believe are natural. I propose that the decolonial is the effort to discover ourselves, to uncover ourselves from beneath the layers of "do this," "do not do that," "those kind of people are x," and "we are y." The decolonial is the effort to be real to ourselves, to have integrity, unity, and wholeness with respect to our own desires and heartfelt beliefs. This cannot help but be the heart of the decolonial process because the decolonial process is the reclamation of our humanity against dehumanization, whether at the hand of others or our own internalization of those "(neo)colonial orders," full of sadness, shame, rage, and the desire to "mete out justice."

To midwife the process of "making face, making soul," as Gloria Anzaldúa puts it, following an ancient Mesoamerican expression, *in ixtli, in yollotl*, is fundamentally creative work.[3] It is the potential power of art making to the degree it concerns itself with the artist's own truth-telling, sometimes against hegemonic ideologies. Ancients across the globe are said to have considered creative intentional production, whether material or mental/conceptual, what today we commonly reduce to only "art," as a means of harmoniously attuning, helping in the constant transformation toward self-realization, guided by the higher purpose of balanced coexistence, toward which humans and all life-forms naturally tend. But as we know, artists and straight-up political ideologues, whether overtly or subconsciously, can also work toward inequity, parasitism of one group over another, and the construction of a compliant, frightened, guilt-ridden, and self-policing semi-citizenry. After all, it is we, accompanied by the ghosts of our ancestors, who create human society and its ills.

Face, heart, face, soul, body spirit, body as inspirited, spirit as embodied.

For after all, the body performs, does it not, the mind or the soul?

Body as mediator,

as laboratory,

as neighborhood,

as community,

as theater,

as prison,

as bedroom,

as attic,

as closet,

as heaven,

as hell.

As spring

fall

winter

summer.

As . . .

Equal?

Equivalent?

Like?

In space-place of?

As *difrasismo*. Diphrasm, two different beings yoked by comma and invoking
a third.

Tú, yo. You, me.

Body itself as my other me. As your other you.

As therefore the first cell of re(ignited)evolutionary action for change.

For individual, necessary (r)evolutions.

How about the body in different conjugations, not as the individualistic,
atomized, alienated, socially love-starved home of the hungry ghosts called
me, myself, and I? Different equations . . . through and with and in and
because of my body as mind and spirit too and as changing as life itself is,
in continual transformation, permutation, hybridization, death, rebirth . . .

To practice the body differently.

To practice the mind as the body

the spirit as the body,
the body as poetic writing on the social landscape.
Me the pen, you the paper, then next time, me the paper, you the pen.

Knowledge through the body in the body from the body.

The circuit gains importance from personal experience to abstraction to reason to objectification and generalization and back again. This circuit, with all of it meaningful, all of it having social and political and, if you wish, spiritual effects, is one of interdependence.

Politically, ideologically, the practice of interdependence and coalition is countercultural in a positive creative way if it involves constructing our own sense of what is decent, ethical, and correct against norms of so-called appropriate behavior that have ensured the hierarchical domination of groups of people against others and parts of the human psyche, such as the materialist and rationalist over other parts of the psyche.

Interdependence and coalition are perhaps, ultimately, the refusal to have our selves dehumanized by the myths of unjust power, congealed, codified into what has been handed to us as society and that we either reproduce as is or that we re-express from our particular, hard-won truths, our hopes, our visions for how to live now and in the future. At the core of the decolonial, of the call to just societies and respectful and good international global relations, is the recognition of our interdependence and the refusal to dehumanize our oppressors, those who negate our full humanity, as they have negated parts of their own humanity in order to subjugate, exploit, and violate others.

Thinking beyond the false binaries of us versus them, of older dichotomies between a good Left and a bad Right wing, or the reverse, is the direction I am pointing to: the idea of "eros ideologies" as politically and socially relevant ideologies that we can recraft and fine-tune to our personal, local, communal, and global lives. Eros ideologies are those that refuse to dehumanize the dehumanizers and refuse to continue internalizing the disempowering pictures about humanity, life, and nature that previous idea banks — that is, ideologies — have imagined. We can imagine, act, and make life differently. Currently nondominant peoples have preserved ways of thinking about life on the planet that are based on the balancing coexistence of differences, re-calibration of the constantly changing activity of all life-forms, and continual reharmonizaton. Ancient lineages of human wisdom about well-being of mind, body, society, and ecosystems exist now in the philosophies, worldviews, sciences, and other knowledgeable practices of different cultures, such as those of the Maya and other traditional indigenous peoples of the Americas, Buddhism, Hinduism, and the African diaspora, and have been reimagined by European neo-pagans. What has survived into the present from the ancient past is durable and necessary. We can learn from each other and create mutually beneficial and healthy ways of being in more harmonious coexistence (Gandhi 1956; Martínez Parédez 1960, 1973; Trungpa [1984] 2009; Hanh [1987] 2005, 2006, 2007; Cajete 2000; Vega 2000; Nagler 2001; Cordova 2007; Naranjo 2010; Boggs 2011; Maffie 2014).

Eros ideologies allow us to operate simultaneously within our skins, our apartments and houses, our neighborhoods and towns; to reclaim scattered, closeted, banished, unknown parts of self and community, where we strive to bear in mind the humanity of "the enemy" within our own hearts, in spite of betrayal, of absences, of violence. It is to know the self, as you, to know the self, my self, your self, freer of conceptual constructs that lack nature-based, reality-based truth, such as "race," "white," and "people of color"; "feminine" and "masculine," even "male" and "female," and therefore "straight" and "queer"; lovable and unlovable, known and unknown. It is to know myself as none of these, and to know you in this way, too. This is where we meet in partial crossings, and in the absences that our words cannot yet name or have not yet remembered.

The social body is love, in its stories of successful social relations. Ultimately, social love is the same element or energy or embodied practice as the love we hold for our lovers, and those who have been good to us. Love and human relationality, eros, is essential, abiding, unifying, the "glue" of interdependence, of a world of differences constantly crossing, meeting, embracing, transforming.

What are "eros ideologies"? They are ideologies that center eros in positive relationships of interdependence and identity with humanity as a species that shares a common life force with the rest of the natural world. Eros ideologies are plural. They arise in different cultures and time periods, and with different forms of specific expression to a people and to individuals. They have social and political effects. However, they are not the expression of one class of people, whether defined socially, economically, culturally, nationally, religiously.

If talk of love, respect, and harmony is fundamentally religious or spiritual (nonuniversal as these latter terms may be), then eros ideologies are ultimately spiritual, yet also philosophical in nature. If one rejects "God-" or "spirit-talk," then eros ideologies may simply be thought of as the product of ancient philosophies or of ethically driven yearning for peaceful, purposeful, just coexistence. Although essentially philosophical in their focus on understanding the nature of being and the meaning of life, eros ideologies are not, however, abstract philosophies, or neocolonizing, imperialist orderings of knowledge, or prescriptive social-political analyses and social action agendas.

Since long before the fall of the Berlin wall, Perestroika, and the revelations of the "excesses" of socialist, communist, Maoist, and Marxist regimes, the Left has been in crisis. But so has the Right, and the so-called center of the modern, Western, and Westernized worlds. It is not merely governments that are in crisis but humans, certainly the vast majority of us in the Westernized worlds, and for many centuries, and not just the last five hundred years since the invasion of the Americas.

Psychiatrist Carl Jung (1875–1961), who witnessed the horrors of two world wars as a medical doctor, the invention of weapons of mass destruction, and the inhumane pathology of Nazism, observed that nearly all Westerners could be described as neurotic. Modern Western people suffered psychologically, as he saw it, precisely as a result of extremely materialist scientism and the consequent decline of religious and mythological thought and the ensuing repression of other ways of understanding human life and purpose. The dogma of materialism over other, including ancestral, ways of knowing led, Jung felt, to the split within the psyche between good and evil, and the denial of the existence of evil as defined in Christian Western cultures within the individual, and therefore its projection onto various others. The scapegoating, subjugation, and extermination of the so-called other would only become worse, Jung predicted, because of *unnatural*, socially derived intrapsychic repression of not only that deemed evil but more generally that which was considered wild, uncivilized, or in some other way undesirable.[4]

Jung and the female analysts who worked closely with him — Emma Jung, Toni Wolff, Marie-Louise von Franz, among others — pointed out that as a consequence of patriarchal culture, energies that could be called "feminine" were repressed in men and energies that could be called "masculine" were repressed in women, with various complex crisscrossings within each individual's psyche. These psychic forces, which the early Jungians gestured toward through the concepts of anima and animus, were regarded as fields in vital need of further study, not least from women themselves. The anima and animus were intrapsychic energies personified as archetypal figures somewhat provisionally in order to better understand the complexity of the human mind and being beneath or beyond socially imposed, rigid, unnatural gender roles, and to heal the psychological and somatic disease arising from their repression by reintegrating these types of energies within each person (Jung [1945] 1953, 99–101, 202). However, Jung also felt that the unconscious was much more than the content of social repression. He felt that it held the slowly unfolding roadmap, as it were, of a person's individual path to unique self-realization, of coming to know and possess the self in a lifelong process of "individuation" that he believed analytic psychology could assist, rather than only focusing on pathology, as did psychoanalysis. Through comparative study of Buddhism, Hinduism, Jewish mysticism, Christian mysticism, and European medieval alchemy, Jung came to believe that there was a shared human species consciousness, which he called the collective unconscious, and that processes of self-knowledge leading to self-realization, akin to individuation, were ancient and cross-cultural (Jung 2012, 75, 87–89, 125). His recently published *The Red Book: Liber Novus* makes his views particularly clear in this respect and constitutes a careful pictographic journal of his decades-long experiment on himself as he tracked the process of individuation and expansion of consciousness of a greater self beyond the egoic I (2009; 2012, 59).[5]

In Jung's thought, it is quite plain that political ideologies of the modern Westernized worlds did not go far enough in their analyses, and therefore in their solutions to human individual and social suffering, or to understanding the basis of exploitation of fellow humans and ecosystems. He feared that without a psychology that could address what was natural to humanity, and to the particular individual, pointing us beyond the so-called human as delimited in Western thought, more internal and external war awaited us (Jung 1990, 55; 2012, 199–200). "Love of neighbor," he wrote, "is not superficial sentimentality. . . . Where love stops, power begins, and violence, and terror" (1990, 57), and "man appears to see the outer quarrel, but not the one within, which alone is the wellspring of the great war" (2012, 199).

The work of Claudio Naranjo has also led him from the diagnosis of mental illness to the critique of the social values and conditions that give rise to it. In *Character and Neurosis: An Integrative View* (1994), a work of synthesis of modern science and ancient non-Western understanding of mind and illness, Naranjo argues that the basis of all psychological suffering can be understood as arising from the lack of sufficient love and care in the shaping of the psyche from infancy throughout adolescence. The lack of good-enough primary care in the early years of a child's life is largely the legacy of unconscious, repeated, and culturally learned dysfunctional behaviors. The remedy therefore lies in the process of self-awareness, of coming to know the self as a specific individual against the grain of normativity and integrating all aspects of being. In Naranjo's *Healing Civilization* (2010), he argues that the basis of all violence and war is in patriarchal cultures' (plural) shaping of a "patristic mind," deleteriously out of balance with its own "femininity."

The feminist Latina Jungian psychologist Clarissa Pinkola Estés (*Women Who Run with the Wolves*, 1992) frames the issue of binary oppositional thought as a problem beyond patriarchy but inclusive of it: the suppression of the "wild," or what is actually natural to human beings, notwithstanding that the natural is not fully knowable and is changeable. Although primarily concerned with developing a psychology for women to survive and overcome patriarchal thought, Estés's creation of an archetype (based on cross-culturally recurring symbols) that she calls the "wild woman" can also be usefully seen as the undomesticated surplus of uncolonized being within humans.

Jungian and post-Jungian psychologies, particularly those from feminist, people of color, and queer perspectives mindful of the specific pitfall to "individuation" or self-realization presented by racial, gender, and sexual normativity, are useful to decolonial thought, alongside U.S. women of color feminist thought, ancestral cross-cultural "theo-philosophies" (philosophical thought rooted in spiritual worldviews), and other Third World decolonial thought. Deeply understanding human peace and freedom from the perspective of not just mind but the knowledges arising from mind-body-spirit, and in ways that challenge gender and sexuality binaries, is core to a deeply decolonial thought. Decolonizing thought arising from nondominant and noncolonial perspectives is vital to analytics that avoid unintentionally repeating the privileging of patriarchal and post-Enlightenment Eurocentric biases.

As Audre Lorde observed, the master's tools — his or her logic, method, and practices — will not dismantle the master's house (1984a). Gloria Anzaldúa, Grace Lee Boggs, Leela Fernandes, AnaLouise Keating, Audre Lorde, María Lugones, Lata Mani, Chela Sandoval, and Linda Tuhiwai Smith are among the many artists and intellectuals creating decolonial thought and practices analyzing the "simultaneity of oppressions" and complex notions of identity as multiple, tactical, mobile, and interdependent that have allowed us to rethink gender and sexuality as core to decolonial being and practice, and not just to women or the queer. Theirs is a politics of self-love, love of community, democratic hope, and creative praxis. Their work stands beside the important poststructuralist thought of French thinkers — critiquing power from within dominant cultural ideology, language, and culture, and identifying desire and the artistic as important potential zones of resistance (e.g., Michel Foucault, Pierre Bourdieu ([1979] 1998), Michel de Certeau ([1984] 1988), Gilles Deleuze and Félix Guattari ([1972] 1983), Luce Irigaray ([1974] 1985), Giorgio Agamben ([1995] 1998, 2009) — and the critiques of Eurocentric neocolonialism and the "coloniality of power" of sociologist Aníbal Quijano (2000a, 2000b), philosopher Enrique Dussel (2000, 2009) and cultural theorist Walter Mignolo (2011). Women of color feminist and queer thought is a powerful, visionary, courageous, and creative body of diverse thought emerging from the cultural hybridity of African diasporic, indigenous, Buddhist, and other non-Western ancestries or affiliations with which they negotiate and navigate the dominant cultures that have historically oppressed, silenced, and marginalized them in racially gendered patriarchal and heteronormative ways (see also Vidal 1971; Martínez 1972; Del Castillo [1974] 1997a, [1974] 1997b; Nieto-Gómez 1974, 1975, [1976] 1997a, [1976] 1997b; Sosa Riddell 1974, all reprinted in García 1997; Combahee River Collective [1977] 1983).[6]

The logic that sees human beings as inferior or superior racially, by gender, class, ability, or other categories, to other humans also sees humans as superior to the rest of the natural world, and likens other human beings and other cultures to the less civilized and, ultimately, to the dangerous. This type of thinking (re)produces human subjectivity as split, fragmented, lacking, and wounded as if by nature. But the psyche is in part the product of human imagination, perception, and narratives that have social and political effects that matter. The psyche is part of that "real," but as Jung and ancient theo-philosophies observe, the psyche is also beyond the human as such, a borderland between human and nonhuman, between the perceivable and conceivable, and what is not.

Why speak of ideologies? Ideologies are defined by Marxian (though not strictly Marxist) philosophers, including poststructuralists, as the worldviews within which a culture's thought makes sense, particularly narratives regarding social reality and the ordering of people within it.[7] U.S. people of color and Third World intellectuals have argued that the dominated also operate by ideologies of their own — that is, that ideology is not merely a matter of who owns and controls the means of production, communication, and education. The poor, the colonized, and the oppressed are said to also operate by ideologies of resistance, in the social-economic margins. But if ideologies are meant to point to coherent enough systems of thought, albeit changing and fluid ones, then we can also think about them in ways that are not pinned only to political, economic, social, cultural, religious, or "racial" or ethnic axes of power struggles.

There are ideologies based on the belief that humans and other life-forms should be treated respectfully, in part because we are made of the same matter and life force. Pragmatically, then, behavior creates social effects that affect the actors, directly or indirectly, sooner or later. Environmental pollution of the planet is an example of the inescapable consequences of irresponsible, disrespectful, and inharmonious actions in the living ecosystem. Crossing Jung, Naranjo, and Estés with traditional philosophies, the effects of humans on such behaviors are widespread depression, alienation, fear, and violence.

"Eros ideologies" is therefore an umbrella term that means to illuminate different threads of thought, a body of philosophies across time, space, and different cultures that emphasizes the identity between humans and other life-forms, and the psychic, social, and political promise such beliefs hold. Thich Nhat Hanh, Mohandas K. Gandhi, and many other spiritual elders express various eros ideologies grounded in an awareness of unity-in-difference, the respectful coexistence of differences as the nature of nature and therefore as what is natural in ourselves as humans. The psyche therefore is the first territory in which we enact a politics that has "real" effects.

A political ideology of eros is personal and interpersonal, a politics of relationality based on understanding of shared identity and treatment like that which we desire for ourselves.

Eros ideologies are the multiple, timeless, yet also historically specific worldviews and practices that some people have received and reformulated in our times in order to better live in our own skins and with each other across the room, the nation, or the globe.

I call the socially consequential healing practices of loving awareness and respect of self "eros ideologies," as these are defined in the life and writing of Thich Nhat Hanh and Chogyam Trungpa; in traditional Maya thought, according to Mayanist (and Maya) Domingo Martínez Parédez; and in the writing of U.S. women of color such as Audre Lorde and Gloria Anzaldúa. To speak of love in our era is to supposedly be apolitical and merely private and personal, emotional, or sexual, that is, supposedly, unwittingly acquiescent to hegemonic social orders.

But before, after, and within the erotic in sexuality is eros — the energy of attraction, of complementarity, of identity across difference, the desire to merge, to unify in various degrees, from good connections, to the blissful loss of self, to orgasm, and to peaceful abiding within nature.

To speak of eros ideologies is to map many "third" ways of conceiving of politically, socially, and globally meaningful realities. It is a way of nonpolar dualism, a way rooted in an identity politics that traditional Mayans have called *In Lak'ech*, but where you are my other me, *tú eres mi otro yo*, a theo-philosophy echoed across cultures and times and useful to us now perhaps as never before, where "identity" is plural, friendly, transformative, attracted, and attracting.

How do we "speak" these eros ideologies and enact a politics of the eros ideological, understanding the "ideological" appendage as an indicator of social-political awareness and critique? The arts are one way, and more generally, the creative and the experimental are gateways beyond unnatural normativities. Zones of natural wilderness are within us, are living underground springs, ways through the socially narrated as "this is how it is," "this is how it's done," or "this is how it has to be." Jung's conceptualization of the "collective unconscious" connected to a much larger, "collective" awareness than that of individual repressions (i.e., Freud's "unconscious"), Estés's "wild" knowing and intuition, Anzaldúa's *conocimientos* of *la facultad*, or the knowings of an instinctive and psychic faculty — which are all winding journeys of being as becoming, through various forms of experience, various relations and exchanges with people and objects, and various types of knowing.

2

EROS IDEOLOGIES AND
METHODOLOGY OF THE OPPRESSED

FIGURE 2.1 Mariana Ortega, *Cómeme el corazón* (2007), detail.

THIS PIECE DIALOGUES with and further explores Chela Sandoval's important and beautiful idea of the "social physics of love" and its possibilities, given "liberal exhaustion" among even progressive intellectuals since its publication, in *Methodologies of the Oppressed* (2000). Using the metaphor of emotional wounding and betrayal in personal relationships, I ask how one comes back from these, and why one should.

The unnamed.
Lo que no tiene nombre.[1]
The unnameable.
The uncolonized. The wild-erness. The ecstatic.
The barely connotable, The hardly visible.
The uncanny, the ghostly. Haunting social, political orders.
The space, the place, the existence of the differently existent.
    The *khora*.

(C/Khora, Greek, proposed by Plato, seized by Derrida, plumbed by Kristeva:
    Originary, abiding, constitutional existential twilight.
Barely conceivable fund of possibility.[2])
The distance between feelings, intuitions, and the verbal, visual, even bodily
    languages at our disposal.

The existence of distance, of between, of difference, of the unfathomable.

The politics and the poetics of transformation, personal as well as social, hinge
    upon our experiential forays into the zones of not only yearning and ecstasy but
    also pain, sorrow, loss, and, perhaps most significantly, the how of our return,
    after we ourselves have suffered, nay, been casualties.

For how does one return from being violenced, violated, betrayed, wounded — individually, socially, culturally, historically — with a game plan for social justice? Or more immediately, for carrying on through hope rather than despair? If no longer intact, at least rebuilt?

Throughout the ideological spectrum, dissent has been viewed as unbridgeable difference, a potentially mortal wounding to be preempted. Torture, confinement, death. At a minimum: exclusion, silencing, loathing, exile.

How to *not* dehumanize the dehumanized dehumanizer further? How to *not* self-righteously dehumanize ourselves?

These questions have been the quandary of the post-Stalinist Left as Deleuze and Guattari put it in *Anti-Oedipus* ([1972] 1983), as Sandoval reminds us Foucault saw when he spoke of our own internalized fascisms, as Anzaldúa (1987) put it when she described the parts of herself that are always on disciplinary patrol, ready to bust the most tender, least domesticated, most yearning parts of herself.

How does one heal the wound that is the lack of love?

How does one learn to love the beribboned scar tissue across our own face and that of the redneck gringo, the sadistic guerrilla, the selfish ex-lover, the treacherous pseudo-friend, the self-satisfied haves of First and Third World alike, whose comforts and comforting self-image are built upon the impoverishment of the have-nots?

How does and why should one bounce back? What if one refuses relationality?

"Methodology of the oppressed," as Sandoval calls the capacity to navigate differences, is an option not only for social justice but for humanization, against a politics that would, perhaps unwittingly, dehumanize us.[3]

They are the vigilance of the consciously but sincerely modest. "There is so much we do not know, so much we must learn, so much more we could do . . ."

Sandoval's theories of differential consciousness and the methodologies of the oppressed, gleaned from the creative, theoretical, and everyday tactics for negotiating existence of women of color in the U.S., remind us that they/we have survived fragmenting, postmodern-like conditions through the colonial and neocolonial ordeals with *facultades*, spiritual and embodied knowing, or *conocimientos*, with integrity or the "making face, making soul" of, again, Anzaldúa, and of so many African American and Native American women and men.

With hearts *strong* from the courage of facing such terrible odds against racialized women and from so much loving in the face of so much lack of it directed at us, century after century, day after day.

To not choose hate is a primal, primary methodology of the oppressed.

Love itself is the uncolonized, ever-streaming excess from the place before creation, radical by definition, heroic because ultimately unmappable though we must navigate it, and as such, a zone of differential consciousness if ever there was one.

Sandoval's own love machine, a theory of social action conceived through the erotic as the socially, ideologically disordering, because of more ethical relationality between self and other, illuminates what she poetically whispers as *"Amor en Aztlán,"* love in a place we hallucinate.[4]

Love, in the nowhere that is the contestatory, imagined community of Aztlán, Black and Queer Nations: collectively imagined spaces of resistance and creativity (Sandoval 2000, 147, 183) that are, by definition, hardly merely ethnically or culturally specific.

"Amor en Aztlán," Sandoval's kindred concept to the middle voice, the oscillations behind meaning, Derrida's *différance*, Anzaldúa's Coatlicue State, *mestiza* consciousness (1987), African American signifyin' (Gates 1988) and W. E. B. Du Bois's double consciousness (1903), Roland Barthes's unconventional, unpossessive loving (2010).

In deed. That is, in practice. To love in Aztlán is perforce to love differently, because Aztlán does not exist.

It is the mythical homeland here, the *khora* among us, within us, in the further north of all our forebears and future kin.

It is a utopia whose outline is daily redrawn in the discursive struggles of our own moment.

Although to love in Aztlán *is* about queerness with respect to dominant orders, it is nonetheless not about sexual, ideological, cultural, political queerness reinscribing patriarchal and other hierarchies of inequality, under new guise.

It is to love at the damning crossroads of your own safety nets, among your own gaping cronies, as you fall in love with a man, after you have come out as a lesbian.

It is about desire across even righteously erected barriers. Where the erotic is and is not bedding. Where love is simply friendship. Where we do not know, in truth, what love is and what it demands of us now.

Anzaldúa's *Borderlands* (1987), imagined by the late Chicana queer writer as an imperfect girl child of a hybrid text, was perhaps also an image of the author herself, as a kind of Frankenstein made deeply human through the pain of so much scar tissue, so much gratitude for borrowed limbs and organs — a human quilt commemorating herself as salvaged from the rag heap, and now a compelling, thoughtfully, uniquely crafted thing of strange but certain beauty.

Eros ideologies would seem a contradiction in terms, as if ideologies could only signify the systematized reason and irrationality of hegemonic, subjugating powers.

But what of the powers of relationalities that bubble up from within, against dominant orders and disciplinary formations of self and desire? These are the concern of Barthes, Foucault, Sandoval, of those of us plodding through the ingratitudes of the day, the new burdens, the fresh humiliations, the ongoing injustice of it all, the real, actual evil systematized behind aestheticized, differently eroticized powers that no longer pretend to be benign.

From the perspective of females and the femaled within patriarchy, of the minoritized, of the socially, culturally, economically down and out: affirmation of an erotics of disordering desires, beginning with love of a self, once shorn of self-regard.

To love thusly is an act of *ofrenda*, of offering, in the face of the other's negation. To love that offending, wounding other is to dis-other him, to her him, to me him, to *tú eres mi otro yo* him, you are my other self him . . . The glimmer of identity across the gulf of differences, across a cavity torn asunder.

A politics of hope can only be a physics of love, as Sandoval calls it, or a hermeneutics toward love, toward social change.

Love is always a practice: the ultimate space of unknowability, the ultimate *khora*, yes. Partly social and cultural construct, historically specific artifice, but also always otherworldly, like spirit, creativity, notions of God or gods, in equations that are beyond our calibrations.

Love, like air, like water, like fire, is a fluid property of spirit/consciousness/the unconscious, an entity, yes, but knowable only in our unique crossings, and then only, partially, so imperfectly, and thus so hopefully . . .

To speak from the wound.

To speak because of the wound.
To not speak because of the wound. And yet, to be more than wound.

Love itself wounds.

I have hobbled, thereby I have been humanized beyond my own self-righteous judgmental othering of the one who oppresses as merely oppressor.

I have wounded myself in this not loving; therefore, I can love again, more deeply.

This is like breaking up. It is about cannot live with, cannot really live without. About boundaries and allowances. About lover as enemy, enemy as lover, about self as enemy, self as lover.

The historical, real enemy won over not by retaliatory violence in kind but transformed by the shift in discourse, politics, feelings, attitude, action. Something has to give because that kind of struggle is breaking *me*. I give, ofrenda. We might give, then. A change of heart. A heart has changed.

This one is broken anyway.

Receptivity, relationality in spite of the other's refusals.

Refusal to repay intolerance and arrogance borne of fear with the same.

Amor con amor se paga, love is repaid in kind, but the lack of it?

To translate, to transcode, to listen, to extend, and to *ofrendar*, to gift, and to receive. To recognize us all, not just the fathers, the golden boys, the momentarily exalted Saint Sebastianed women of color, the queer, the other.

Love is repaid with love, but it also pays itself before the silence of the indifferent heart, before the refusal to acknowledge you or your terms.

Yes, relationality as deindividualization. Deindividualization that produces us anew, as hybrids of ourselves.

3

LONG NGUYEN

Flesh of the Inscrutable

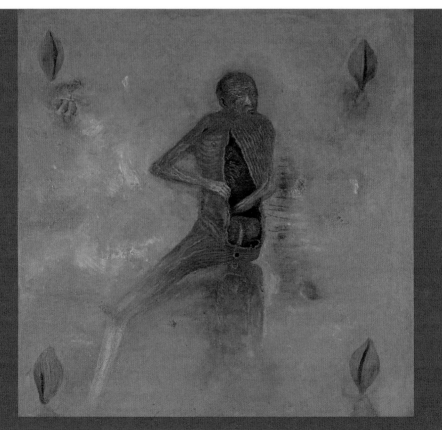

FIGURE 3.1 Long Nguyen, *Tales of Yellow Skin #2* (1991).

THIS BODY IS AN enigmatic sign, a hybrid whose impassivity is at odds with the itinerary of pain recorded on its skin.

One hand further opening the gaping hole in the trunk of the body, the being reaches within as if searching a bag or drawer, lips pursed in concentration.

What does it seek to discover? What does it uncover?

There is another visible hole, an anus, like an Oh or a zero, that is perhaps also the mark of missing genitalia or limb.

If it is a he, he is femaled in a map of opened and torn tissues. This form of being, this s/he, is remnant, scar, hole.

Yet, a hole that if wound is also aperture; a flesh that if scarred is also luminous; a remnant that remits as much to what is missing as to what is not.

A skin meticulously stripped away by self or other, or both.

A flaying, a mutilation, a vivisection that is perhaps none of these.

Inside and out, the being is made of the same evanescent sea of light into which an unfinished limb fades.

Framed by shells in each of the corners, the painting pictures a fluidity where external and internal, surface and interior, limit and limitlessness, manifestation and nothingness merge in a sea of precipitating and dissolving forms.

The painted canvas is also a s/he: the body as parchment, bearing the inscriptions, excrescences, uneven colorations made in embodiment, through stories of being as s/he.

A codex-like parchment, recording the simultaneity and imbrications of the sublime and the historical, in the strange hieroglyphic of a serene, bloodied figure, afloat in yellow waters.

Yellow waters, yellow canvas, yellow parchment, yellow histories, yellow skins.

Yellow: the color of the occident's cultural unknowns, colored through both attraction and repulsion, like all that seems enigmatic.

The inscrutable, once presumably illustrated in bodies colored yellow; indeed, painfully inscribed as such.

Moments and ways of being, some so raw, some so luminous that they are only partially told in tales of yellow skin.

HIDDEN AVANT-GARDES

Contemporary U.S. Latina/o Art

FIGURE 4.1 Asco, *Spraypaint LACMA* (East Bridge) (1972).
Photo by Harry Gamboa Jr.

IF WE EMPLOY CURRENT ART HISTORY categories for understanding contemporary art, or art since the historical avant-garde period of the first four decades of the twentieth century, we are left without useful categories by which to understand Chicana/o and other U.S. Latina/o art as anything other than "political art," a way of minimizing both the conceptual and the aesthetic projects in this diverse body of art as it emerges in the 1960s and continues through the present.[1] Within Western art history, developed as part of a cultural evolutionist discourse, there is a catch-22 described well by intellectuals and artists in late 1990s publications like *Beyond the Fantastic* (edited by Gerardo Mosquera, 1996) and *Santería Aesthetics in Contemporary Latin American Art* (edited by Arturo Lindsay, 1996). This conundrum — that of being judged as always playing catch-up, ostensibly without the originality or the training environment of the "First World" capitals (Paris, New York City), or of not being authentic enough (i.e., recognizably "ethnic," "folkloric," "exotic," "fantastic," "primitive," etc.) — remains the culturally disciplining "place" of minority art and its scholarship today: always other, always marginal, and, at best, a flavor of the month.

If this is so, then these discourses cannot be of use to decolonizing artistic or scholarly practice. What then might be of more use? Certainly thinking of art production as a cultural practice that produces or reproduces or interrupts meaning in dialogue with its time as visual cultural studies attempts — in distinction to an aestheticizing and depoliticizing traditional, Eurocentric art history — has been useful. Analysis of gendering, sexing, and racialization through a broader visual culture, including but not limited to art, is part of the published work that we can now draw upon, and that itself draws upon earlier Third World and oppressed minority thinkers, such as W. E. B. Du Bois in his concept of double consciousness ([1903] 1994) and Frantz Fanon's observations regarding the colonizing adoption of the cultural value system of the colonizer culture by the colonized ([1952] 2008).

But how do we deal with the constant preeminence, the tautological and continual re-centering of the "center" in terms of both art practice aesthetics and theories, and scholarly theory about these, as art critic Nelly Richard asks, for example, in her essay in *Beyond the Fantastic* (1996)? There is a very basic question of cultural visibility even before we can formulate the problem of access to the canon. How can what is proscribed as culturally abject be recognized by a system that defines what it is, *against* the perceived cultural difference of the "Third World," difference that is furthermore racialized, classed, and gendered? How can it be acknowledged, and then, if it is, how can it possibly be seen in a way that does not reinforce or confirm that which is expected and projected culturally, racially, and in terms of class, gender, and sexuality?

Defying expectation and rupturing received and expected discourses — of reason from the Enlightenment, Christianity, capitalist order and progress, and so on — are what the historical avant-gardes of the first four decades of the twentieth century are celebrated for: Surrealism's championing of the oneiric, the irrational, the insane, the occult, and the infantile; Cubism's exploration of multiple, simultaneous, and unexpected perspectives; Dadaism's destructive impulse to wipe clean the cultural slates and begin anew with childlike babbling and messes; and the Italian futurists' crafting of verbal and other languages to express the effects of then-new technologies such as planes, trains, telegraphs, cars, and overall increased mechanization and speed on urban sensibilities. All these vanguard movements functioned via formal (that is, aesthetic) and conceptual ruptures, albeit from at times different ideological positions among different groups.

The first reactions to this work by the uninitiated were incomprehension — as intended. "What does it mean?" was precisely the meta-textual project of this work. Why can't we read it easily? Why don't the codes we received as normal and natural, visual or conceptual tools, work to decode this stuff? The work embraced the need to move beyond these received languages and, most importantly, the worldviews, the perspectives they narrated.

It is this basic strategy of what French philosophers would later call deconstruction that profoundly affected postwar French intellectuals and gave rise to poststructuralist projects that, like the historical avant-gardes, would question received cultural traditions and the epistemologies that underwrite even the possibility to pose questions that make sense within a given culture:

and thus the notorious difficulty of reading Jacques Derrida or Jacques Lacan, who structure their writing and thinking through complexity, paradox, and creative intellectual and linguistic play. The historical avant-gardes and the poststructuralist philosophy and cultural theories that grew out of these focused on the political effects of verbal and visual languages and their artistic, social, cultural, religious, and political orders and, in turn, led to critiques that disorder(ed), in order to allow reconstruction of new social relations, new human dispositions and sensibilities, new political orders, in short, new forms of consciousness and thus new kinds of relationships and community.

The association of the new with the productively disruptive has remained with us for more than a century, since at least Futurism (1907). In the 1950s and 1960s, Jackson Pollock dribbled paint nonrepresentationally and Andy Warhol made mass media's creation of celebrity and consumer desire his themes and methodology. These things were new, unseen, a new "avant-garde," that is, a(nother) front guard battalion eventually incorporated into an art history that lionizes the new as cutting edge, following in the tradition of productive disruption.

From these criteria, how could the representational, realistic murals of Diego Rivera and his cohorts, or Frida Kahlo's self-portraits as mestiza, be viewed as vanguard too? This newness, not born in the "first world," is somehow illegible because somewhat autonomous from the dominant capitals. They have indeed "made it" into Western art history but generally not as part of the historical avant-garde projects of the era. How then could the resurgence of muralism in the post-1965 period in the United States be viewed as vanguardist rather than as merely derivative? In fact, how could this yoking of a depoliticized emphasis on the technically new and a merely formal disruption do anything other than confirm the culturally underdeveloped nature of Latin American and Third World art in the U.S. as art historically naïve, as conceptually unsophisticated, as backward and not new? But understanding the significance and the novel contributions of U.S. Latina/o art conceptually and ideologically can be yoked to something other than the difference of a newness defined or visible within Euro-American and Eurocentric cultural horizons.

Miguel León-Portilla's translations of conquest-era codices recording what we call in our own Westernized language "art" or "artists" are relevant to understanding U.S. Latina/o art, like that of Cuban American Ana Mendieta, or of Chicana/o and other art using both Western and non-Western philosophies of art and aesthetics. The codices León-Portilla translated and studied tell us that *tlacuilo*, scribes and glyph makers, were highly trained in the content and technique of the pictographic scribes who preceded them, but that their job was nonetheless to make it newly relevant. And the artist who failed to bring relevance to old truths in new times was considered a thief, a waster of other people's time, one who had failed to produce greater harmony between the "face" and the "soul" — that is, the integrity — of the beholder or audience of the pictographs and their performance by the *tla-matinime,* their sage interpreters.[2] There is philosophical depth to the idea of making things new among the pre-Columbian tlacuilo and tlamatinime that reading in that literature reveals, albeit reading today with the necessary caveat that most known existing codices were recorded as a project of colonizing Christian culture. Making what was understood of indigenous pre-Columbian philosophies and aesthetics new in the 1960s was in fact innovative and kindred in spirit and intent to the project of the European and Latin American avant-gardes of the World War I and II eras.

The questions that the historical avant-gardes attempted to pose about art and about culture, more generally, were not dissimilar to those attributed to the pre-Columbian tlamatinime: Is it relevant? Is it meaningful to the individual, society, and as future legacy in the world we leave behind? Although the new was celebrated in itself given the effects of new technologies on human sensibilities among the European and Latin American historical avant-garde movements, the search for new formal expression was itself a technique, a method to introduce new sensations, experiences, perceptions, and, most ambitiously, to broaden awareness. The Western art historical notion of the avant-garde as the meaningfully new can be a useful category by which to think about art production nationally and globally, mindful that commodification of art because it appears "new" rather than as a necessary sign of new sensibilities undermines the creation of the new as methodology rather than decorative bell and whistle. In the latter, form is dissociated from meaning. Scholarship and art making that are not Eurocentric, or solely so, in their aesthetic philosophy or visual language references also remind us that we must carefully disentangle the meaningful creation of "the new" from mistakenly cultural evolutionist, elitist, Eurocentric art historical discourses that now often serve the commodification of art.

For a moment in the 1980s and early 1990s, as in the 1930s and 1940s, when Latin American art was the new flavor of the month in New York, "multicultural" art was interesting to some because it was perceived as new and productively disruptive. The thrill is now gone, and we have been lectured that all such work was "identity politics" art — questionable in its merit, conceptually and formally, and ostensibly simplistic in its notions of "identity."

The bringing to visibility of the aesthetic, philosophical, ideological cultures of oppressed ethnic minorities in fact circulates the new with respect to Eurocentric art history. The intertwined structures of racializing, imperialist, capitalist culture that Peruvian sociologist Aníbal Quijano (2000b) describes as the "coloniality of power" prevents real aperture toward generative difference and yet helps to produce the continuing "newness" or productive difference of oppressed ethnic minority art.

Thus, without fetishizing newness for its own sake, as evidence of Darwinian, racialized cultural evolution in the arts, much self-designated U.S. Latina/o art of the present continues to be a hidden avant-garde because it is for the most part neither culturally visible nor visually intelligible. Mexican and other Latino cuisine is culturally very familiar now, and even very "in" in some places, but artwork conceived through Western, indigenous (e.g., Mexica, Maya), and African diasporic hybrid aesthetics, for example, are not; nor is work depicting or dealing with poor people of color issues, even when delivered in wholly Western idioms viewed as sufficiently valid subject matter (i.e., as "interesting," "new"). It is often dismissed as too narrow, too parochial, and (the old sawhorse) "too political." Yet artwork largely focused on white male heterosexual cultures and concerns is still represented as if universal, though it can be strikingly gender-, sexually, and culturally specific or "parochial," and in spite of dominant culture's own still largely unacknowledged historic and ongoing cultural hybridity. I would like to frame Latina/o art from a decolonizing politics that resituates Eurocentric perspectives and aesthetics as such, as perhaps mainly relevant for European and Euro-American cultures. The latter might indeed achieve universality of concerns, but it might also amount to the more honestly perceived reality of being simply one cultural perspective and aesthetic among many other distinct or hybrid possibilities of what constitutes art, good art, relevant art, and, most to the point, a socially, historically, and humanly meaningful avant-garde of our times.

There are historical, cultural, and practical differences in the Latina/o communities with respect to dominant and mainstream cultures that they challenge, borrow from, and transform at local and unacknowledged/undocumented levels, sometimes in very culturally specific ways. One area that cuts across pan-Latina/o arts is the nature and role of post-1960s spiritualities that are engaged in politically oppositional and decolonizing ways. Feminist Chicana artists, as I have written elsewhere (1998b, 2007a), since at least the 1970s have not just criticized the sexism, racism, and heterosexism of traditional in-stitutionalized religions; they have considered neo-pagan, Buddhist, African diasporic, feminist goddess, and diverse ancestral indigenous worldviews, crafting culturally hybrid spiritualities that are meant to be individually and socially meaningful in contemporary times through decolonizing aesthetics. The reemergence of these types of spirituality are politically relevant in cul-turally avant-garde ways given the values they hold regarding the meaning and possibilities of life and art that are at radical odds with consumerist, corporate-driven ideas about what art should be, do, and serve.

Living amid the massive carnage of the world wars; the rise of militarized, violent fascist governments; the persecution and genocide of Jewish, queer, and "gypsy" people in Nazi Germany; the invasion and occupation of many countries by Axis powers and the oppression of local national and ethnic cultures by the occupiers and right-wing governments elsewhere in Europe; and in too many cases the complicity of the bourgeoisie and the Church, his-torical avant-garde artists of the first four decades of the twentieth century criticized the duplicitous or deluded dominant mainstream cultures of their world. U.S. people of color artists, and Latina/os among these, continue to do this very thing under conditions of varying physical, economic, social, cul-tural, and psychological violence. They too strive to create not just commod-ity art but art to create a new world through new forms of consciousness.

5

FREEDOM AND GENDER
IN ESTER HERNÁNDEZ'S *LIBERTAD*

FIGURE 5.1 Ester Hernández, *Libertad* (1976).

BASED ON PENCIL-AND-INK versions and a drawing sold some two years before its definitive production as an etching in 1976, and subsequently as a silkscreen print,[1] *Libertad /Liberty* is today one of Chicana/o and U.S. feminist art's most familiar images. It embodies that era's racial, gender, and sexual civil rights struggles and pioneers a culturally decolonizing melding of Euro-American and Native American visual cultures and a U.S. women of color–centered politics of solidarity across cultural differences.[2]

In *Libertad*, Ester Hernández pictures herself carving a regal Mayan female figure from the Statue of Liberty, one of the most recognizable symbols of the United States and of freedom. The monument was given to the U.S. by France in 1886, on the occasion of the centennial of the signing of the Declaration of Independence. Standing on Liberty Island in New York Harbor, the massive 151-foot icon, reaching 305 feet from the foundation to the top of the torch,[3] has been reproduced as a public statue hundreds of times throughout the world, as an image of freedom's certain, strident step against oppression. The words of "The New Colossus," an 1883 sonnet by Emma Lazarus engraved in 1903 on a plaque within the interior of the "Mother of Exiles," have given voice to the democratic ideals identified with the copper and steel figure: "'ancient lands / . . . / With silent lips, Give me your tired, your poor, / Your huddled masses yearning to breathe free.'"[4]

The symbolism of the national public monument harkens back to Europe's ancient religious and visual cultural roots, to Libertas, Roman "goddess of freedom from slavery, oppression, and tyranny." Officially named *Liberty Enlightening the World* (*La liberté éclairant le monde*), the statue holds high a torch in her right hand and a tablet of knowledge in her left, and tramples upon shackles at her feet as she steps forward. The figure's flowing tunic and seven-spiked crown, representing the Greek and Roman sun gods, bestows ancient pedigree and dignity to the struggle of the former colonies against political oppression and domination and to those seeking refuge in the new nation.

It is to this cultural and political legacy that Ester Hernández laid claim in 1976, in her visual reworking of the national icon during the bicentennial. In Hernández's version, "Libertad" smiles contentedly as an image of the artist chisels away at her, revealing a visually continuous and harmonious Maya female figure. The legs of the Maya carving, roughly in proportion to "Libertad"'s figure, serve them both, as does the right arm, thus identifying the two figures to some extent. Three-quarters of the "statue's" body (excluding the upraised arm) is composed of the Native American figure, yet Hernández's print does not efface either the recognizable visage of the national monument or the upraised arm and torch. Hernández allows for the visual coexistence and hybridization, the mingling and melding, of the two figures drawn from different cultures, art histories, religions, and philosophical worldviews. In art historical and feminist "sisterhood," they stand together (on the same legs!) for the struggle for greater social and political freedoms.

Given their juxtaposition, Hernández's drawing/print illuminates and resignifies the received symbolism of these historic images. Both are images of power, represented through females, and both would seem to suggest female empowerment in ancient Greco-Roman and Maya cultures, among divine and, at least, elite social orders. Within the context of the civil rights social movements against racism, sexism, and homophobia of the 1950s through the 1970s in the United States, the invocation of these ancient figures in *Libertad*, however, brings into focus the ongoing legacy of patriarchy and heteronormativity within Freedom's so-called birthplace.

The Maya figure, selectively copied and altered from the carved depictions of "royals," is rendered by Hernández as a strong and beautiful gender-bending warrior figure with baby. The Maya "royal" is atypically clothed and adorned in *Libertad*, "wearing the clothing of a Classic Maya elite male. The belt and loincloth worn with bare torso is a distinctly male practice. The shoulder wrap could have been worn by either sex, but women wearing them at Yaxchilan wore them over full-length Huipil. The sandals and wristbands were worn by both sexes."[5]

The artist has explained that she wanted to decorate her figure lavishly and that she gave herself the liberty to adorn her as she found attractive from the imagery available to her at the time as a student of pre-Columbian art, anthropology, and feminism.[6] Therefore, Hernández bared the breasts of the commanding figure, and replaced traditional accoutrements, such as the presence of a "vision serpent," with an image of the artist herself at work. While a relationship between the two figures is made manifest visually, it is not clear that the substitution of vision serpent as such by the artist was conscious. If it was, it would suggest that the contemporary artist is the ancient figure's future. The continuity of the figures, in any case, is arrived at in other ways, as we shall see momentarily. In the crook of the other arm, the artist transformed what in the archaeological lintels might have appeared as a deity image, representing social status, into a baby. The artist explained that the baby came out of her memories of the empowering religiosity of the strong women of her childhood rural community, centered around the Virgin of Guadalupe, which she also drew upon for her other well-known print of that period, *Virgen de Guadalupe Defendiendo los Derechos de los Xicanos* (*The Virgin of Guadalupe Defending the Rights of Chicanos*).[7]

Ester Hernández's image enacts, on the visual level, the "U.S. women of color" thesis of the imbrication and simultaneity of gender, "race," class, and sexuality oppressions, born in the 1960s and 1970s, and continuously elaborated through the present: that is, that there is no universal experience of gender because women experience gender differently, according to class, racial, heteronormative, and other forms of social privilege or its lack, which allow them different degrees of freedom.[8] And while gender cannot be understood without the effects of racialization, neither can racialization, sexuality, or class be understood in isolation from each other or apart from gender privilege, or its lack.[9] Chicana feminists of the late 1960s and the 1970s were fascinated by accounts of pre-Columbian female social life not only as a decolonizing antidote to the cultural Darwinism of Eurocentrism that propagated the self-serving idea that European cultures, particularly those of English and Germanic extraction, were superior but, as importantly, because they offered alternative models of gender and sexuality to those brought by the Europeans and imposed, by the colonization of the Americas, onto people native to the continent.

From this perspective, the Statue of Liberty, a gift from one patriarchal republic to another, is ironic in its seemingly simultaneous celebration of liberty and "the female." But it is also ironic that the female monarchs of Spain and England led the colonization of the Americas, where patriarchal social, economic, and political privileges were extended beyond aristocratic nobles to European men and their male descendants who would not have received them in their own highly and rigidly stratified "mother" lands. And while "liberty for all," for the "founding fathers" of the U.S., actually meant liberty for property-owning men, preferably descending from English "stock," by the nineteenth century, the gendered racialization of "white" men was a "democratic" privilege of even the most criminal of "white" men.[10]

In contrast, the seemingly more empowered and fluid gender roles for women of pre-European indigenous American cultures represented to Chicana feminist and queer artists and intellectuals models of greater social democracy. And indeed, queer studies scholars from the 1980s to the present believe gender roles and sexual practices prior to colonization among many of the different peoples of the American continent to have been less binary and more fluid than in Europe, with such phenomena as cross-dressing and androgynous people socially recognized rather than repressed.[11]

Thus, Hernández's *Libertad* hybridizes different visual cultures and thereby the social imaginaries out of which they emerge and within which images, symbols, color, media, material, and other tools acquire culturally and historically particular meanings. In simultaneously staging female gender as free and creative (e.g., the artist as female), as androgynous and institutionally recognized (e.g., the cross-dressing Maya elite female), and as a deity representing human freedom (e.g., the goddess-based Statue of Liberty), Hernández lays claim to multiple visual imaginaries in order to broaden the social imaginary, that is, our national culture's general assumptions about freedom, democracy, justice, gender, sexuality, and racialization.

The image could be said to enact a postmodern aesthetic that anticipates the architectural and art manifestoes of the 1980s, in its cutting-and-pasting of historically disparate styles. But *Libertad*'s visual bilingualism more precisely and meaningfully represents that era as the beginning of respectful engagement between different cultures that emerges from direct experience with each other and knowledge about the historically silenced from their own perspective, as democratically necessary correctives to the tales told by the socially dominant. Hernández does not obliterate the European goddess, nor does she collaborate with a colonizing effacement of an equally magnificent Native American womanhood. The two ancient female figures and the contemporary woman are shown as simultaneously different and yet also one with each other in their stand for freedom for all, regardless of gender, sexuality, and racialization.

At the heart of *Libertad*, American and European ancestors are shown as visually continuous with their "racially" and culturally mixed progeny, the Chicana feminist artist, who dynamically stands on the outstretched palm of the one and, chisel in hand, within the crook of the outstretched arm of the other. Hernández pictures herself as she creates her version of the ancients, and as they cocreate with her a liberated notion of being for the present.

6

'GINAS IN THE ATELIER

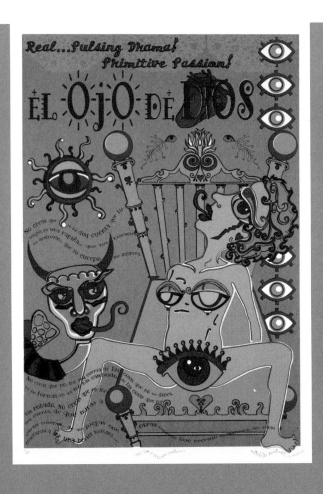

FIGURE 6.1 Favianna Rodriguez, *Del ojo de Dios no se escapa nadie* (1999).

THE MAESTRAS ATELIER XXXIII was the first all-female silkscreen "master" workshop to be held at Self Help Graphics in Los Angeles, in 1999. Under the direction of Yreina D. Cervántez, seven Latina and one African American women, at various stages in their career as artists and with different levels of experience in the medium, came together in a collaborative process, from January through April of that year.[1]

The 1999 Atelier was loosely organized around the figure of Sor Juana Inés de la Cruz, the seventeenth-century polymath and writer, and other feminist icons, heroines, goddesses, and sexuality (e.g., figure 20.1). Some truly remarkable pieces emerged from that gathering. Given that hosting an all-female atelier constituted a historically significant moment for Self Help Graphics, if a strikingly belated one, it was rather surprising to be invited to write about this workshop and arrive in Los Angeles only to find we were restricted to a total of four pages — that is, two 8½" × 11" pages, back and front, including images — in lieu of a catalog. Alongside the images that would be inserted next to my text, that left two pages for my curatorial essay, or barely a few lines for each. Rereading that mini essay afterward felt like a breathless fifteen-minute race through a museum before a flight. Happily, I was able to write elsewhere about five of the pieces from the series of which these were part. After being interviewed by *#Emerging US* of the *Los Angeles Times* (June 12, 2015) about the Atelier's youngest and least-exposed artist at the time, the Oakland-based Favianna Rodriguez and her new "Pussy Power Imaginary" project, I decided to return to her earlier, related workshop piece, and then to explore other vagina-centered feminist art. It seemed to me the importance and courage of this work becomes clearer in the context of ongoing widespread and common gendered sexual violence.

Rodriguez was an undergraduate at the University of California, Berkeley, in the 1990s and one of my and Yreina D. Cervántez's students while Cervántez served as a visiting artist and lecturer at Berkeley in 1998. At the end of the semester, Rodriguez gave me a print, *Eva y Eva en el Paraiso hacienda el amor ante Dios: Hahaha!,* of two nude female lovers before the long-lashed "eye" of God peering at them from a hand mirror. What Rodriguez created for the Maestras Atelier one year later—*Del ojo de Dios no se escapa nadie* (figure 6.1)—was related. Now the "eye of God" emanated from within the lid-like labia of the vagina of a nude figure, from where, Rodriguez explained at the time to me, it saw all, everywhere, including men's objectifying and abusive sexual behavior.

In December 2015 Rodriguez announced on Facebook the "Pussy Power Imaginary" project and its three-pronged approach: a series of silkscreens; a traveling interactive installation of a giant vagina that viewers could interact with, touching it and walking through it; and a website where people could share their feelings, experiences, and thoughts publicly.[2] A project apparently still-in-progress, and circulated through Twitter and Facebook, the artist's website said the "Pussy Power Imaginary" project would open and hopefully travel in late 2015. Rodriguez's project to de-pornografy and unshroud patriarchal imagery and thinking around the vagina forms part of a larger body of powerful pieces and histories of women protesting rape, such as Take Back the Night, INCITE! Women of Color Against Violence, and the recently emerged college campus–based movement to bring campus rapists to justice beyond the historic male-centered culture of higher education that lingers in spite of more equitable female enrollment figures (Burroughs and Katz 2015). The emergence of transgender activism also represents an important critique of socially and historically specific conceptions of gender, particularly those that rely on anatomy. Instead, transgender activists point us toward understanding that personal feeling and identification are at the crux of the matter, regardless of genitalia. Such thinking is in solidarity with, not opposition to, feminist artists' attempts to de-pornografy the social imaginary in terms of women's bodies, most particularly with respect to the vagina.

Women's bodies have not always been viewed as objects of heterosexual control, pleasure, or violence. Rodriguez's "Pussy Power Imaginary" silkscreen imagery of the anatomical vagina viewed frontally stylizes multiple references: fluid, flowery, and winged shapes, as well as abstract Virgin imagery that draws on a forty-year history of Chicana feminist revisions of the mixed-race Virgin Mary/Guadalupe (Pérez 2007a), including the parallel made between the shape of the vagina and the Mother of God (Trujillo

1991). Rodriguez's imagery also brings to mind ancient representations of nude figures with clearly marked vaginas — such as the wooden sculptures of "fertility" or maternity figures from various parts of Africa; so-called Venus figures, including the "Venus of Willendorf," found in Austria; Mesoamerican pictographs of Tlazolteotl and the "Aztec Birthing Figure" sculpture; and Celtic carvings of the wide-eyed Sheila-na-Gig, holding her labia open widely — and twentieth-century art by women.

In the early decades of the twentieth century, Frida Kahlo's frontal, open-legged view of the vagina in *My Birth* (1932), her lithograph *Frida and the Abortion* (1932), and her painting about miscarriage, *Henry Ford Hospital* (1932), were immediately recognized by Diego Rivera as historically groundbreaking images of women's experiences (Herrera 2002, 158). Carolee Schneemann's performances of the *Interior Scroll* (1975 and 1977) featured the nude artist removing a thirty-six-inch folded scroll from her vagina that she proceeded to read as truth to patriarchal power in the art world of the ways women are "USED and MISUSED," diminished, appropriated, belittled, and minimized through eroticization, advising, "NEVER justify yourself just do what / you feel carry it strongly yourself" (Schneemann 2002, 151–61). Judy Chicago's collaborative and multimedia *The Dinner Party* (1974–79), a monumental installation of a triangular table in the abstract shape of the vagina, held painstakingly crafted individualized ceramic plates, most in flowerlike vaginal shapes, honoring 39 women, and rested on a floor of tiles with the names of 999 historical and mythical women written in gold (Chicago 1979). Such an archaeological project simultaneously countered myths of the lack of great women in the making of world culture, de-eroticized female genitalia imagery, and visually expanded an alternative social imaginary about vaginas beyond that dominated by violent heterosexual pornographic thought. Parallels are drawn between the form of vaginas and deeply crevassed stone walls (*Primordial Goddess*), vegetal, fertile landscapes (*Ishtar*), floral and mandala shapes (*Sophia*), Fleur de Lis heraldry (*Eleanor of Aquitaine*), African Masks (*Sojourner Truth*), and a winged, all-seeing eye in astronomer Caroline Herschel's (1750–1848) tribute, to describe but a few.

If the erect penis is the symbol of male creativity in language and art, theorized by Freud as the ostensible object of female and male child envy, and if semen is the metaphorical ink of the fertile, powerful patriarchal "phallic" social imaginary (Johnston 2013), in the work of these feminist visual think-ers, the vagina is resymbolized to signify every form of creativity, innova-tion, and human contribution. From Kahlo's painted vagina, in *My Birth* (1932), issues self, artist, art. From Schneemann, interiority, symboli-cally accessed through and connected to her vagina, come knowledge and critique about art and relations under patriarchy. From Chicago's collaborative team, we witness a historical record of women's accomplish-ments across time and cultures and all branches of human activity, sym-bolized through the most shrouded of women's body parts, the vagina, a metonymic reference not only to women but to their shrouding as such within patriarchal cultures.

Sandra Cisneros's fifty-eight-verse "excellently / female" poem "Down There" flowed in response to John Updike's poem published in *Playboy* about sex with a menstruating woman, as she informs the reader in a note at the end of the poem (*Loose Woman* 1994). Cisneros was not impressed by Updike's poem and rendered his brag adolescent. She broke ground describ-ing the smell, texture, and color of menstrual blood through a woman's cycle with evident glee, from early-day watery wisps to the thickening and darken-ing of gelatinous discharges and the rich, dense smell of the female body's period ("Think / Persian rug. / But thicker. Think / cello. / But richer"). It was a virtuoso poetic performance about "Men-struation," claimed as a monthly art form, the "inkwell" from which she would do something really new: own pleasure in her menses against its view as nasty and dirty.

Unfortunately, the late 1980s and early 1990s saw a backlash against femi-nist and queer freedom and equity struggles, as it did against those of people of color (e.g., anti–affirmative action policies and anti-multicultural "culture wars"), that the late 1960s through the 1970s had advanced. In the arts, cen-sure against women's and queer control of their own bodies and sexuality took the form of the fight against immorality and indecency in feminist art by the Religious Right and neoconservative government in the United States. Public legal cases were made, attacking federal grants to institutions show-ing supposedly obscene and immoral artwork (e.g., a Robert Mapplethorpe retrospective and *Immersion [Piss Christ]* by Andres Serrano), and against "the NEA Four," which included feminist performance artists and writers Holly Hughes and Karen Finley. Under pressure from outspoken conserva-tive members of Congress (Jesse Helms, Newt Gingrich), the director of the

National Endowment for the Arts vetoed the grant applications of the four artists selected by their peers on the grounds of "indecency" in 1990.

These highly publicized cases marked the downward spiraling of federal support to individual artists and art institutions, and in public primary and secondary education, where among the first things to be cut were art programs. As to the NEA appropriation, it went from $175,954,680 in 1992 to $97,627,600 in 2000, and in 2018, to $152,849,900.[3] But one important way to understand these repressive measures is as a confirmation of the power of art, and in particular of the importance of feminist, queer, and people of color critique and creativity in the cultural transformation of society. Tellingly, this era of Religious Right politicians' and evangelists' performances of conservative, family-values morality ended in well-documented revelations of infidelities, closeted homosexuality, closeted mixed-race liaisons, and financial abuse.

It is also telling that it was not the truly immoral, sadistic criminality of "snuff" film pornography, in which persons, largely females, are literally killed, or child pornography — both of which are in themselves sexual violence, and contribute to it, against women and children — that were made into public object lessons on morality and decency. As to pornography in general, the *Huffington Post* reported, "Porn Sites Get More Visitors Each Month Than Netflix, Amazon, and Twitter Combined," that is, "30% of all data transferred across the internet."[4] To be sure, images and literature recording sexual erotic pleasure should not be confused with dehumanizing pornography that stages domination over, torture of, and death of females, children, and males humiliated through sexual assault. Sexuality and its pleasures are natural functions of the human body not to be confused with nonconsensual sadistic or patriarchal versions of these.

The present movement of college women and their allies across the country is exposing sexual violence on campus and its hidden management in higher education institutions (Burroughs and Katz 2015). But institutions of higher learning are not alone. Sixty-plus years of feminism and the high numbers of enrolled and graduating female students have not yet changed a culture of male-centered privilege, and the corruption that such power imbalances breed and cover. This struggle against the sexual violence against women that male privilege gives rise to is in reality part of a global movement that includes exposure of sexual abuse of children and women in the

Roman Catholic and other Christian churches, and to the still insufficiently exposed culture of sexual violence and torture in the U.S. military, and the more recent revelations of sexual harassment and violence, including rape in the entertainment industry and in politics.

But sexual violence is not universal, divinely sanctioned, or the product of a healthy human being, in spite of it being widespread in patriarchal cultures. Patriarchal culture is neither natural nor divinely mandated. Like racism and homophobia, it is achieved and maintained through physical violence and its implied threat, and psychological violence. Violence of every sort, including gender, sexual, and racial, appears natural because it has been common for so long in so many places. Unwarranted physical assault and murder are also common in human history but clearly seen as immoral, universally and across time. It is important that we register that the outcome of gender, sexual, and racial violence in their extreme forms are not just avoidable, physical and psychological suffering but murder.

The desacralizing objectification of women's bodies as inferior is an important basis for rationalizing and sanctioning sexual violence against females and queer beings viewed as inappropriately "feminine." This was one way of reading the July 1997 performance in Los Angeles of Patricia Valencia, at the time a member of the Mexican Spitfires feminist art collective. The piece, *The Virgin Vagina*, featured the seemingly unconscious artist on a table, legs splayed, with an image of the Virgen de Guadalupe over her vagina, and a small placard nearby reading "$5 a ~~pop~~ prayer." Alongside the still widespread valorization of female virginity, and the legacy of the economic exchange of virgin brides for power and wealth, Valencia's performance, like Favianna Rodriguez's "Pussy Power Imaginary" project and other Chicana feminist Virgin of Guadalupe–based artwork, asks what constitutes the sacred, which is worthy of respect, care, protection? Valencia's performance also implicates hidden cultures of prostitution and rape within ostensibly Christian mainstream cultures.

Eve Ensler's *The Vagina Monologues*, first performed in 1996 and still performed on college campuses today with scripts and performances by local women, has brought broader public attention to how women feel about their vaginas, including the negative views they have internalized and, in some cases, the achievement of healing new views of their bodies. I attended an early performance in Berkeley and most remember a piece called "The Flood," the story of an older woman remembering how a man who sexually excited her in her youth shamed her because she got wet when he unexpectedly kissed her in his car. She got wet and it clearly disgusted him and he drove her home. After that, she tells the audience, she was afraid to even come close to sexual satisfaction. If she were a house, she mused, her vagina would be the damp, dark cellar. The monologue ends with the elderly woman admitting she has never talked about it before and that she finds she now feels better about it.[5]

In cultures centered around male supremacy, being born female has been a shame, that is, a pity, precisely because shameful. Why shameful? The logic seems to be that to not be the top dog, the bully, the shamer, is shameful because one can then be shamed. It follows that pride due to violence-based might is associated with male difference, as symbolized by male genitalia, and that shame is associated with women, symbolized by female genitalia. Thus, to not satisfy the modern-day mythologies of hypermasculinity is to be a "pussy." In a misguided attempt to equalize the playing board that leaves untouched the equation of females with lameness, some young women today still call each other out as "pussies," "cunts," or "bitches." Rodriguez's reclamation of the word in her "Pussy Power Imaginary" project, however, follows the movement to resignify "cunt" positively as recorded in such publications as Inga Muscio's *Cunt: A Declaration of Independence* (1998).

Bringing pejorative gendered views into the public is an important antidote to the silencing, hiding, and shaming prescribed as the proper social and psychological space of women, the queer, the poor, people of color, the differently abled, the non-Christian, and so on. It is no mistake that being shameless, a moralizing judgment, hinges on public performance of atypical, nonconforming gender and sexual identifications. It is interesting that disclosure of the private in the form of public autobiographical work is considered naïve or unsophisticated because it is taken as inappropriately personal rather than socially relevant, and it is assumed to be unreflected expression rather than the product of self-reflection, research, and creativity. However, the autobiographical, performed publicly in whatever medium (literature, visual art, or performance art), is paradoxically the moment of exposing the social and cultural nature of being and experience, and implicitly breaks with personalizing phenomena such as sexual violence as "one's own fault," due to one's own character flaws or random bad luck. The autobiographical mode in art allows for a distancing reflection about the constitution of feelings of inadequacy, shame, and self-loathing as the result of specific and intersecting personal and culturally specific histories.

Women shamed into talking about vaginas in whispers between themselves, if at all, unfortunately enables the cultural hiding of sexual violence against women, children, and the queer. How personal, private, and secret should it be that one out of six women will experience attempted or completed rape in their lifetimes and every 98 seconds someone is sexually assaulted? The RAINN website states that 82 percent of all juvenile victims and 90 percent of adult rape victims are female; ages 12–34 are the highest-risk years for rape and sexual assault; seven out of ten rapes are committed by someone known to the assaulted (59 percent acquaintances, 34 percent family members, 7 percent strangers), except for Native Americans, who are 50 percent more likely than other "racial" groups to experience sexual assault (41 percent by strangers, 34 percent by acquaintances, 25 percent by intimate or family members). Against the stereotypes of racist racial profiling, 57 percent of rapists are white, 27 percent black, 8 percent unknown, 6 percent other, 1 percent mixed, and although 310 of 1,000 sexual assaults will be reported, 994 out of 1,000 rapists will never spend a day in jail.[6] "Transgender, genderqueer, and nonconforming" (TGQN) youth are at highest risk of assault among students (18 to 21 percent of non-TGQN female and 4 percent of non-TGQN males). Furthermore, sexual assault is also high in prisons and jails, where 60 percent of all sexual violence is committed by staff. It is important to acknowledge that even though some believe we have full equality of women in the United States, it clearly is neither postfeminist — that is, beyond the need for feminist struggle for institutionalized equity in all spheres between men and women — nor a gentler, safer patriarchy than those of other countries frequently held up in comparison in the Middle East or Latin America. Taking into account that many rapes are not officially reported, as of 2017 the United States ranked third highest in the world in the number of rapes, after South Africa and Sweden, and ahead of England and Wales, India, New Zealand, Canada, Australia, Zimbabwe, Denmark, and Finland.[7] The economically "developed" world is in fact far from being developed as a democracy — if by this we mean structurally, legally, economically, socially, and culturally equitable for all human beings, including the half that identify as women.

The public rise of the transgender movement has helped stimulate useful discussion of the psychological and physical violence and intimidation that transgender people experience and what constitutes being itself, as a "woman" or a "man." The former point was particularly made in season 3, episode 12 (June 11, 2015) of *Orange Is the New Black*, a Netflix series that premiered in 2013. The transgender character Sonia (played by transgender actress and activist Laverne Cox) is beaten by female inmates, with her attackers asking if she has a vagina and wondering whether she has a right to claim a female identity and placement in a women's prison. Identity based on feeling and conviction rather than on genitalia arose in a nationally televised interview on April 24, 2015, in which Caitlin (previously Bruce) Jenner discussed her lifelong identification as a transgender female. Diane Sawyer's questions led up to "the big question": Will you have an operation? In other words, will you have your penis and testicles removed and a vagina surgically constructed? Jenner said she did not know yet and made clear that for her, this was not the crux of the matter. She was excited to be able to finally and first of all live openly as a woman, something that clearly did not depend on having a vagina. An Olympic Men's Decathlon gold medalist in 1976, Jenner hoped her going public with her identity would create greater understanding and acceptance of transgender people.[8]

From Native American studies of the continent, north and south, particularly that recording precontact culture and that of the colonial eras, we have learned that gender was constituted within a complex spectrum of possibilities rather than a male-female binary. There is evidence of many Native American peoples having what we might think of as "third" or multiple genders (*berdache*) and not simply the male and female social identities that Western cultures that colonized the Americas soon imposed (e.g., Roscoe 2000). Today, the legacy of the Christian patriarchal homophobic cultures that colonized the continent from the late fifteenth through the eighteenth centuries continues to dominate. Females, femme males, transgender, and other nonbinary queer people who cannot or refuse to pass as identifiably male or female according to heterosexual perspectives are still castigated. Butchy queer females, femme male gays, and transgender people, alongside straight females and children, suffer psychological and physical abuse, terror, and murder.

It is, therefore, in cultures where women, the female-like, or the "feminine" are viewed as inferior, exploitable, and expendable that "Pussy Power Imaginary"–themed work matters. The two-year imprisonment in 2012 of two members of Russia's punk activist musicians and performance artists Pussy Riot, for protesting the patriarchal "marriage" of the Russian Orthodox Church and the unpopular yet reelected President Vladimir Putin, made this point across the globe. The documentary film *Pussy Riot: A Punk Prayer* (2014) included footage where Putin and Russian Orthodox self-appointed religious activists refer to the obscenity of the performance art group's name.

Contrary to myths of the caring, benevolent patriarch or head of the family, church, and nation, patriarchal inequity is not a voluntary agreement for the greater good of all. It is an unequal order based on construction of gender as unequal, an order that is forced on females, "feminine" men, and transgender people. That force continues to be used, hidden, and abetted by patriarchal religions of every stripe claiming God is male, presumably cis-heterosexual, and wants women to be subservient to men in family and social life. The Roman Catholic Church attempts to finesse an ostensibly "theological" but clearly biased argument that while we are all equal in God's eyes, Jesus himself indicated the propriety of a male-led social order by choosing male apostles, male evangelists, and a male head of his future church. Feminists in religious studies have little difficulty seeing the unspiritual and instead sinful intellectual and theological tautology of such arguments (e.g., Isasi-Díaz 1996, Althaus-Reid 2003, Medina 2005). That sexual violence is hidden, aided, and abetted by patriarchal religion has been made plain by the global movement of survivors of clerical sexual abuse that continues to expose predator priests and the Christian churches that have enabled and shielded them through morally blind patriarchal bias. The least we can observe is that the hierarchies that privilege men as a matter of orthodoxy or unquestioned tradition promote the undemocratic, injustice, excess, and violence; in short, the conditions "democratic" institutions claim to wish to overcome.

In November 2014 former U.S. president Jimmy Carter delivered a keynote lecture at the American Academy of Religion in which he recounted his personal journey in recognizing racism and its injustice. He described how much longer it took him to see and understand that sexism is also a human injustice around the globe. He pointed out that two places where rape is widespread in the United States are college campuses and the military, and he pledged that he would dedicate himself during the remainder of his life to fighting against this form of human inequality.

As with all stereotypes and myths passed down to us based on error or insufficient knowledge and lack of wisdom, the remedy is knowledge and, through it, the transformation of our views and actions. Straight men have been bullied and even terrorized out of behaviors not considered "manly" enough: that is, being dominating, aggressive, and competitive. Psychologically, patriarchy is not the healthiest culture for heterosexual men either, as Jungian analytic psychology long ago exposed in its development of the concept of the integrated psyche as one balancing so-called feminine and masculine, "anima" and "animus" energies, as discussed in chapter 1.

At the end of his life, my father had journeyed from probably the kindest form of patriarchal upbringing to a transformational deep understanding of the inequities his wife, daughters, and other women experience. His love, support, and respect, based on his intellectual and spiritual willingness to learn, grow, arrive at truth, and be just, make me grateful to have been my father's daughter. Together we were able to become nobody's stereotype.

7

THE POETRY OF EMBODIMENT

Series and Variation in Linda Arreola's Vaguely Chicana

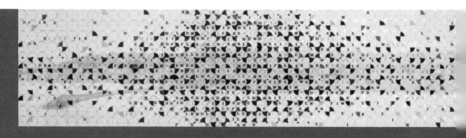

FIGURE 7.1   Linda Arreola, *Wildfire* (2007).

AT THE HIDDEN HEART of what the European West has claimed as its intellectual core lies the classical Greek world of Pythagoras, the mystic and artist who inspired and informed the work of later figures such as Plato. Pythagoras taught of the harmony of the spheres and developed systems of harmony in music and drawing as a reflection of the natural world and the principle of sacred geometry: God's or the gods' signature through the formal beauty and hidden codes, decipherable numerically, in the natural world.

When I look at Linda Arreola's work, particularly the collection presented in *Vaguely Chicana*, I am reminded also of the cross-cultural principle of harmonious balance of differences, derived from the observation of nature, and the gentle tension between core patterns and variations within these. A lush landscape in spring, variations of green, speckled with the yellow of new daffodils, the blues of irises, red tulips, of random variation held, as it were, within the bosom of a green (or brown or yellow) hillside — this is what Linda's work brings to mind: a capturing of essential unity and, in the stillness of closer observation, noticeable individuation.

In this, Linda's work is like that of Joan Miró and of the Russian constructivist Lazar Markovich Lissitzky (El Lissitzky). Form serves to anchor poetry: disciplined, repetitive geometric shape, pattern, and color series alongside the random splash of color, a sudden reversal of color and shape distribution, letters floating in all directions, and organic waves and globular figures cutting across the rest.

Linda's work reveals beauty in the constancy and essence of geometric form, the stencil, and minimal color palettes, yet crucially allows for the witness of the human trace, the signature of the unique, the unrepeatable, the unexpected.

The poetic in itself is sign of the enigmatic, of the unsayable: the cipher and the undecipherable. For me the power and beauty of Linda's work rests in this liminal sensibility. And in so many of her pieces I find an irrepressible joy and energy, an affirmation of the constancy of change, inserted in what could be dry, cerebral exercises. Some minimalist sculpture, for all its stark beauty, for example, speaks anorexically of a binary, dogmatic aesthetic of skeletal purity. But beauty and purity are also lush, baroque, unmappable.

Poetry does not serve form. It is form that serves, that follows, the intuition of the poetic. Linda's work in *Vaguely Chicana* embodies a pleasure in structure, in the materiality of the embodied, and in its knowability, but it also witnesses that which is glimpsed beyond, between, alongside that which has a name, a figure. Her work captures the unexpected hybrid, the sudden birth of new forms, evoking in this way the birth of all form. Constancy, repetition, identity giving way in a sudden emergence to difference, variation, serendipity.

Linda's work opens before me like a landscape, like the spirit of a historical epoch, like a ten-year cycle of past life, only now beginning to take shape, to become meaningful, coherent. I cannot perceive it all. I see some of it only at a distance as the dance of color and shape that reminds me of a swarm of bees (figure 7.1), the organic dance of two strands of DNA, a core of microparticles dancing in space (figure 7.2).

Part and parcel of these forms is their porosity, their commingling, their promiscuous transgression of borders, their essential hybridity. Poetry obeys natural, not social, laws. Miró, Wassily Kandinsky, El Lissitzky, Robert Motherwell — these are names that come to mind when I think of the primeval joy of the visual, the birth of color, the birth of form, birth itself, spoken of through the sculptural in paint. Geometry and poetry, the grid and serendipity. This is the stuff of which the living and its poetry are made. *Vaguely Chicana* registers the search for meaning, the capturing of that meaning as "flower and song," *in ixtli, in cuicatl*, that is, as the poetic, as the Mesoamerican

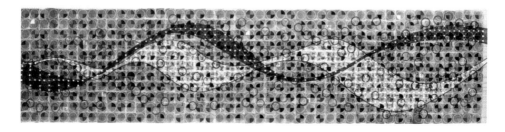

FIGURE 7.2 Linda Arreola, *Double Helix* (2007).

king, philosopher, and poet Nezahualcoyotl mused in the fifteenth century, shortly before the colonial invasions of the continent. How can a marker of cultural-ethnic and gender forms such as the word *Chicana* or Irish, Polish, or English woman be anything other than vague, even while it is also quite historically and culturally specific? The natural world shows us both essential identities through repetitious forms and variations within these. Difference and identity simultaneously, playfully, mysteriously.

55

8

ART AND MUSEUMS

FIGURE 8.1 Emma Amos, *Tightrope* (1994). © Emma Amos. Licensed by VAGA, New York, NY.

WHAT COUNTS AS ART? Who gets to decide? What do museums do with art? How do we define and value it? What are museums anyway? What functions do museums serve? How do art pieces get into museums? Who runs museums? How are exhibitions put together to create a show? Why does art matter? How do different artists try to make art matter?

Is there a universal way to understand art? That is, does everyone in the world, across time and cultural differences, understand what we call "art" and "artist" in the same way? Is art a decoration, a valuable investment, a mirror of the times we live in? Can it take political stands, that is, can it be overtly political and still be art? These are questions that have been asked by count-less scholars and writers. Can we have any impact on what gets to count as art, what appears in a museum, the function that both art and museums play in society, the social role of the artist and artwork? Who cares? Why should we care?

I have been asked, by people who have little to do with art, why museums are sometimes so boring, and why being in museums can feel like being in a temple or a library, or even a crypt. And I have asked myself, why is some art not straightforward enough for people to just get? Why is it that going to certain museums sometimes feels like getting into an insider's club, where the clothing we are wearing, the money in our wallets, even the color of our skin and our ethnic characteristics make of us objects on display too?

These are the kinds of questions that I think about when I think about museums and the art and people in them, and as I reflect on my own experi-ences navigating museums, and when I teach and write about art, museums, and the role they play in our culture today and have played in the Westernized world since their establishment and development.

Museums are environments that aim to work on us, and artworks are ob-jects that engage and can transform us. The more aware we are about their history, and the more information we have about both museums and the kind of art within them, the more we exercise our own critical capacities to decide whether we wish to be shaped by them or the degree to which we do, or whether we want to set about reshaping the beliefs and values from which they take form.

Throughout daily life in our culture, we hear the word *art* used in a way that assumes that it means the same thing to everyone. Even art historians have assumed, for example, that this category of human activity called "art" in English and in other European languages essentially means the same thing to people of different cultures, on different continents, and even separated by thousands of years: "the art of Greece two thousand years ago," for example, or "the art of Native Americans before Columbus." But this is a mistake. While it is true that we as human beings do seem to share core activities across cultures and times, such as the creation of grief rituals, the making of objects that we would categorize as art is tricky even for a person within the multiple cultures that constitute a single society and nation. What different cultures consider significant, interesting, necessary, of value, or properly made differs according to the purpose and standards of the culture in question.

Even within one culture, such as the French or the Mexican, what we may consider art today we might not have six hundred or even two hundred years ago. In the Middle Ages and the Renaissance, more than five hundred years ago, tapestries or weavings hung on walls were considered high art. If you look at the famous *Unicorn Tapestries*, a series made in 1495–1505, you see why and realize how determining whether something is "high art" based on either its medium or whether its heyday was centuries ago is spurious.

Today, even the finest weavings are more often than not considered craft, not "fine" art. Yet artists like Jean Pierre Larochette and Yael Lurie and Consuelo Jimenez Underwood work beautifully, powerfully, relevantly, beyond such simplistic art versus craft binaries and ideas of "progress" in artmaking that suggest that it is no longer interesting or modern enough if the media has been used before, or used in a similar way in previous epochs.[1]

When a person outside a culture or outside the time period when an object was made looks at it and determines that it is or is not art or that it is or is not "good" art, it is a lot like declaring that a word in a foreign language means something it really does not, because you do not know the language well enough, although you think you do. Judgments based on insufficient knowledge are a form of misrecognition, a miss rather than a hit in terms of cognition, the ability to arrive at proper meaning.

During the first four decades of the twentieth century, from about 1907 through the early 1940s, in Paris, London, Buenos Aires, Mexico City, Granada and León in Nicaragua, Chile, Cuba, and Puerto Rico, as in New York and Los Angeles, artists radically asked themselves, "What is art?" "What gets to count as art?" In a well-known image, Marcel Duchamp, for example, visually posed the question "Is any object signed by an artist and put on display, a toilet, for example, 'art'?" A urinal signed R. Mutt (1917), for example?

The Cubists, active from about 1907 through the early 1920s, had already made the point in their paintings and sculptures that making these forms as lifelike as possible was not all that art could or even ought to do. The work of Cubist artists was literally about perspective, or how we see things. This question was not idle or abstract. It arose out of the time they lived in and its challenges. These artists, part of the generations that constitute what art historians call modern art and, more specifically, the historical avant-garde, lived the four decades before, during, and after World Wars I (1914–18) and II (1939–45). As a generation, they survived these wars and their aftermath, in some cases in their own countries, as soldiers or nurses, as citizens, exiles, or refugees. Pablo Picasso's *Guernica* (1937) is one very well-known response to the bombing of a Spanish village during this era. The art movement known as Cubism explored the difference that different perspectives made, how sometimes what we look at is not really the whole, but one piece over the others, or that our looking is a composite of the different angles from which we might look at something or someone. Two early Cubist images that can be found on the internet that make this point are Pablo Picasso's *House with Trees* (1907) and Diego Rivera's *Portrait of Ilya Ehrenberg* (1915).

During the 1910s and 1920s, the Dadaists (1916–23) and the Surrealists (1924–early 1940s) continued to explore what the possibilities of art were to intervene in their world. The Dadaists tried to strip language down to its basic syllables, as it were, to purify, to show the difference between what could be said and what actually was. Their interest in what was "really" behind the appearance of reality led them to a destructive aesthetics regarding art but also regarding social conventions, more generally. Dadaists sought to defy expectations and interrupt the fashion among the monied classes to appear culturally savvy and liberal. They staged performances that turned into mayhem and intentionally insulted bourgeois audience members (Goldberg 2011; Short 1980, 17). Unable to make heads or tails of the performances and art pieces of the Dadaists, enraged patrons and art critics wondered if it was art, a mockery of it, a fraud, or just plain garbage. Dada was definitely a mockery, but it mocked itself as art, and art history too.

Artists of the Surrealist movement, or admired by it, were disinterested in finding approval from the art-as-usual crowd, and particularly bourgeois art patrons, and instead sought inspiration in the margins of society, among the derelict, among the criminal, among the insane, in dreams and the irrational, and in the art of the non-Western world. (Examples of such work include Salvador Dalí's *The Persistence of Memory* [1931]; Frida Kahlo's *Self-Portrait on the Border of Mexico and the U.S.* [1932], *My Dress Hangs There* [1933], *What the Water Gave Me* [1938], and *The Two Fridas* [1939]; Leonora Carrington's *Self-Portrait* [1937–38]; Lois Mailou Jones's *Les Fetiches* [1938]; Leonor Fini's *The Ends of the Earth* [1949]; and Remedios Varo's *Exploration of the Sources of the Orinoco River* [1959].)[2]

As feminist scholarship of recent decades has shown, official histories and museum collections and exhibitions disproportionately show the work of men, telling us a story about these art movements that end up being from male, heterosexual perspectives or mainly European and Euro-American viewpoints. But female artists were an integral and important part of these art movements in the history of modern art in Europe, the U.S., and Latin America.[3] Women like Leonora Carrington, Lois Mailou Jones, Remedios Varo, Frida Kahlo, and Leonor Fini investigate what art is, what it might be able to do — that is, what personal and social effects artwork might have — and what it might be capable of illuminating, of allowing us to see better, freshly, or even to envision for the first time.

Living during a strikingly similar period, artists who came of age during the era of the 1960s and 1970s witnessed globally visible struggles against colonization in the 1940s and 1950s, when European and U.S. colonies in Africa, Asia, and the Polynesian and Caribbean islands struggled to regain their nationhood from beneath the yoke of imperial forces.

Gandhi's nonviolent struggle against the British for India's freedom in the 1940s, for example, provided Reverend Howard Thurman and other African

Americans, including the Reverend Martin Luther King Jr., with the means for pursuing a spiritually grounded politics of nonviolent active resistance to social evils following an ethics and logic of love in the face of racist hatred throughout the 1950s and early 1960s (Hogan 2007).[4] Through the example and victories of the nonviolent sectors of the African American civil rights movement, César Chávez developed a nonviolent farmworkers' rights movement that in turn ignited the Chicano civil rights movement (León 2014). The Black Power, Chicano, American Indian, and Asian American movements were as a whole deeply inspired by the anticolonial struggles they witnessed around the globe, as were the feminist movements — especially women of color, who also identified as "U.S. Third World" — and the lesbian and gay movement against discrimination.

Art was central to these movements for greater personal, social, and political freedom. Like the artists of Picasso's and Kahlo's time, the artists of the 1960s and 1970s asked what role art could have in helping to guide or even to resolve inequity, injustice, and other forms of mental and spiritual insensitivity (J. González 2008).[5]

Visuality and perception are the principal tools for languages of visual and performance art. But what we see is also a question of what we are able to see: that is, what we are taught to consider worth seeing, what we learn is socially visible, or not. We are also taught to not really see, to only see peripherally, according to what our times and culture think is worth looking at and considering. Dorothea Lange's famous photograph *Migrant Mother* (1936), for example, brought into focus new subjects to "art," though not to the reality of the moment: the dustbowl migrant mother.

We are taught without words by observing the discomfort, the embarrassment, the disdain, even the anger that results in the purposeful decision to not really look at things and people thought unpleasant, dangerous, unworthy, and unimportant.[6] Modern and more recent contemporary art continues to richly explore what is see-able and the why of it, why we see some things well, while others are more ghostlike, instead haunting us through their twilight social and cultural existence as kind of present, kind of not.[7]

Seeing and visibility are in fact so dependent on the historical moment and on the particular culture or even social segment from which the person doing the seeing comes that what art is, to return to the beginning of this essay, cannot be defined the same way for different people across different time periods.

It is not just that one generation might ask, like the Dadaists, Cubists, and Surrealists, what kind of art to make that is not a repetition of what others in previous generations have already made. It is also that how we answer the question "What is art?" depends on who we ourselves are and how aware we are of others who are not like us, who may have a different understanding of what art is or can do.

The Mexican muralists, for example, active particularly from the mid-1920s through the mid-1950s, and the mural movement of the 1960s and 1970s in the U.S., inspired by the former, saw that it was the upper classes — the social, cultural, and political elites or power wielders — that dominated the discussion, the purchase, and the display of art.

Muralists from the 1920s through the 1970s, even into the present to a notable extent, worked against many in the art establishment who disdained a medium available to the poor, with subject matter concerning the poor, as "bad" art, devoid of "class," "sophistication," refinement, and economic value. Diego Rivera's *Man at the Crossroads* (1932–34), destroyed by order of the unhappy Rockefeller patron at its original Rockefeller Center, New York, location, represents one of many murals that exposed the ideological clash of interests between wealthy benefactors and muralists critical of the class inequities that enriched such "art lovers."

Although highly trained, Mexican and U.S. mural movement artists chose to create art that would not serve as toothless decoration or possessions of the wealthy. The U.S. mural movement especially chose to create art in communities that were poor, racially segregated, and unwelcome in museums and the "nicer" parts of town where those museums were located. The muralists reached out to the poor and the lower middle classes and to people of color by collaboratively creating and leaving art in these communities. They painted on local public walls, featuring local people and issues important to them from their own perspective in murals such as *Wall of Respect* (1969, destroyed 1971), by William Walker and the Organization of Black American Culture (OBAC), and *Latinoamérica* (1974) by the Mujeres Muralistas, painted on a wall of the Mission Model Cities office in the heart of San Francisco's Latina/o neighborhood, and their *Para el Mercado* (1974). The Mujeres Muralistas were Graciela Carrillo, Patricia Rodriguez, Consuelo Mendez, and Irene Pérez, often working with other artists, such as Ester Hernández, Miriam Olivo, and Ruth Rodriguez.[8]

When feminist artists, especially women of color artists from the 1960s to the present, have examined the question "What is art?" they have observed that most art books, classes, and museums showed and based themselves on male-centered art, especially European and Euro-American male art, but as if they represented female points of view too, and the views of non-Europeans,[9] as if the work of male white and otherwise privileged artists should be understood to be universally meaningful. African American artist Emma Amos's works *Tightrope* (1994; figure 8.1) and *Worksuit* (1994) captured this widespread feeling succinctly.[10]

A society's double standards cannot help but to show up in the art it produces and in how artists define what gets to count as art, in terms of the media or materials used — paint, barbed wire, spray can, cloth, recycled objects, for example — or in terms of the subject matter, who and what it pictures, revealing the social and cultural perspectives from which such picturing is made. Is the person pictured shown in a humane, respectful way or as a dehumanized object to be pitied, feared, disdained, or subordinated? We observe the visualized implicit power relations in representations of European or Euro-American men, as well.

And finally, what is the work art "does," even when seemingly romantic and apolitical? For example, a nineteenth-century landscape image of peaceful life on a slavery plantation or Spanish *criollo* hacienda itself produces the myth of one culture's superiority to the subjugated other, shown more as object, like an animal or a tree, a subjugated other in harmony with a social order as natural as nature itself. Or art can do the opposite and show that stereotypes are false representations (Berger 2005; Earle 2007; López 2010). Betye Saar's *The Liberation of Aunt Jemima* (1972), for example, puts a rifle in the hands of a happy "mammy" figure, piercing the myth that some slaves were happy in their subservience (see Farrington 2004).

How we understand what art is ultimately depends on the worldviews of the particular, specific culture within which it is produced. For the indigenous peoples of the Americas, especially before the European invasions and colonization period but still into the present in many communities, the media or materials used, and the purposes and therefore display of what we might call art today, were and are different.[11]

Many Chicana/o and other U.S. Latina/o artists, like African diasporic artists, have mixed two or more different art histories arising from different aesthetic philosophies, those of European-descended peoples and those native to the Americas and/or Africas, or other parts of the world, discovering in the process that things like layout, color choice, media or materials, subject matter, and function or purpose differ. Some contemporary artists claim both traditions, innovating for their and our own time, teaching us a kind of visual and conceptual double-dutch, as in, for example, the work of Santa Barraza mixing indigenous Mesoamerican and European painting conventions.[12] In African diasporic cultures of the United States, artists since the Harlem Renaissance and multinational negritude movements of the 1920s through the 1940s, and then again in the 1960s and 1970s through the present, have studied the different values, techniques, and objectives of different kinds of African cultures.[13]

FIGURE 8.2 Ana Mendieta, *Corazón de roca con sangre* (1975, Iowa, *Silhueta* series). © The Estate of Ana Mendieta Collection, LLC. Courtesy Galerie Lelong, New York, NY.

Ana Mendieta, Cuban American artist of the 1970s and 1980s, explored the significance of *ashé*, of sacred energy in fluids like blood, milk, ocean and sweet water, and the ashé running through all of nature, including the physical human body (figure 8.2).

Mendieta attempted to recapture the basic idea that a sacred life force exists in nature, and that human nature and the natural world are interdependent, as I explore further in chapter 12, "Decolonizing Self-Portraits of Frida Kahlo, Ana Mendieta, and Yreina D. Cervántez."[14] Art participates in this sacredness. These were not ideas that were "in" during her art school days where conceptual art and the nonrepresentational were most influential. Her return to the ancestral as an Afro-diasporic Latina woman in the U.S. went against the grain of what the official and even underground art worlds thought of as cutting edge, yet such work was both new and, most importantly, ideologically and culturally visionary, necessary, and transformative. Mendieta's performances and sculptural "earth-body work," as she called it (Viso 2008, 81), were rarely exhibited in museums and instead carefully documented by her in photographs and film, some of which she exhibited. In her work, nature is the museum.[15]

MUSEUMS

Mendieta's work within nature, including the *Rupestrian Sculptures* she carved onto the Caves of Escaleras de Jaruco, as part of the landscape in Cuba, make obvious the point that museums did not always exist, or did not exist as we now know them. The rise of the public museum during the age of European imperialism and capitalism, and its use in constructing desirable middle-class subjects, has been written about very interestingly (Price [1989] 2001; Bennett 1995, Fernández-Sacco 2002). Geopolitical and class considerations and the racialization of Third World others account for different kinds of museums — fine arts, natural science, folk art, and the historically more recent: women's, African American, Latin American, U.S. Latina/o, Native American, Asian, and Jewish art and culture museums. It matters to think about how museums themselves are the first frame around a piece of art. It matters a great deal to ask why work shown in specialized museums may not be well represented in mainstream and major national museums and why this is so. And it matters to think about how modern-day museums came about as an idea and as a practice.[16]

The modern-day museum with which we are familiar can be traced to several sources, including the private and public display of religious relics to the devout, and the display of unusual, rare, or exotic objects in what were called curiosity cabinets, pieces of furniture or whole rooms, dedicated to storing and displaying objects, including those obtained through travel abroad, commerce and trade, and war. Royalty and other wealthy citizens began to accumulate sizeable collections that were privately and eventually publicly exhibited. In time, it is these private collections that became the cornerstones of our oldest, most influential public museums (Ewen and Ewen 2006).

Ellen Fernández-Sacco (2002) writes of the establishment of Philadelphia's Peale Museum, founded in 1786, which openly displayed scalps and other body parts of Native Americans as part of its natural science collection. Such displays were meant to illustrate the supposed inferiority of Native Americans and African Americans, based on cultural differences in worldviews and everyday habits that Europeans and Euro-Americans did not understand but nonetheless regarded as inferior, thereby rationalizing subjugation, enslavement, and even genocide. These early collections and the creation of the idea of a public museum in the late seventeenth century and throughout the eighteenth century are both thus heavily shaped by the private interests of particular donors and, like art itself, embedded within the beliefs and worldviews of their era.

Elizabeth Ewen and Stuart Ewen's *Typecasting: On the Arts and Sciences of Human Inequality; A History of Dominant Ideas* tells us that Czar Peter the Great of Russia purchased private collections, one of which contained carefully preserved plant and animal specimens, and another that included "lifelike human specimens in glass jars, his pieces culled from the bodies of criminals, vagrants, and stillborn infants" (2006, 37), believing that he could now "comprehend the ordering of nature." Czar Peter's opening to the public of his newly acquired collections was meant therefore to educate fellow Russians and visitors as to the supposed natural order of the world. This representation of the personally, historically, and culturally specific acquired tastes of a collector as if scientific, let alone universal, is one of the fault lines of museums, particularly the oldest in the United States and Europe. Another is through the evolutionary narratives they create by their organization and display of objects, as well as through what their gaps are, what they have refused to collect (Price [1989] 2001; Karp and Lavine 1991; Karp, Kreamer, and Lavine 1992).

During the age of colonization, from the sixteenth through the nineteenth century, private collections that became public grew, featuring as objects of curiosity or of natural science the art and even the bodies of Native, African-descended, and other non-European peoples. Such collections presumed to teach about the order of humanity and of nature, and promoted sexist, racist, and classist ideas of humanity, working hand in hand to illustrate dubious ideas about the superiority of one kind of human being over the other.

Public museums were used to inculcate imperial, Eurocentric histories in the museum visitor by such displays. To go to the museum demonstrated having "culture" or knowing enough to aspire to acquire it, thus improving oneself (Bennett 1995).

Two kinds of public museums arose, and the line between the two is only crossed in terms of what they display in our own time. Fine art museums house what has ended up mainly being artwork of the dominating gender and cultures or so-called races, mainly men of European origin and identified with the upper classes. The last one hundred years, and especially the last fifty, since the civil rights movements for racial, gender, and sexual equality, have challenged and transformed this bias. The other kind of museum, the natural science museum, displays artifacts from the natural world, including body parts of vanquished peoples as, in effect, war trophies (Fernández-Sacco 2002). Like world fairs with living dioramas of indigenous, African, and other peoples, modern-day museums still create living exhibitions where "exotic" or non-European people display the making of "crafts."

The civil rights decades of the 1960s and 1970s ushered in an important new era in the history of museums, revising the collections of the older, famous museums of the United States and the logic by which they collected and created exhibitions, challenging Eurocentrism and outright racism and a historic bias toward upper-class culture and the perspective of heterosexual men. This era also saw the foundation of new museums and community art galleries, and seeded the ones to follow in subsequent decades. As a corrective to the exclusion of the artwork of people of color and women, for example, we now see museums dedicated to the work of African Americans, Mexican Americans, and women.

We also begin to see work like that of Los Angeles Chicano art group Asco, David Hammons, and James Luna, reflecting on who supposedly belongs in the fine art museum versus the natural science museum. Asco's

Spraypaint LACMA (1972), for example, responded to a racist remark by a curator at the Los Angeles County Museum of Art (LACMA) in the 1970s that Chicanos do not make art; they only make graffiti (figure 4.1).[17] James Luna's *Artefact Piece* (1985–87), an installation of his own body, challenges the history of expectation that Native Americans get into museums only dead and stuffed or as living oddities of the human race. An untitled installation by David Hammons features toy elephants made of painted dung in the kind of glass jar and white pedestal used to display precious objects in fine art museums. Guillermo Gómez-Peña's and Coco Fusco's *The Couple in the Cage* (1992–93) involved installation of the artists themselves in Columbus Plaza, Madrid. Billed as "Two Undiscovered Amerindians Visit . . . ," the real discovery was that some Europeans believed "real primitives" were caged before them.[18]

YOU, ME, HISTORY

In the same way that a work of art or a museum represents particular moments of history and culturally specific worldviews and value systems, including what gets to count as art, we, those of us who see and experience visual and performance art (to continue focusing on these two types among other art forms), also experience and interpret from our own individually and culturally unique vantage points. We — whoever we are, in our particular place and time — are also changing and growing, forgetting some things and learning others, so that if we were to see the same work every few years, we might significantly change in our understanding of it.

The unfamiliar in artwork, when this is due to different generational, historical, cultural, gender, or other experiences, is like modern art was initially: unintelligible but in highly useful ways. Such work is also designed to scramble unilateral, falsely universal codes of interpretation. The difficulty of cultural difference is part of the message. It interrupts us in assuming we know, so that we can reexamine what we think we know. In visually and conceptually disrupting our ability to easily make meaning, we expand our capacity to see, to notice, to observe, to suddenly put on the map things that were not visible in the same way before. Such work can also turn the tables and point to the history of art and of museums, as we have seen, as very political, in spite of the constant claim that fine art has nothing to do with the political, that it does not take sides. Such art, like more obviously experimental art, must operate to articulate itself against the normative and the naturalized, which exclude it without, in fact, persuasive grounds. It is by necessity experimental in that it searches out new horizons, new value systems, new ways of seeing reality or of envisioning the future. Like Dada, or like Spanish to a racist's ear, it sounds like gibberish because it makes sense only from another vantage point, another value system.

Initial confusion, or a sense of only partial understanding when confronted by the unusual and the culturally, aesthetically, and politically different in modern and contemporary art, is an honest response. Sitting with a piece, opening our mind and carefully observing, having patience with ourselves and with the artwork is what follows: revisiting in our mind what and how it showed us something. What I most appreciate is artwork that invites me to think and dialogue with it and to grow as a person and as a human being. Ultimately, our engagement with art can help us to know ourselves and each other better.

Major national museums and the art they collect and exhibit today are an important "face" of the city or nation in which they are located and an invaluable visual historical and cultural archive. Locals and visitors flock to museums, large and small, as a way of knowing a place, its people, and their history. As such, museums, especially large ones in major cities, are highly lucrative and have been funded decade after decade by taxpayer dollars and private donations for the public good. Art and the museums, galleries, and other places we display art, including school textbooks, therefore should reflect us all, in terms of who makes it, who it is directed to, and what it is about.

9

THE@-EROTICS IN ALEX DONIS'S

MY CATHEDRAL

FIGURE 9.1   Alex Donis, *Untitled (Jesus and Lord Rama)* (1997).

FROM AUGUST 19 THROUGH SEPTEMBER 27, 1997, Galería de la Raza in San Francisco's historic Mission District neighborhood housed a gallerywide multimedia installation called *My Cathedral*, which included exterior window "light-box" 2' × 3' enamel and resin paintings on Plexiglas and, entering the gallery, a 10' × 20' × 18' horseshoe-shaped "apse" of more images on translucent Plexiglas, a soundtrack of moans, and in a separate alcove, a video by the Los Angeles–based artist Alex Donis. I first learned about the show in a newspaper article noting that the gallery's windows had been broken twice and the light-box artwork displayed in them destroyed.

Other newspaper articles recounted at the time that in the twenty-seven-year history of the Galería, only one other artist's work had touched such a raw nerve—Yolanda López's feminist Virgen de Guadalupe imagery in 1978 and 1981, which had garnered threats to the artist and the gallery, broken windows, and a bomb scare (Cisneros 1997; Laird 1997)—and that it was the Galería's most attended show to date (Carstensen 1997). I mentioned it to a friend, Norma Alarcón, and it turned out that she had been invited to speak at a community meeting that the gallery organized to discuss the show and what seemed to be community vandalism. Some two hundred people showed up,[1] including, I recall, a Latino gay artist who identified himself as such and then chastised Donis for what he phrased as "disrespecting the community" by showing images in the gallery's storefront windows that were offensive to it. The artist peaceably responded by asking who gets to count as the community and noted that homophobic violence against children, such as he had experienced growing up, reflected a notion of community that would benefit from being interrogated.

The artwork in the gallery's windows, smashed after hours twice, consisted of illuminated paintings with text below these, offset against blackened windows, that featured Martin Luther King Jr. and a Klansman, Madonna and Mother Theresa, Jesus and Lord Rama of the Hindu pantheon, Pope John

Paul II and Gandhi, and, finally, according to then-marketing and development director of the gallery, Dino Piacentini, apparently the most incendiary to the vandals (Laird 1997, 5): César Chávez and Che Guevara. Each of these paired iconic figures, garbed in their signature costumes, were shown in erotic embrace, single-pointedly kissing. The last painting, along with *Untitled (Jesus and Lord Rama)* (1997; figure 9.1), were damaged by objects thrown through the windows, evidently aimed directly at them. Both Piacentini and Donis speculated to the press that male resistance to feminized representations of male figures seemed to be the point around which offense was particularly taken. I think that by feminized they referred to both the homoeroticism and more generally, the vulnerability and intimacy of these heroic men being pictured tenderly embracing.

One entered the gallery into a U-shaped 10' × 20' × 18' apse of translucent Plexiglas sheets imprinted with black-and-white drawings of more same-sex pairings of historical adversaries or culturally opposed figures: Queen Elizabeth and an indigenous woman, Mao Tse Tung and the Dalai Lama, Mexican revolutionaries Pancho Villa and Emiliano Zapata, Hitler and an African man, Columbus and an Indigenous man, Mary Magdalen and the Virgen de Guadalupe. Multicolor text on the gallery's exterior walls included lyrics to a famous romantic Mexican bolero, "*bésame, bésame mucho*" (kiss me, kiss me a lot), and pleasurable exclamations ("UUUUUUUY! and !AAAAAAAYY") that were continued visually in ribbons of undulating, multicolored lettering throughout the curved installation (e.g., "UUUYUYUYYOOOMOOOHOMOOOOMOO" or "OOHOO-HAAAAAAAY"). Splashes of color (pale pink, honey, blue, yellow) across the images spoofed the idea of "stained glass" by literalizing it into Plexiglas splashed by love juices, a gently humorous relay of orgasms across time, and political and cultural differences. Like the textual ribbon of lettering that embedded "homo" within its exclamations, a repetitive loop of pleasurable moaning sounds stretched "Ay, sí," oh, yes, into Assisi, and "a sissy."[2]

The artist had been commissioned by the gallery to create an exhibition (Coile 2007), and to its credit, the Galería remained fully behind Donis's proposal in the hope that it would generate productive discussion around ongoing homophobia in the Latina/o community (Laird 1997, 5). In the press, Piacentini identified himself as a Latino gay male and declared that the show's controversy "could be a good thing if it broke down taboos about homosexuality in the Latino community" (Delgado 1997, 3). For his part, Donis, exhibiting the equanimity he had during the community forum, made the intriguing observation that "hatred is a better response than not even noticing" (Delgado 1997, 3).

My Cathedral had a powerful effect on me the moment I entered the transformed gallery space and realized that the artist was suggesting some zone of convergence between the gallery and the church, between art and spirituality, between spirituality and sexuality, and between politics and sexuality, and all the variations arising from further conjugations among these. I decided to write about it and contacted Donis by telephone several months later, then gave a presentation about his show at a conference the following spring. Body and sacredness seemed a particularly important linkage to me, given negative racialization, sexism, and homophobia in the dehumanization of some bodies over others.

"Donis's work," I wrote (Pérez 1998a), "explores the limits of the politics of love and liberation in leftist, nationalist, and religious discourses.... The borders of art and the spiritual [are] blurred in this show, through a common politics of love.... In transgressing the limits of religious and diverse political ideological discourses of liberation, Donis exposes their rather lame and contradictory claims to a politics of love."

"He seems to ask," I continued elsewhere, "what would history and culture have been or be if MLK, Jr. and the Klan, if Kennedy and Castro, if Madonna and Mother Theresa embraced — and erotically so?" In addition, "What effect would a politics of love that could openly express itself as homo- or gynoerotic have on the histories of struggle and violence that define patriarchal and heterosexist cultures? [That is,] [h]istory as a no holds-barred loving encounter?" I further observed, "*My Cathedral* spoke to history and political opposition through an erotic politics rooted in the nonviolence of Gandhi, Martin Luther King, Jr., and the Dalai Lama, the latter of whom was quoted at the entrance of the show in the gallery: 'Anyone who puts all their energy into destroying anger will be happy in his life and in lives to come.'" I concluded my thoughts in that conference paper by observing, "In *My Cathedral* Donis pursues as natural rather than unnatural, the fluidity between spirituality, eros, and politics, and challenges intolerant notions of community, in each of these spheres, to practice what they preach" (Pérez 2008; see figure 9.2).

FIGURE 9.2 Alex Donis, *My Cathedral (Pope John Paul II and Gandhi)* (1997).

One reviewer of Donis's show during the controversy hastily scoffed that his show did little beyond aiming to shock (Milos 1997). It struck me, however, that the reviewer herself refused to succumb to shock of any sort, and did not take religiosity in the Latino community of the Mission District or of the artist in the installation seriously. She regarded same-sex sexuality likewise as resolved or old hat like "Fridamania." This intellectual ennui and boredom, the inability to find anything authentic, serious, or brave in Donis's show, seemed a particularly impoverished reflection on the exhibition.

At a minimum, *My Cathedral* and the controversy and community forums it generated revealed that religions, sexuality, art, and political ideology are a varied landscape in the process of transformation. Donis's show *did* shock to the degree that his representation of religious or spiritual love includes and embodies homoerotic love, short-circuiting the heteronormativization of spirituality, the divine, and the way love itself has been conceptualized.

Further, *My Cathedral* scrambled the colonial legacy of interwoven *casta* (caste, a pre-race social category), "race," sexuality, gender, and religion that upheld a hierarchal social order on the basis of the ostensibly unbridgeable differences of colonizers and colonized. Violence imposed and maintained the racialized heteronormative patriarchal, colonial culture by physical punishments and death.[3] Racialized heteronormative patriarchal violence continues to be enacted through disproportionate violence against and the murder of queer people. This violence is also psychological, leading to high suicide rates by youth made to feel like deviants, misfits, and evil.[4] Social violence is widespread in discrimination and belittling stereotypes.

Donis's artwork reminds us that artificially imposed divisions on naturally fluid states of being and relationship do not permanently succeed, as eighteenth-century casta paintings show, tracking and naming people of different global ancestry collectively constructing the colonial social body of New Spain. Indigenous, European, and African people and their descendants mixed intimately in spite of social prohibitions aimed at racial separatism (Katzew 2005).

The hybrid crossings, especially religious, in Donis's show foreground gender, sexual, and cultural meetings. Personified as Jesus and Rama, Christianity and Hinduism on the one hand and two men on the other are shown in intimate, loving contact. Eros, both emotional and sexual, is the underlying zone.

The sacred itself in Donis's *My Cathedral* is hybrid: crossing religious leaders, popular cultural icons, and social justice heroes. The good and even the bad meet and mingle in a third space, as Anzaldúa (1987, 37, 46, 78–79) called for, which goes beyond reactions against violence and oppression that remain within dominant culture's dehumanizing logic.

Donis's images suggest that his cathedral is love itself, that which escapes and confounds and contradicts and leads by the nose religious and ideological dogma. Love itself is the radical signifier, the energy of constant slippage and loopholes, the fund of that which can never be colonized, and from which we resist neocolonization and oppression of human device in contrast to the fluidity, variety, and constant hybridity and movement of nature and therefore of our human nature as well. Love's realm of performance, the erotic, is a practice, not merely an idea, nor an ideal or a guiding principle, but rather an energy, a politics, present in its various forms of enactment, whether intention and thought, feeling, touch, or other act forms.

My Cathedral performs not only as an *eros ideology* (as I have discussed in chapters 1 and 2) that challenges self-designated revolutionary, radical, and democratic ideologies to envision the dismantling of racism and the hatred that breeds it by embracing interracial love, homoeroticism, and love across the wounds of racism such that, following Gandhi, we refuse to "dehumanize the dehumanizer."

Donis's culturally hybrid spirituality and gender hybrid sexuality also manifest in themselves an eros ideology, that is, a politics of love tested at its present-day limits. Together, the erotic spiritual politics of *My Cathedral* are, in effect, salves to heal the wounds of mutually exclusive binary oppositions: whether it is cross-racial hostility, male versus female dislike, straight versus queer distrust, one form of queerness versus another, or, as Anzaldúa (1987, 48) put it, whatever part of ourselves is policing another part of ourselves.

From this perspective, Donis's installation is both a barometer of the visionary within our time and place and an inquiry into the limits of love; the meaning of sanctity; the role of the material, via the body and sexual expression, in the spiritual. And finally it is an inquiry into the degree to which all these categories are identified, are somehow connected to each other and through each other. What this bold, brave, and insightful body of work by Alex Donis envisions is community as communion among its varied, nonidentical elements in pairings predicated on a remainder that cannot be erased, for it is our common essence: the erotic, which perforce is the sacred.[5]

CON O SIN PERMISO
(WITH OR WITHOUT PERMISSION)

Chicana Badgirls: Las hociconas

FIGURE 10.1   Maya Gonzalez, *Self-Portrait Speaking Fire and Flowers* (2008).

CHICANA BADGIRLS, *hociconas*, big mouths, loud mouths, women who talk back — they are the ones who will not stay quiet, who will not make nice, will not pretend everything is okay when it is not. Badgirl hociconas do not behave in a world of double standards, whether these be men over women, heterosexuals over queer folk, haves over have-nots, "white" people over those "of color," and so on. They should not.

Chicana Badgirls: Las hociconas was a jubilant show. It was a celebration of the courage and vision of Chicana and other Latina women artists attending to their bodies, their spirits, and their minds to discern truths when everyone else lays claim to defining them, when the difference between right and wrong, truth and falsehood, selfishness and selflessness are not only blurred but upside down.

This was a show of solidarity between California-based artists and local New Mexico– and Texas-based *artistas*, between exhibition newcomers, midcareer artists, and those whose work sits in important collections and has earned them prestigious awards, all of them breaking ground in their media or subject matter.

Con o sin permiso, they speak out on behalf of the hidden strengths that have allowed women, and Chicana/Latina women in particular, ways to survive and even thrive against adverse conditions of racist, classist sexism rooted in the historic misogyny that accompanied the European invasion and settling of the Americas.

For if prior to and during colonization European women were hounded as witches if they displayed healing and other skills contrary to Christian patriarchal orders, in the Americas, Native American and African diasporic women were construed as even more frightening and threatening by the male-centered social and religious powers than their Euro-American counterparts were.

Although this was a gathering of Latina women artists, in recognition of the need to continue creating more equity in the art world, where women "of color" still receive marginal attention and support, the exhibition's topic was universal, ancient, perennial. Standing up for the vision of something better in the here and now is what the pursuit of greater democracy on the collective level and spiritual growth on the individual are made of.

History is full of s/heroes labeled as outlaws for challenging unjust law. It is interesting how many are gender-bending figures, individuals loving enough to step beyond socially invented notions of gender into zones of greater complexity, ambiguity, and truth.

The "father" of Greek thought, Pythagoras (sixth century BCE), a spiritual and philosophical luminary, was chased from his monastery-like school and hounded aboard a ship, where he was starved to death by order of his enemies. Hypatia, the Alexandrian mathematician and philosopher, some nine centuries later, was dragged from her chariot to a macabre death at the hands of fanatical Christian monks. Jesus, a Jewish ethnic minority member under Roman rule, had the courage to challenge religious tradition, refusing to discriminate between people of different classes or genders, refusing to bow down to the kingdoms of earth, though it cost him his life. And St. Francis, a one-time party boy, stood up to the ruling Catholic Church hierarchy, steadfastly turning his gaze from material and political power to the mission of serving the poor, the sick, and the despised.

The centuries are lit by such luminaries whose spirits refused to bow down before injustice, and it is to them that we turn for inspiration.

From the Maya we receive the principle of *In Lak'ech*: *tú eres mi otro yo*, you are my other me. Not only are we interwoven; we *are* one. I *am* you and you *are* me. To harm another is thus to literally harm one's own being. This is a basic spiritual law in numerous traditions.

For the purposes of this show, it meant that there is a Chicana badgirl in every one of us, speaking truths, visions, hopes, and criticisms necessary to greater individual integrity and to the acceptance of seemingly irreconcilable differences within our own selves and thereby our families, our communities.

The work in this show, through various media, offered individual and collective food for thought regarding inherited legacies that dehumanize women, and in so doing also dehumanize men. But it also offered up ways to unthink and rethink braver, more truthful, and more deeply human understandings of being and existence.

The eighteen artists of this exhibition offered visions of a humanity healing in a balance of so-called female and male energies. They illuminated the

FIGURE 10.2 Diane Gamboa, *Supreme Spirit* (2006, *Alien Invasion: Queen-dom Come* series, 2006–12).

links between eros as spiritual love and eros as sexual or physically embodied spirituality. They raised questions about when women's bodies get to count as holy and who gets to interpret and define female sacredness, asking why not women-loving-women? They showed the tension between inner and past gendered violence and present struggle to maintain spiritual and psychological balance. They shared with us their excavations into pre-Columbian, non-Christian notions of deity, where the Creator and gods are also imagined as female, indeed as twinned male-female energies (see figure 10.2).

They exposed the myth of female inferiority for what it is in figures like the polymath Sor Juana Inés de la Cruz (1648–95) of colonial New Spain. They held up like a mirror the religious and cultural archetypes we have received such as women as bearers of evil (Lilith, Eve, La Llorona / the Wailing Woman, witches), as if we were "aliens" to humanity. They suggested that we draw the links between the women we know and these ingrained specters of a human imagination that is ultimately self-loathing.

This loathing of the female body is made abundantly clear in crimes against women, from rape in the home to the war camps, from the Inquisition's so-called witch burnings of *curandera* or healing women, to the ongoing Juárez murders of young Mexican women today.

The cultural fear attached to figures we symbolize as female was the subject of some of the work in the show, as is the transformation of that fear into a fountain of speech and other energetic action (figure 10.1). In some of the artworks, this energy is a cry against war and for deeper spirituality. In other pieces, it was a cry in favor of the poor, the undocumented, the historically wounded and exploited. The self-loved and thereby loving body of women, of a "feminine" sensibility, of that considered specifically the territory of females, even if socially constructed — these are topics that recurred in the various pieces of the show.

Who gets to count, the artists seemed to ask? We all do. And that is a we that strives for personal integrity of a body no longer demonized for being female and fleshy, a body no longer castigated as witchy because intuitive and blessed with piercing visions, a body no longer loathed because it is darker or non-European looking, or not male, or not straight. And the show seemed to say that the inner, deeply personal level is a prerequisite for the search for justice on any score in the outer world, for we are, indeed, each other.

11

MAESTRAPEACE

Picturing the Power of Women's Histories of Creativity

FIGURE 11.1 Juana Alicia, Miranda Bergman, Edythe Boone, Susan Kelk Cervantes, Meera Desai, Yvonne Littleton, and Irene Pérez, *Maestrapeace* façade (1994).

MAESTRAPEACE IS A MONUMENTAL MURAL, five stories at its highest, covering two walls of the Women's Building, in San Francisco's vibrant, historically Latina/o and artist's Mission District neighborhood.[1] Designed and painted by a seven-woman multicultural, multisexual collective, and completed in 1994, *Maestrapeace* was commissioned by the community service organization housed within the building that has served women and children for more than twenty-five years. Created in a collective, multiple-stage process involving the local community, the Women's Building staff, and the artists, its painting permanently celebrates this feminist landmark and the power of female creativity across cultures and time.[2]

The mural process was a testament to community involvement and artistic collaboration. In 1992 the Women's Building administration formed a committee to plan a mural project. Funding strategies were implemented and questionnaires on possible themes were distributed to eight thousand building visitors, neighbors, and community organizations. The results from this survey were compiled. About a year later, enough funds were in place to begin. Fund-raising was ongoing throughout the two-and-a-half-year span of the project, including several special events.

A call was put out to artists to apply: "The committee decided that the selected artists should reflect cultural diversity and artistic excellence. Out of the numerous applicants, seven women were selected. . . . The muralists . . . collectively possess over a hundred years of mural experience. They play an active and integral part in the Bay Area mural movement. [They reflect] ethnic diversity (two African-Americans, two Latinas, one East Indian, and two Caucasians, one of them Jewish); [and] sexual diversity (lesbian, straight, and bi-sexual), ranging in age from 26 to 56, including two grandmothers" (Soriano and Sánchez 1996, 2–3).

Maestrapeace is not a piece of art meant to court the approval of the art world or other institutional hierarchies. Its concern is not with the views of elitist arbiters of culture, trading on the bankrupt Darwinian idea that only the formally "new," generated in the Eurocentric capitals of the world, represent artistic "progress." Rather, *Maestrapeace* is a genuinely vibrant and generous visual work that exuberantly proclaims the legacy of women's creativity and the importance of art in the everyday lives of people. A coalitionary art and activist project, *Maestrapeace* is beautiful in its conception, its design, its color palette, and its relationship to the building on which it is painted, harmonious both architecturally and in terms of the building's function as a woman-centered social services resource.[3] In the overall significance of its subject matter and its execution, the two-walled mural is an uplifting gift to the users of the Women's Building and the residents of the community in which it is located.

Like the creators of the prehistoric wall paintings of Altamira (Spain), where mural art is said to have been born, and the ancient murals of Egypt, Phoenicia, pre-Columbian America, Europe of the Renaissance, and 1920s–1950s Mexico, the *Maestrapeace* artists — Juana Alicia, Miranda Bergman, Edythe Boone, Susan Kelk Cervantes, Meera Desai, Yvonne Littleton, and Irene Pérez — capitalize on the sheer power of walls as a medium. A wall's larger-than-human dimensions boldly proclaim artists' perspectives on their subject matter, here appropriately illuminating the enormity of women's contributions the world over to the well-being of humanity, making art relevant to everyday existence and an active interlocutor within the social environment.

In this, muralism is a remarkably generous art medium, subsuming to some degree the individual vision of artists to those of the art collective and the community in mindful negotiations of representations important to the larger whole. The mural is also a courageous medium, in light of the classist and racist snobbery still surrounding those of our own time, since the community-based Chicana/o– and African American–led mural renaissance of the 1960s and 1970s. *Maestrapeace*, like other Mission murals since the civil rights era, consciously and steadfastly resists art's appropriation as bauble of the rich and the powerful.[4] In an uninterrupted history since the 1920s in Mexico, then the United States, and now across the globe, murals, alongside other wall art, such as graffiti and stenciling in urban spaces, render the public environment a museum, and more than this, a forum for the masses. These murals bring art as a medium of thought and debate to the community and incorporate the community's vision and creativity. In the present era of the increased commodification and privatization of art as economic investment, and against the dominant proposition that art does not matter socially beyond decoration and personal taste, *maestra* or masterful murals demonstrate spiritual and intellectual ambition and artistic virtuosity. They communicate necessary truths, uplifting and inspiring us to strive for what is in the interest of the greater good.

The various generations of Mission murals from the 1960s to the present are widely different in terms of the artists' ambitions and skills, the murals' subject matter, and the level of technical and conceptual success of the pieces as works of art. But against the shallow and uninformed generalizations by some that murals are historically naïve or insufficiently tutored, that is, the work of amateurs, is the reality that they continue to be a strikingly effective genre of choice among world artists, who are among the most acutely savvy about visual culture in our image-saturated globe. Given the increasing privatization of art, public space, and even of forums of public inquiry and commentary, murals and other wall art implicitly contest this silencing homogenization of the collective within the public sphere by private corporate interests and their ideological allies. In countless murals today, *Maestrapeace* among these, we see the best of what artists have to offer technically and, as much to the point, ethically, in a medium that has proven itself remarkable in its longevity, its visual and intellectual sophistication, and its politically effective agency.

Moving politically and aesthetically beyond the legacies of the Renaissance, and even the Mexican muralism of the twentieth century, for all of the latter's populist subject matter, *Maestrapeace*'s production, visual language, and subject matter are characterized by a feminist decolonizing ethos that seeks to empower negatively racialized, gendered, and sexed communities. In this, *Maestrapeace* continues the legacy of the first all-woman mural collective, Mujeres Muralistas, a Latina, Mission District neighborhood–based group of the early 1970s that sought to celebrate the life-giving force of Latin American and U.S. Latina women's activities in vibrant, joyous murals throughout San Francisco's Mission District neighborhood. These works baffled Chicano male muralists and critics who could not grasp the political oppositionality and the significance of atypically placing women's everyday labors as nurturing, life-affirming work at the center rather than in the margins of the viewer's and, eventually, the larger collective social consciousness.

Maestrapeace's own Irene Pérez was part of the foundational core of that historic feminist collective, alongside Patricia Rodriguez and Consuelo Mendez, with the collaboration of others such as Ester Hernández.[5]

Each of *Maestrapeace*'s seven collaborating artists contributed formally and conceptually to the design and its execution. Drawing on the thousands of surveys taken by the Women's Building staff, the artists cooperated in combining their individual sketches in a collective vision based on this gathered information. The painting itself was executed with the help of more than one hundred volunteers, without whom the process would have perhaps quadrupled in the time (one year) it took to complete.[6] The result is a powerhouse of ideas, knowledge, and visual fireworks. Against the odds, the massive, two-wall mural is a harmonious, visually complex, rich compendium of women's accomplishments, featuring minute reproductions of unique patterns of weaving, needlework, and painting from traditions across time and countries, many of which are storybooks in their own right about the families and communities among which they were created. Who but a collective could have produced, for example, the list of more than 470 women poets, writers, doctors, scientific researchers, native healers, painters, political leaders, social revolutionaries, community activists, musicians, and intellectuals? The names of these historical, seemingly largely-than-life, female "superheroes" are painstakingly inscribed throughout the mural on images of golden ribbons of fabric that tie together the two walls of the building, and the building itself, symbolically embracing the social service organizations within it that serve women in need and their families.

At the foot of the mural, which is awe-inspiring both as a feat and in its content, viewers are on eye level with children peeking out from among swaths of fabric, as if from the swirling skirts of their elders. Positioned at the four corners of the mural walls are the monumental heads of humanity's symbolic foremothers. Representing the four corners of the globe, the two-story-high Olmec-like heads, drawn as if etched in stone, steadily and respectfully hold each other's gaze. The dimensions, the sculptural-style drafts(wo)manship, and the sensibility conveyed in these profiles evoke the durable presence of the powerful legacies symbolized in the archetypal grandmother: love, wisdom, meaningful knowledge, and responsibility for future generations.

If it is true that our gendering — the ways we have been taught to be female and male, but not transgender — are largely cultural conventions, and that therefore we are hardly explained by stereotypes of so-called femininity and masculinity, then it is also true that within the constraints of millennia of patriarchy in so many cultures of the world, women of unequal social, political, economic, and cultural power have managed to produce and protect not only life but our most noble human sensibilities. Against the cultures of death, war, and the anxiety of greed-driven cultures, the mural celebrates the cultures of life, creativity, and responsibility for others, and accountability to the communities of our present and future. From the ancient forebears to goddesses and historical figures, power is evoked not through violence or the arrogant gestures and expressions of those who consider themselves superior to others but through the serenity imparted by a life of integrity, equanimity, self-discipline, and spiritual nobility. And in this, the representation of women here is significant, as part of the history of feminist revisions of racist and patriarchal views of females as ancillary breeders, sexual playthings, and inconsequential contributors to the history of human achievement.

The history and courage of women's struggles are remembered in the names of women like Joan of Arc, Sojourner Truth, Rosa Luxembourg, Lucy Parsons, Susan B. Anthony, Rosa Parks, and, from our own epoch, Angela Davis and Audre Lorde. This history is also recovered in the form of images such as that of Puerto Rican nationalist Lolita Lebrón, standing before a cell of imprisoned women activists, and in the cultural, social, and political leadership of figures like Niuta Teitelboim, the Warsaw ghetto resistance fighter; Lillian Ngoya, leader in the anti-passbook movement in South Africa; Hanan Ashrawi, the Palestinian diplomat; and Rigoberta Menchú Tum, among many others.[7]

On the Eighteenth Street side, fish-filled waters stream down from a nude, pregnant figure, identified in documents available in the entryway of the building as "the Goddess of Light, Creativity, Rebirth," blending gracefully into the ribbons of patterned, painted, and stitched cloths of African, Asian, Scandinavian, American folk, Native, East Indian, and many other traditions. On Lapidge Street, the intertwined, flowing bolts of fabric originate, or end, depending on where the viewer starts, above the poised brush of a full-sized rendition of Georgia O'Keefe, bringing full circle the celebration of all forms of women's creativity.

The legacy of the life-giving power of women's artistic, intellectual, and social creativity is expressed through huge hands, located midsection on

FIGURE 11.2 *Maestrapeace* (1994, detail).

both sides of the building and at eye level at the corner, over an entryway. Along one wall, the oversized hands of Rigoberta Menchú Tum,[8] the Nobel Peace Prize–winning Guatemalan Indian human rights activist, hold the figures of Yemayá, African diasporic goddess of salt waters, and Coyolxauhqui, the Aztec moon goddess (figure 11.2).

As explained by Chicana artist Juana Alicia, both deities represent resistance to oppression: Yemayá embodies resistance to slavery during the Middle Passage and beyond; and Coyolxauhqui symbolizes defiance to patriarchy and war. Coyolxauhqui's body, traditionally shown dismembered and imprisoned within the moon's disc by her brother Huitzilopochtli, the god of war, is now whole, breaking out of the patriarchal imagination, in a groundbreaking image by Irene Pérez. Rising out of a maguey cactus, symbolic of fertility in Nahua cultures, including that of the Mexicas (Aztec), the warrior daughter emerges, paint brushes in one hand. Like other goddesses and historical women depicted, she is shown as a creative spirit of the mural she illustrates.

On the adjoining wall, the huge heads of Laplander and Asian women elders face each other, one visible hand outstretched toward the other's, each holding the streaming cloths emanating from the goddesses, ancestors, and women's legacies of enriching life. The monumentality of women's contributions to the rich "fabric" of life is made evident in the sheer size of the one- and two-story-sized heads of the four ancient foremothers, of Menchú Tum, and of the animated golden figures of goddesses (Yemayá, Quan Yin, Coyolxauhqui, a dakini), one or more stories high, and of slightly larger-than-life women in the lower half of the mural. The richness of colors and patterns suggests the richness of women's lives and their work as a continuous history of creativity. The mural is truly a *maestra* piece, a masterpiece by accomplished women at the height of their artistic skills working in coalition to center and honor women's contributions throughout the world and across time. Like an intricate weaving or embroidery, the mural is a glorious piece of "handwork," descended from great art traditions as much as from those of more recent vintage, such as canvas painting, that have been unnecessarily supervalorized against the "mere craft" of women's and Native people's artwork. Thus, part of the uplifting effect of the magnificent *Maestrapeace* lies in the full-hearted embrace of the still silenced or belittled histories of women of all ethnicities and their contributions to the arts, as in other realms of social life.

Maestrapeace, furthermore, is visionary in its embrace of the varied spiritualities of San Francisco's multicultural communities, refusing to lionize ethnocentrically one over the other, and interrupting, rather than reinforcing, patriarchal interpretations of them. As powerful deities in their own right, the dakini, Coyolxauhqui, and Yemayá all help to authorize women's empowerment on the earthly plane, balancing a male-centered imagination that colonizes the religious imagination and its practices in order to justify a self-serving, male-gender-biased social rule.

In many ways, the mural is very much a product of San Francisco's Bay Area and, even more specifically, of the historically multicultural, immigrant-influenced, youth-identified, and artist-rich Mission District. It enacts an integration of our different cultures through their respective arts, their religious traditions, and their healing practices, into a global activism for human rights, not just those of women. The community-accountable collective process, the inclusive painting team, and the cross-cultural subject matter focused on women's lives throughout the world — with many of their descendants coinhabiting the Mission District neighborhood — all work toward an equitable plurality rather than an exotification of culturally specific characteristics as exceptional differences to white culture. We are shown that we do indeed come from the same source, all of us: women, a benevolent planet, and the spiritual world beyond the imperialist and elitist hierarchies misogynistic cultures have projected on it.

As a work modeled on the artistry of women everywhere, the Mission District mural offers us an image of our interwoven human origins, and our increasingly re-entwined, joyous, creative future. A paean to the enormity of women's contributions to life, *Maestrapeace* is a public national art monument, on par not only with contemporary pieces like Judy Chicago's *Dinner Party* and the AIDS Memorial Quilt but with the lasting tributes to the human spirit of great achievement everywhere.

12

DECOLONIZING SELF-PORTRAITS
OF FRIDA KAHLO, ANA MENDIETA,
AND YREINA D. CERVÁNTEZ

THE SELF-PORTRAITS OF Frida Kahlo (1907–54), Ana Mendieta (1948–85), and Yreina D. Cervántez (b. 1952) grapple with representing the material absence of the hidden or unseen that makes up our interiority — the self as a spiritual being, the ghostly social figure of the racialized and female(d), and the self as part of nature — a not fully knowable being that exceeds socially constituted versions of self or "identities" yet is simultaneous to these. They worked, and in Cervántez's case work, through this paradox by hybridizing Western and non-Western notions of the self and perspective, and employing visual languages and materials, particularly natural elements, whose meaning is informed by non-Western cultures. All three artists chose self-portraiture — in Mendieta's case through the *silhuetas* (silhouettes) she called self-portraits and "earth-body work" (Viso 2008, 94, 81) — as the terrain upon which to investigate the limits of representation and perspective, reaching beyond what is overdetermined by cultural and historical specificities. While fluent in the dominant Western art histories of their times, but as students of non-Western thought and art, all three work against the grain in examining being in ways that unmoor gendered, racialized, and other dehumanizing identities through recontextualizing the historically, socially, and culturally specific against the natural world of flora and fauna, and the life energies connecting these. In their self-portraits, all three artists center representation of the physical body or its identifiable trace within or surrounded by vegetation or animals, or in the earth, drawing on their study of non-Western art and non-Western philosophies of the energetic (or "spiritual") interdependence of all forms of being. They ultimately represent their self, and self more generally, as nature, that is, as a part of the larger natural world, opening the personal self of self-portraiture to more general reflection on the nature of being as unknowable, as excess with respect to the social, and as literally interdependent to all other life-forms.

In traditional European portraiture and self-portraiture, objects adorning and surrounding the subject typically supply information about the social life and character of the person pictured (Schneider 1994, 6–9, 24–28). In Kahlo's and Cervántez's self-portraits and in Mendieta's *Silhueta* series, when nature is the environment in which they place their images or more abstract references to their bodies, the identity they point to in a sense is elsewhere, even as it unflinchingly records the appearance of the physical self in Kahlo's and Cervántez's paintings, or the outline of Mendieta's body. And while not reserving to women a particular relationship to nature as one that reinforces sexist and racist pseudoscientific assumptions about women as essentially more animal-like, and therefore farther from reason and civilized impulses, Kahlo, Mendieta, and Cervántez embrace self as nature, interrupting binary and human-centric assumptions. Nature functions in their work as a way to un- or redefine self and being. In turn, nature is imbued with intelligence and pictured as animate, while relations between human, plant, animal, earth, and cosmos are rendered porous.

The image of Cervántez's face in *Big Baby Balam* (2017) is covered with hybridized glyphs and genetic codes that signify water and different forms of vegetation, suggesting that we literally are made of the same matter as the rest of nature. Furthermore, in this piece, as in other self-portraits by her, the image of the artist's body is marked by symbols of an animal with which she identifies, thus picturing herself as a were-jaguar. Given that the jaguar is said to be symbolic of the coexistence of spiritual and physical being in Meso-american cultures, the image of a human-jaguar hybrid emphasizes transformation or transformed being, something in-between the human and the jaguar (Miller and Taube 1993; Pérez 2007a, 85; Navarro 2017). In hundreds of earth-body works that Mendieta produced between 1972 and 1985, including the *Silhueta* series (1973–81), the artist covered her body with grass, blood, flowers, feathers, stones, and mud, or sculpted her shape out of sand and earth and filled these forms with natural matter such as fire, water, blood, and flowers. At other times, Mendieta blended her form into the diverse natural landscape she worked in, allowing the works to be recuperated into nature (see figure 8.2 earlier, and here figures 12.1 and 12.4). While Kahlo, from early on, and increasingly in her work, pictured herself framed by plants, animals, and insects, adorned by them, dressed in foliage, and as a hybrid of human and plant and of human and deer (e.g., *Self-Portrait with Thorn Necklace and Hummingbird* [1940; figure 12.2], *Roots* [1943], *The Little Deer* [1946]), by *The Love Embrace of the Universe, the Earth (Mexico), Diego, Me, and Señor*

FIGURE 12.2 Frida Kahlo, *Self-Portrait with Thorn Necklace and Hummingbird* (1940). © 2016 Banco de México Diego Rivera Frida Kahlo Museum Trust, Mexico, D.F. / Artists Rights Society (ARS), New York.

Xolotl (1949), the spiritual interdependence of all life-forms is represented through the anthropomorphization of the planet and the cosmos lovingly embracing vegetal and animal life-forms, including the human.[1]

All three artists have been misread on their use of self-portraiture. One of Mendieta's critics viewed the use of her own body in her art pieces as a period of entrapment in identity politics that she was said to have fortunately grown out of in later work.[2] Meanwhile, an art critic writing of Los Angeles–based Yreina Cervántez's self-portraits suggested her ongoing use of the genre represented some sort of narcissistic rut.[3] And Kahlo's self-portraits have been used to psychoanalyze the artist as narcissistic, with her art, persona, and relationships reduced to signs of pathological fragmentation, neediness, and insecurity, ostensibly crucial keys to interpreting her artwork.[4] Even in more recent publications, her artwork continues to be read as if it is a diary page documenting her emotional life, something the psychiatrist and Kahlo critic Salomon Grimberg openly asserts regarding her self-portraits and still lives (2008b, 22). Kahlo's life is exotified by many as a woman of the exciting 1920s–1940s postrevolutionary Mexico City, yet it is also judged as inauthentic, as employing a personal style in her attire and artwork that aimed to draw others to her to fulfill her neediness, especially Diego Rivera, who is credited with formative, persistent, and extensive influence on her (Herrera 1983; Grimberg 1998). Helga Prigntiz-Poda (2010) even elaborated a Eurocentric and homophobic theory suggesting that Kahlo's sensuality, which she judges as excessive, was inauthentic and, further, was associated with evil and sadism. Kahlo's "primitivist" identification with indigenous culture is also viewed as inauthentic, an appropriation in keeping with the fashionable primitivism of the nation-building era's intelligentsia. Wendy B. Faris, for example, assumes that Kahlo's identification with the indigenous, nature, and psychologically regressive narcissism are givens, but she argues that "the nature and arts of pre-Columbian and indigenous Mexico are important props in that drama of self-fashioning," which along with her beauty "lead her to fetishize her body, painting it repeatedly . . . often making it into a primitivist idol" (2000, 229–30), "a self-constructed and self-worshiping nature goddess in the body and on the canvas" (234). And although she offers many valuable observations regarding Kahlo's "intense personal connection to nature" (225), Faris reads self-portraits where Kahlo is "less contiguously connected to the natural world, as if acknowledging her growth out of the primordially mirrored self" (234). Less identification with the natural world, which Kahlo is read to impose herself on rather than to be subsumed into it, is viewed as sign of psychological health through a Eurocentric lens of binary oppositions between nature and human, the indigenous and the mestiza(o)/European, and the "primitive" and the "civilized" (Faris 2000, 221).

In the work of many prominent art historians and critics, biography and painting in Kahlo are reduced to the struggle to ostensibly cover up her insufficiently mothered (and hence pathologically narcissistic), fragmented, needy being through masking, subterfuge, makeup, dress, and general deception, which she nonetheless is said to have revealed herself, as if slyly, by signing some of her letters as "*la gran ocultadora*," and noting in the diary of the last ten years of her life that "*las apariencias engañan*," appearances deceive, next to a drawing showing her damaged spinal cord and leg beneath long skirts, blouse, and shawl. Apart from it being quite a stretch to suggest that it was deceptive of Kahlo to choose to minimize attention to the life-long pain she endured that was marked by scars, prostheses, and leg brace, a more fruitful route to exploring Kahlo's identification with "*la gran ocultadora*" is likely through Ixmucane, one of the ancient creator "grandmothers" of humanity in the *Popol Vuh* and also known in one of her epithets as "*la Antigua Ocultadora*." Dora Luz Cobián, in *Génesis y evolución de la figura femenina en el Popol Vuh*, writes that "Ixmucane was respected for her wisdom and her experience, knowledge expressed through her magical art, her capacity to transcend her corporality, and her access to knowledge hidden to other gods, and of course, to mortals," and that "her function . . . is to preserve and protect by 'occulting,'" that is, veiling (1999, 37).

Kahlo's self-portraits are understood as impassive, impenetrable masks that hide the artist's lack of a sense of integrated self. Even her arrival at a belief in the interdependence of all life, which she records in her diary, letters, and paintings, is judged as psychologically "compensatory," rather than the result of genuine and hard-won, lifelong intellectual, philosophical, and spiritual study, reflection, and significant integration. The patriarchal bias of psychologizing women artists as narcissistic has been noted by scholars such as Jane Blocker (1999), writing about Mendieta, and feminist psychologist Danielle Knafo, in her study of ten women artists, including Kahlo and Mendieta, in *In Her Own Image: Women's Self-Representation in Twentieth-Century Art* (2009). Knafo's illuminating study concerns itself with what women under patriarchy have been able to achieve through their artwork toward psychological health or integration and, notably, what these artists' investigations offer the patriarchal field of psychology, alongside the work of feminist psychologists. With respect to Kahlo, and to the theme of "*la gran ocultadora*," that is, the ostensible personal deceptiveness that her masklike self-portraits are said to reveal, Knafo instead concludes that Kahlo's masklike self-portraits ultimately represent the achievement of a humanly necessary stoicism in the face of the human condition: "She also demonstrates that it is possible to transcend one's pain by drawing the self-torture out of it and meeting it with forgiveness and healing awareness. She thus turns into that force of nature that goes beyond the human condition; she becomes a goddess archetype — focused, indifferent, looking beyond the personal. She exists outside of her physical pain and outside of her lover's infidelities. Frida's work, in the final analysis, consists of the same 'unemotional' self-portrait: a mask of strength and fortitude, a mirror of survival, and a flamboyant fête of pain and suffering" (2009, 82–83).

Gannit Ankori also criticizes the implicit sexism inherent in largely biographical approaches to Frida Kahlo's artwork. Ankori's careful scholarship, encompassing the study of Kahlo's library, argues that the highly intelligent artist, a lifelong voracious reader, could be characterized as erudite in the breadth and depth of her knowledge. On the basis of her library, her activism, and numerous other sources, Ankori illuminates Kahlo's serious identification with her Jewish ancestry and identifies the influence of Hindu thought in Kahlo's ideas of interdependence (2013, 2002).[5] Ankori also remarks on the insensitivity with which Kahlo's lifelong physical pain has been treated by some critics. Indeed, some critics have gone so far as to suggest that even Kahlo's constant physical pain, illness, and disability were part of her arsenal of deception and manipulation so that others might become attached to her. However, Kahlo's life might as easily be read as so appealing to so many for so long into the present because it is a testament to self-love and self-creation beyond a woman's — and a "Third World" one at that — place on the margins of patriarchal Mexico, the U.S., and Europe. As early as her teen years (1925), Kahlo wrote in defense of herself to her then-boyfriend (Alejandro Gómez-Arias) that she loved herself as she was, in response to his sexist accusations based on gossip that she had become a loose woman (see Kahlo [2003] 2006, letter dated December 19, 1925). Kahlo's niece, Isolda Kahlo, who lived with her mother, Cristina, and her brother in Kahlo's and Rivera's house, attests to her aunt's spirit and courage, her lack of self-pity, and her care for others, as have many others who knew the artist well.[6] Indeed, wounds to the healthy development of self, as Jung believed, were widespread in the modern Western world, as noted in chapter 1, and not characteristic of its women only. It is the lifelong work of healing wounds to a healthy "narcissism" or self-regard that is of vital interest, and that, as Knafo argues, self-representational artwork has allowed powerful female artists.

The significance of Kahlo's genuine and gradual embrace of her indigenous ancestry as a mestiza woman and her coming to respect the predominantly indigenous living culture around her, as well as the pre-Columbian past, is also insufficiently accounted for in its transformative effect on her views of nature, the essential equality of all human beings, and the interdependence of human beings within nature. She was not a cookie-cutter product of the condescending and still Eurocentric views of the Mexican intelligentsia of her day, like that of influential figures such as José Vasconcelos, minister of education from 1921 to 1924, who viewed the indigenous as an inferior "race," or the many others who viewed the living indigenous people of their era as degraded descendants of once great indigenous civilizations (Vasconcelos [1925] 1997). Kahlo's journey of decolonizing transformation of her views of the indigenous from a neocolonizing education to decolonizing respect for the living indigenous people as well as the historical cultural legacy of ancient Mexico is traceable from her teenage apologetic letters requesting visits to her town, though it is full of nothing but Indians, "*indios y [sic] indios*" (Kahlo [2003] 2006), through her adult letters, the diary of her last ten years, her paintings, and her collections of diverse artisanal objects.

Kahlo's postadolescent refusal to Europeanize her appearance and instead to embrace, enhance, and give center stage to her indigenous ancestry was a politically significant and transformative choice of identification and representation in a culture where "having culture" meant people identified culturally and "racially" as mainly or fully European. For the Mexican state and its intelligentsia, building a postrevolutionary nation meant championing an abstract notion of past indigenous greatness (Earle 2007; López 2010; Coffey 2012) while lamenting the ostensibly degraded condition of living indigenous peoples. "Progress" was based on pseudo-scientific racialized models of Eurocentric modernity that by definition were anti-indigenous, and thereby anti-Mexico, whether Mexico was understood as mestiza/o or indigenous. Kahlo's *My Grandparents, My Parents and I* (1936) delineates her ancestry, including the indigenous, explicitly and respectfully through her maternal grandfather. Kahlo's identification with her indigenous ancestry is evident, however, in earlier self-portraits, her written "Portrait of Diego" (Kahlo [2003] 2006, 344–57), her letters (Kahlo [2003] 2006), and her diary (Kahlo 1995). Together they document a decolonizing trajectory of serious identification with her maternally ancestral indigenous culture rather than a fashionable nationalist adoption of the popular, the folkloric, and the indigenous while performing an everyday identification of Eurocentric *mexicanidad.* To reduce the complexities of negotiating hybrid or mestiza/o identities under neocolonial Eurocentric regimes to idealized positions outside of contradiction and refuse to acknowledge the significance of transformation of views through time is to miss how processes of decolonization function and the difficulty of disentangling more liberatory views from those imposed by dominant culture from childhood.

THE INSUFFICIENTLY EXAMINED assumption that representation of a self that is rendered invisible precisely because gendered and racialized through visual cues (skin color, features, attire, ornamentation, etc.) is merely "narcissistic," a psychologically wounded "self-absorption," an artistic and intellectual "dead end" (Grimberg 1998, citing French painter Jacqueline Lamba), or dangerously "essentialist" misses the significance of conscious, politically aesthetic, performative self-representation, spanning decades in the lives of these highly intelligent, original, and independent artists. For negatively racialized artists, particularly for women and the queer, self-portraiture and self-representation hinge on the inescapable quandary of how to represent one's own complex, changing, and socially excessive or transgressive subjectivity and agency — precisely against the history of static, homogenizing, and culturally specific gender and racial stereotypes. Kahlo, Mendieta, and Cervántez were not meant to be visible as artists or, more broadly, subjects with self-determining agency within the patriarchal cultures of their time and ours. Thus, part of the politics — the social significance and effects — of their practice of self-portraiture and use of their own body in their artwork lies in the disregard and potential/actual transformation of the various dominant gazes and the accompanying interpretive discourses that shape these — an ideological transformation of which the artwork is the enzymatic agent in the viewer and the larger culture from which visual and intellectual legibility and legitimacy are drawn. Seemingly only about the self, the self-portrait in the work of such women is intimately about the social production and disruption of selfhood. Nonetheless, as self-portraiture or self-representation announces, the artists speak first but also to themselves as audience, critic, intellectual; beholder as well as beholden; subject as well as object of their own interest, daringly, productively out of step with the dominant culture of their times. The self-portrait allows these women socially disruptive and creative self-authoring. When one is *fuera de serie*, outside the serial, the meaning of self-representation is pointedly, if paradoxically, not the obvious.

ALL THREE ARTISTS were concerned with incorporating non-Western notions of identity and self, informed by non-Western spiritualities, into their work. Mesoamerican indigenous cultures were and remain spiritual cultures, that is, their philosophies of being and therefore of nature, science, and human creation are viewed through understandings of the divine and energetic interdependent nature of all life (Caso 1958; Martínez Parédez 1960, 1973; León-Portilla [1961] 1988, [1963] 1990; Maffie 2014). In "Portrait of Diego Rivera," Kahlo approvingly describes Rivera's solidarity, respect, and love for the indigenous people of Mexico, whom he considered "the living flower of the cultural tradition of Mexico," and his view of pre-Columbian art as "the living heart of true Mexico" (Kahlo [2003] 2006, 351, 356). Based on Kahlo's contemporary, Mexican-born Anita Brenner, a promoter of Mexican popular crafts and pre-Columbian arts and author of *Idols behind Altars* ([1929] 2002), and quoting diary entries in which the artist described herself at one with Rivera and nature, Hayden Herrera early on observed Kahlo's "feeling of oneness in all living things" and related notions of interdependence (1983, 357; see also 315, 327, 328; and Kahlo 1995). Kahlo's respect for Mesoamerican indigenous art and the worldviews or philosophies from which these sprung was further evident in her and Rivera's collections of pre-Columbian and contemporary popular crafts and in their love of the clothing and egalitarian gender behavior of other mestizas of the south of Mexico in whom cultural indigeneity was dominant, the Tepehuan and Juchitlán women (Covarrubias 1947; Turok 2007).

Mendieta identified with indigenous and African diasporic notions of the interdependence of all being and ashé, or life force, and explored these in relation to the power of art making as a living, interactive conversation within a world of natural forces. Alongside African American and Afro-Latina/o contemporaries in New York, she studied Afro-diasporic cultures, as well as the indigenous cultures of Mexico and Cuba.[7] In 1978 Mendieta wrote admiringly of the "inner knowledge" of Santería in Cuba and of Afro-Cuban culture's seeming "closeness to natural resources. And it is this knowledge which gives reality to the images they have created." She described her own work as "exploring the relationship between myself, the earth and art. Using my body as a reference in the creation of the works, I am able to transcend myself in a voluntary submersion and total identification with nature. Through my art I want to express the immediacy of life and the eternity of nature" (Viso 2008, 296).

Also deeply read in the scholarship and art of pre-Columbian America, and other indigenous peoples of the world, and a participant in living indigenous spiritual practices, Yreina D. Cervántez has deeply identified with and researched indigenous visual languages as the ancestral, from colonial-era glyphs to disposition of space, color, figuration, perspective, and the spiritual-philosophical worldview from which these are derived (Pérez 2007a; interview, 2015). Cervántez, like Celia Herrera Rodríguez and Santa Barraza, has developed culturally hybrid visual languages that aptly describe being as multiple and changing, as opposed to essentialist, static notions of self and existence. In Cervántez's self-portraits, produced since 1970, pre-Columbian and other American indigenous imagery appears often and points to culturally different notions of the self, reality, and perspective than the modern Western world's.

When self-portraits are produced in a series, or over a lifetime, as in German Expressionist Käthe Kollwitz's work, a source Cervántez has mentioned many times in conversation with me, or in Rembrandt's famous series of self-portraits throughout his life, they manifest the desire to see better, to more fully capture what was not managed before, such as aging, character, and other marks of time. Repeated self-portraits figure a spiral of returning, repeated ruminations about repetition with a difference, and together they make evident the nonidentity of the seemingly same through the changes of time. Although Cervántez began her lifelong exploration of appearance, identity, and being via the mirror before encountering Kahlo's work for the first time in the early 1970s, when she finally saw the corpus of self-portraits rather than the few pieces she had seen in books, a magazine article, and an exhibition, she, like other Chicana/o, and especially Chicana feminist artists, experienced a strong sense of identification and validation for the work she, like her peers, was engaged in already.[8] Thus, while Cervántez's *Homenaje a Frida Kahlo* (1978) pays tribute to the artistic forebear, it does so precisely through self-portraiture, with the artist's reflection shown in a mirror the older artist holds up. (The image can be seen in Pérez 2007a, 283, fig. 75.)

A perduring theme in Cervántez's self-portraits is the illusory nature of life, particularly as understood through Mesoamerican notions of the duality of life and death, of the continuity of life ("spirit") beyond human (enfleshed) life, visually represented through partially skeletal forms, hybrid were-creatures, and particular glyphs. In *Despedida a las ilusiones* (*Farewell to Illusions*, 1985), this philosophy appears through Aztec poetry, inscribed on a hand, and a half-skeletal face and finger. In *La vida es una ilusión* (*Life Is an Illusion*, 1989), one of two skulls sitting on a vanity-like altar before the young artist is emblazoned with the title's words. And in *Disfrutamos la fruta de nuevo* (*We Enjoy the Fruit Again*, 1993), a skeleton inserted into an otherwise lush tableau repeats this same message. The theme reappears in the pair of 2014 mixed-media works *Do You Know Where ITZ'AT? Searchin' for My Mojo* (figure 12.3) and *Wiri wiri con nagualito*. In these pieces, Cervántez's linguistic play in three languages (*itz'at* = Mayan: wise one; *wiri wiri* is onomatopoeic Spanish slang for "chitchat") resonates with the play between culturally different selves that she stages as a humorous internal dialogue. In *Searchin' for My Mojo*, a mature Cervántez and her jaguar self are pictured within a Mesoamerican setting. The jaguar asks the artist if she has seen its "bag of tricks," while the artist asks her "*nagualito*," her spirit guide, for her "mojo." Presiding from a shelf, an animated skull intones, via Mayan pictograph-based "speech scrolls," a version of fifteenth-century philosopher-ruler-poet Netzahualcoyotl's well-known verses, "It is not true, it is not true that we came to live here. We came only to sleep, only to dream." In *Wiri wiri*, chitchat with her nagualito is a reflection on "postidentity" debates from the Mesoamerican philosophical framework that guides her work. Her undomesticated spiritual trickster jaguar self slyly asks, "Are you Post-Xicana? Or Post-Chicana?" A mature Cervántez pointedly replies, "Por favor! Obvious isn't it? So are you post-Jaguar? Post-Ocelotl? Perhaps a tribe of a different stripe?" As in many of her other pieces, talking or labeled skulls function as a kind of chorus to contextualize the seemingly specific within the larger social and historic or cosmic contexts. "A jaguar is a jaguar is a jaguar," one remarks, and another, "¡Por eso sufre Aztlan. Can't we all just get along?" In *Wiri wiri*, one of the jaguar self's paws is human, while the artist's dress is the stylized jaguar pelt skin. In *Searchin' for My Mojo*, one of the jaguar's paws is an elongated, long-nailed humanoid hand and the artist's left hand is the

FIGURE 12.3 Yreina D. Cervántez, *Do You Know Where ITZ'AT? Searchin' for My Mojo* (2014).

complement to the jaguar's right hand, rather than the round-fingered more human hand of the artist. In this pair of self-portraits, whether a jaguar is a jaguar or a human a human depends on whether you think jaguars are also human, and humans, jaguars. As a kind of abstraction, what is pictured is the were-jaguar, the paradoxical nature of being to which talk of "spirit" points, as undefinable, exceeding the humanly knowable, exceeding definitions of the human that are solely material, too circumscribed. Defined by mutability, were-beings give body to traditional, living indigenous philosophies such as those of Mesoamerica, of the interdependence and identity of all forms of being, at every level of existence: physical and seemingly invisible or energetic. The fleshless identity of being is also marked in the self-portraits by the skulls, which function as witness and also appear in multiples of Death as irreverent observer and advisor.

Chicana/o artists like Cervántez identified with Kahlo's dramatization of racialization and gender nonconforming strength pictured in her self-portraits, and in her personal life or autonomous bisexuality, political activism, and commitment to social justice. However, as Cervántez has pointed out to me, there is an important difference between artists marginalized as minorities and negatively racialized for being Mexican and Latino in the United States and artists who are part of the dominant culture (if not classes) as Kahlo as a mixed woman was, unlike full-blooded indigenous people in Mexico. Although Kahlo only temporarily lived in San Francisco, Detroit, and New York, and for no more than about two years in total, it is certain that she was aware of Euro-American racism and anti-Mexicanism in spite of the progressive views of artists and collectors around her during her stays in the U.S., or theirs in Mexico. Anita Brenner, only two years older than Kahlo and a good friend of hers, returned to Mexico, her birthplace, after living in the U.S. for seven years, in part due to the anti-Semitism and anti-Mexican racism of Texas (Glusker 1998).[9] Isolda Kahlo, Kahlo's niece, writes of being told by Kahlo and Rivera not to allow anti-Mexicanist and anti-indigenous sentiments from foreigners and recounts their support when she hit a foreign classmate for such views (I. Kahlo 2004, 100).

Many of Cervántez's pieces deconstruct racializing, colonizing semiotics of appearance by working to transform what we think we see and thereby "understand." We do not easily understand the worldviews from which some of her visual language or written texts are culled. Kahlo embraces the indigenous within the mestiza, whether her own or other subjects. Her moustache and connected natural brows are also negatively racializing marks of nonbinary gender identifications, of more androgynous or "manly" femaleness that she also embraces. And Mendieta, from early on in her work, removed all identifiable external traces of the self, leaving only the silhouette, refilling its volume symbolically with elemental fluids and matter that, following African diasporic and indigenous worldviews, carried sacred power and life force, in this way, giving body to both the question "What is the substance of identity?" and its response: nature — but a nature greater than the humanly graspable. All three artists knowingly refuse(d) the performance of expected socially conforming identity in their self-representation, and instead investigate(d) fuller notions of the human by exceeding racializing gendered stereotypes and ideals, and working toward decolonizing perceptions of themselves and in the viewer.

Note to this effect the enormous difference between Kahlo's first self-portrait, *Autorretrato con traje de terciopelo* (*Self-Portrait with a Velvet Dress*, 1926), and those that followed, such as *Autorretrato con collar* (*Self-Portrait with Necklace*, 1933). In the latter, Kahlo no longer represents herself as desirable to a male heterosexual and Euro-identified racializing gaze through idealized femininity and Europeanization. Her masculinizing and indigenous self-representations effectively reject racialized norms of social decency and propriety.[10] This awareness is evident in her dual self-portrait in *The Two Fridas* (1939) and in *Self-Portrait with Cropped Hair* (1940). Her unconventional gender behavior and her standing behind her transgressive behavior is evident from her teen years, as previously mentioned, in a letter where she refuses to be shamed for her sexual behavior, unsurprisingly for that era, by the very person with whom she had had sexual relations (Kahlo [2003] 2006, December 19, 1925).[11]

Unlike the male muralist masters, Kahlo dislodged the still-idealized, "white-washed" mestiza female figure from its place as symbol of the nation, whether as so-called backward indigenous or as brave new proletariat of a mestizo future, which her own image was made to represent in some of Diego Rivera's work. Read against the idealized use and misuse of female bodies in the Mexican muralist movement, and its foundational concern with the monumental, greatness, and historical legacies (Coffey 2012), Kahlo's own self-aware concern with the personal, the concrete, and the nonidealized was striking. It is clear that she admired muralism. She directed her pupils at the experimental art school La Esmeralda to paint on the walls of a collective of laundry women, and in her Coyoacán neighborhood on the walls of a *pulquería*, and her diary attests, as does her painting in her later years, to her wish to be useful to social justice revolution through her art. Nonetheless, more than once, including in 1945, Kahlo spoke of wanting to paint what she knew best — those she personally knew, the travels and experiences she had, and, of course, herself.[12] The overwhelming bulk of self-portraits in her *obra* attest to that knowledge as a quest, which, in spite of physical and emotional pain, she did not abandon.[13] If her project is by genre and square footage of work produced more modest than that of the three great muralists Rivera, David Alfaro Siqueiros, and José Clemente Orozco, and less obviously socially meaningful, its staging of self-awareness of identity as a terrain of inquiry into self as something more than performance of the socially inculcated self may prove to be more vital, in that the transformation of self beyond neocolonial gendered and racialized forms of being is politically and socially significant, and the basis of lasting social change.

At the core of self-representation in the artwork of all three artists is how to perform the apparently self-evident, the self-portrait, in a culturally defamiliarizing way, precisely in order to render the subject human, against centuries of dehumanizing gendered and racialized representation and erasure. How can one peel away the social as mask? Cervántez stages this pointedly in *Danza Ocelotl* (1983). The Nahua spring ritual of symbolic flaying, symbolized in the print through a transparent glove as hand and face as mask, functions not only as a metaphor of natural, seasonal renewal but in this early self-portrait as a stripping away of projected façade. Although structured as a "head shot," an identifiable face is absent. In its place, the artist pictures herself holding up a mask, a mirror, a disc, colored and inscribed with numerous images and symbols. An open third eye within the glyph of *ollin*, a were-jaguar nose, and other personal symbols, as described elsewhere (Pérez 2007a), render "self" as *ollin* (Nahuatl): complex, continual movement and transformation and being as multilayered. The paradox of a self-portrait with one's biological eyes closed but one's "third" or spiritual eye open speaks to a different kind of reflection than that based on physical or literal visuality. The "big baby" of the title resonates with tears on one side of the mask and on the other, a child, enclosed in an ex-voto-like heart. Opposite these images are stars raining from the other eye, and a skull. Flowers at the base of the disc mask render it a kind of altar, a self-homage, while nine growling *balam* (jaguars) protectively surround the artist's body within a thick black frame. The frame's inability to contain the self-portrait is evident as well through the hand that reaches around the frame to hold up the mask.

In Cervántez's self-portraiture she is more than a U.S. "woman of color," the screen of unfriendly, dehumanizing projections. She is in, but also beyond, the repertoire of Western visual signifiers regarding so-called race and gender, as her *Nepantla* triptych (1996) in particular explores through considering the possibilities of visual decolonization, and as the Mesoamerican glyphic world she animates in *Searchin' for My Mojo* suggests. She has visualized self and being through registers of meaning not readily intelligible to a dominant cultural gaze, an "otherness" about the nature of being, as both larger than socially constricting understandings of the subhumanity of a woman of color and more broadly about the "spiritual" or cosmic aspect of being as part of nature's nature. Thus, the idea of the being of humans as spiritual as well as material, and through these in identity with nature and all other beings, is not reserved for indigenous or mestiza/o peoples, though it is introduced and centered through visual cultural and linguistic references from these philosophies as they still prevail there. It is a view of all of humanity. Through art making centered in Mesoamerican philosophies of being as interrelated to other life-forms, Cervántez has visualized her flesh as more than the scar of colonization, victim of or reaction to neocolonizing, dominating powers. Instead, she has pictured herself and helped us to see her, and through her, perhaps ourselves, as part and parcel of the enduring power of a natural world that is not immobile, passive, mute material that is ostensibly unalive and therefore can be ravaged by greed. From a vantage point beyond some post-Enlightenment and poststructuralist denials of spiritual essence, Cervántez's self-portrait strives to capture a sense of self that returns us to awareness that we are nature and that individuals are part of a larger human and planetary community by virtue of the nature of being itself as nature. Self here is quite literally my other me, and you, the seemingly other that is captured in the Mayan expression of the Mesoamerican concept *In Lak'ech*: *tú eres mi otro yo*, you are my other me (Martínez Parédez 1973, 19, 120, 153).

MENDIETA'S PERFORMANCES, earth-body work, natural wall carvings, and carved wood sculptures insistently erase the demarcations between human and nonhuman life-forms. Thus the human body is covered and silhuetas filled with mud, grass, flowers, feathers, hair, water, blood, milk, or fire. The body or its shape — typically, the artist's own throughout the 1970s — was also nude beneath superimposed, glued, dripping, slathered surfaces, kinds of new skin or extensions of skin. Early performances of 1972–74 involving the application of male facial hair to her own face, feathers to her body, or blood dripping down her forehead register her fascination with the intermingling of identities and of forms. Mendieta seemed to be exploring where one form began and others ended, and to what degree the idea of discrete identities was a conceptual limitation and human, limited projection of reality.

In sculptural performances in nature making use of her body as part of the surrounding environment, a zone of ambiguity between human and non-human is created, as it is between what seems alive and what does not. In many of the untitled pieces Mendieta performed at Old Man's Creek in Iowa, but also elsewhere, the human figure anthropomorphizes natural forces, such as that of trees — whether limbs, trunk, or root — the soil, sand, and bodies of water. Mendieta's views of the sacred life force, ashé, in the African diasporic Yoruba tradition of Santería were present from the beginning of her work. In a 1982 grant application, she stated, "For the past twelve years I have been working out in nature, exploring the relationship between myself, the earth and art. I have thrown myself in to the very elements that produced me, using the earth as my canvas and my soul as my tools" (Clearwater 1993, 41).

From this perspective, the movement from embodied performance as a kind of still life and of silhueta as human trace when covered in or filled with organic matter perhaps is not absence so much as a different kind of presence (figure 12.4). Still, and covered with natural materials, the recognizably human form is no longer a personal body, nor is it a corpse, but rather another life-form within a field that is full of other natural forms that might be performed alive through the performer as sculptural natural form. Kahlo's paintings have a similar quality. In *Self Portrait with Braid* (1941), tufts of her hair seemingly free themselves from their tight braid, and in many of her still lifes, color, moist ripeness, and movement capture vibrancy. *The Love Embrace of the Universe, the Earth (Mexico), Diego, Me, and Señor Xolotl* (1949), like Remedios Varo's fantastic and whimsical paintings of animated objects, explicitly anthropomorphizes the seemingly inanimate.

Mendieta's silhuetas and other earth-based performance sculptures stage a partial erasure of the familiar human form and of the specific, identifiable person. What one sees instead (through photographic and video documentation) is a differently materialized presence, one that insists on identity with the surrounding landscapes. The performance when the artist's or a model's body is used is a performance of human as nature, as well as of nature as animated. Covered in mud, standing against a tree, in *Tree of Life* (figure 12.4), the performance sculpture lends body to other life-forms. Hollowed out or carved outlines of the human body, when filled or covered with matter, together constitute the earth-work's body or its skin.

FIGURE 12.4 Ana Mendieta, *Tree of Life* (1977, Old Man's Creek, Iowa). © The Estate of
Ana Mendieta Collection, LLC. Courtesy Galerie Lelong, New York, NY.

As much or more than functioning like the photograph, as a trace of what is now absent, the silhuetas paradoxically address persistence, precisely because they are designed to be ephemeral, to be washed away with the returning tide, to melt with the return of spring, to dissolve under the rain, scatter with the wind, or like the *Rupestrian Sculptures* in Cuba, to slowly vanish across the centuries back into the elements. Disintegration, dissipation, and decomposition are compositional elements of the pieces. Made of natural materials, the silhuetas are to dissolve into the materia prima from whence they came.

Identification with nature is literalized in Mendieta's performances as nature, as part of tree, soil, roots, and fields. Perhaps this is another way of thinking of the shamanic concept of the capacity to identify with other life-forms to the point of transforming into them, as in Cervántez's self-portraits as were-jaguar, symbolic of the nonmaterial self that is in identity with an inspirited natural world whose vitality is characterized precisely by constant movement and transformation.

I WANT TO RETURN TO Kahlo's self-portraiture. In addition to approaches to her work discussed earlier, critics have noted that the exuberant, highly social artist had in self-portraiture an outlet to express the constant physical pain with which she lived since a bus accident during her adolescence, or that it revealed the sadness and isolation of a psychological sense of solitude, explained in diverse ways. But alongside her still lifes and especially in the self-portraits of the 1940s, and in some of the portraits, Kahlo begins to surround or even dress the sitter in vibrant vegetation (as in *Portrait of Mariana Morillo Safa* [1944] and *Self-Portrait with Braid* [1941]). Vegetation and animals are not merely a backdrop and props, or framing devices. In the 1940s, Kahlo's identification with indigenous dress as resistance to negative racialization of the indigenous (*My Dress Hangs There* [1933], *Me and My Doll* [1937], *Escuincle Dog with Me* [c. 1938], *Self-Portrait* [1940]), not withstanding that it was a politically correct sartorial statement of the time for others too, makes way for self-representation through and as nature. In *Thinking about Death* (1943), vibrant vegetation, animals, and the external natural world are the principal signs of her inner or true nature. In *Roots* (1943), she explicitly paints herself as nature, a cut-out in her chest allowing red-veined leafy vines to grow through and from her amid the barren cracked surrounding landscape. In *The Dream* (1940), she pictures herself sleeping in her canopied bed, covered by a growing vine. Atop the canopy, a Judas skeleton wired with firecrackers and holding a bouquet mirrors her sleeping frame, life and death both a kind of sleep, of being in another time-space of fleshless consciousness.

Identity as nature — a nature of constant movement and transformation — and the transitory nature of the human, especially in its social embodiment, is an important part of the process of self-reflection and self-possession that the self-portraits of Kahlo, Mendieta, and Cervántez record. But rather than constituting a pointless archive of the traps of narcissism and self-absorption as various critics have argued, they allow meditation on the nature of being in the face of social and physical suffering, and more generally of the inevitable mortality of the flesh. Profoundly philosophical, if by this we mean reflection on the nature of being and thereby conceptions of self and identity, the self-portraits of Kahlo and Cervántez and the performance sculptures and silhuetas of Mendieta explore the nature of self as not-(social) self, as multiple, as matter and nonmatter, as specific, socially circumscribed identities alongside identity as nature and cosmic being. Beyond asking what is self, their work asks what is life, what are its forms, what constitutes lasting being? Their work powerfully responds. As Gloria Anzaldúa observed, "For images, words, stories to have this transformative power, they must arise from the human body — flesh and bone — and from the Earth's body — stone, sky, liquid" (1987, 75).

13

UNDEAD DARWINISM AND THE FAULT LINES OF NEOCOLONIALISM IN LATINA/O ART WORLDS

FIGURE 13.1 Gloria E. Anzaldúa, *Untitled (The Forbidden)* (n.d.), box 131, folder 14, Gloria Evangelina Anzaldúa Papers, Nettie Lee Benson Library, University of Texas Libraries, University of Texas at Austin.

CULTURAL DARWINISM IS THE Eurocentric premise that the cultures of politically, economically, and socially dominant peoples are the result of nature's own law of survival of the fittest "races," as demonstrated by domination itself, and that all other cultures should, and will, if exposed, progress or modernize in the footsteps of the presently dominant. The least desirable should be discouraged from populating in eugenics. Cultural and racial Darwinism, decisively elaborated by Charles Darwin's cousin Francis Galton (1978, 357), is about as intellectually and rationally unsound, and self-servingly Eurocentric, that is, ethnocentric, as racial phrenology and the theory of "race" have been. Cultural Darwinism is a master tool of post-Enlightenment thought, rationalizing geopolitical imperialism and the devaluation of the cultures that colonizing empire represses, marginalizes, or supplants. In dominant cultural art world discourse(s), as in other forms of dominant cultural humanities and social sciences thought, the burden of proof of relevance, adequacy, universality, impartiality, truth, and importance rests on the presumably inferior, backward, naïve, parochial, non-European, or insufficiently Euro-Americanized other.

Cultural Darwinism is like patriarchal sexism and heterosexism, where respect and acceptability depend on definitions created by patriarchy and heteronormativity to legitimize themselves over women and the queer. It is a catch-22. Cultural Darwinism is tautological: what constitutes equal from its point of view is only what it validates to begin with. It cannot recognize difference with respect to itself as anything other than lagging, and to the degree it is able, it inculcates what it projects: the yearning, the anxiety of those it marginalizes to become like the dominant cultural. This is methodology of the neocolonial, as Chela Sandoval (2000) might put it, and precisely what the "methodology of the oppressed" brings into view and exposes as dominant, historically and culturally specific ideology rather than the universally true cultural outcome of nature itself. It thus covers up its own ahistorical and false essentialisms.

Two important anthologies of the 1990s, *Beyond the Fantastic* (Mosquera 1996) and *Santería Aesthetics in Contemporary Latin American Art* (Lindsay 1996), laid out the quandary for both Latin American and U.S. Latina/o artists with respect to the possibilities of inclusion in a global art world still dominated by European and Euro-American art. With few exceptions, even Latin Americans raised as dominant cultural found that the global art world, like the global economy and intellectual production in general, was still dominated by the legacies of European imperial powers, even those in decline. How Latin American and U.S. Latina/o arts' historical, aesthetic, and conceptual or thematic concerns are received, artists and critics in these collections pointed out, is embedded within the logic of imperialist binary logic: either/or-ism. Latin American and U.S. Latina/o art are only visible, legible, or intelligible as mimicry of the so-called First World, where "First World" is understood without need of explanation as superior, as most modern, let alone postmodern. Such imitation is understood as stigma, as second-rate. Or the concerns and methods of this art are to be read as "authentic" if a naïve performance of the folkloric, the non-European as precondition. This either/or binary of inauthentic imitation of dominant art or so-called authenticity via nationalism and folklorism functions as a condition of legibility for dominant culture but from which dominant cultural artists are somehow exempt.

In essence, this is the reenactment, the repetitive performance that reproduces a colonial legacy of more than five hundred years in ever-modernizing ways as the neocolonizing, the translation of the unfamiliar into the familiar and thus its management, its disciplining, its repression, if not its erasure. With respect to the Americas, it is the willful or unconscious but in all cases methodical recodification/scrambling/replacement of the worldviews of the indigenous, and the African diasporic, and of other non-Europeans and mixed peoples. To share a historical anecdote from Serge Gruzinski's *La guerra de las imágenes: De Cristóbal Colón a Blade Runner (1492–2019)* ([1989] 1994) regarding initial cultural struggles in what would become Mexico, colonization exercises itself at the moment in which the culturally unfamiliar indigenous sacred bundle named through an unfamiliar indigenous word is translated from admitted cultural unknown to the ostensibly knowable and familiar by the colonizers as a foolish, superstitious, naïve fetish, the "zemi."[1] The unfamiliar is dismissed as unimportant through the performance or guise of universal knowing, through translation of the culturally different into the culturally same.

In a similar manner, because overdetermined by the legacy of colonizing thought in so-called postimperial, postnationalist, postracial U.S. and European cultures, the Latin American and U.S. Latina/o become legible, that is, tolerable, through the either/or of translation into dominant cultural worldviews and power dynamics. Whether supposedly mimicking the dominant cultural worldview or performing what is actually more authentic to it, both versions of the binary are Orientalist ideological projections of the dominating culture rather than realities of the subordinated one, and perform and reinstall domination. To the degree that "we" (in all our varieties) buy into them, they are disciplining versions of the Latin American and U.S. Latina/o that reproduce the racially based inequity of the cultural, intellectual, and economic landscapes within which the art worlds function.

GATOS-POR-LIEBRES, CATS PASSING AS HARES

The prefix "post-" continues to proliferate, as if the yearning it captures could perform the leap beyond the reality it wants to leave behind, but to which it is bound by the phenomenon itself: postcolonialism, poststructuralism, postmodernism, postindustrialism, postfeminism, postrace, and the very slippery "postidentitarian." In 1977 Mexican novelist María Luisa Puga engaged Kenyan writer Ngugi Wa Thiong'o, later the author of *Decolonising the Mind: The Politics of Language in African Literature* (1986), in a conscious not-choosing of Europe and Euro-America as intellectual and political interlocutors, in spite of their global hegemony, in an effort to undermine the colonizing binary I have referred to above, emanating from global powers even in its liberatory forms. In her novel *Las posibilidades del odio* (*Hatred's Possibilities*, 1977), Puga observed that independent — that is, politically postcolonial, multiracial — Kenya, and by analogy mestizo Mexico, were not necessarily decolonial or beyond the Eurocentric. Puga presented the complex multiethnic culture of postcolonial Kenya as a mirror of a Third Worldism in order to illuminate the still unfinished work of decolonial postcolonial cultural and social realities in Mexico.

In the early 1990s, when postcolonial theory began to circulate widely in the U.S., scholar Frances Aparicio observed (in my presence) that Puerto

Rico was a case in point as to why neither the United States nor Latin America was in fact postcolonial. In a graduate seminar I taught on the history of U.S. women of color (WOC) thought of the late 1960s through the first decade of the twenty-first century, one student offered that the difference between U.S. WOC feminism and that of postcolonial feminists was precisely the "post-": the ostensible development, progress, in sophistication of analyses, in complexity, in advancing beyond earlier essentialisms with respect to the complexity of identity. Jasbir Puar's *Terrorist Assemblages: Homonationalism in Queer Times* (2007) concludes on such a note; what is becoming an all too familiar analysis posits that we need to move beyond the language of intersectionality to something more fluid, mobile, savvy: the language of assemblage and disassemblage.

In a campus presentation at UC Berkeley after the publication of her book, Puar exhorted U.S. women of color thinkers to get with the program and read the same people she had been reading: more European male thinkers whose thought, unlike women of color's, we were to assume, remained evergreen, never needing to be publicly upbraided for intellectual backwardness and datedness. Puar enters feminist thought at a time when white feminist historical accounts, as Sandoval (2000) has carefully shown, appropriate and renarrate the little it knows of WOC thought in mainly self-serving ways, preserving hegemonic racial privilege, even if rendering it difficult to detect in homogenizing narratives of development. In accounts where "feminism" as a whole ostensibly progresses through stages of contradiction such as essentialism and from lesser ideological awareness into new resolutions of greater democratic and inclusive thought, the complexity of Chicana, African American, and other 1960s and 1970s WOC thought is ahistorically redated to the 1980s, well after second-wave white feminisms' own reemergence in the 1960s, and in a derivative way with respect to the latter, and, finally, insufficiently examining the game-changing theoretical and analytical contribution of WOC thought — the project Sandoval maps in her masterful *Methodology of the Oppressed* (2000). At least from 1969, Black, Chicana, and Native American feminists point to the histories of female resistance to racialized slavery, colonialism, and occupation in individual publications and anthologies (Beal [1969] 1970; Moraga and Anzaldúa 1981; Hull et al. 1982; Brant 1983; Smith 1983; García 1997). Even today, "postmodern" or "poststructuralist" white feminisms' indebtedness to the black civil rights movement of the

1950s and to U.S. WOC thought of the 1960s and 1970s remains insufficiently acknowledged as intellectually powerful analyses of social reality in the U.S., and other multicultural countries created through the tensions and inequities of imperial histories between "First" and "Third" Worlds. Women of color's hard-won concepts, as they elucidate, emerge from their unsanctioned analyses of their and their communities' own existence. But these are appropriated and misrepresented in the 1990s and thereafter, turning WOC critiques of the essentialist gender identity politics of white feminist essentialisms against them, in a wholesale judgment and dismissal of the theoretical naïveté of pre-European poststructuralist thought in the United States. Women of color's complex analyses of dehumanizing identity formations created by racializing, patriarchal, and heteronormative colonial and neocolonial cultures, captured in Combahee River Collective's "simultaneity of oppressions" (1977), is unread, erased, absorbed, or rendered so self-evident that they may be absorbed unattributed and shallowly engaged if at all, and instead U.S. women of color's complex concepts of social identity and its construction are attributed solely to European and derivative Euro-American poststructuralist thought. The much later concept of "intersectionality," developed from the more complex earlier formulations of identity and social reality to pragmatically serve in courts of law (Crenshaw 1991), is both taken as a (belated) origin of important women of color thought proper and literalized spatially as descriptive of less fluid movements beyond graph plottings. But this misunderstanding of Kimberlé Crenshaw's formulation is only possible in the absence of knowledge of WOC thought before her apt critical legal studies formulation necessary to real-life transformation of the legal system.

The allure of the "posts" is embedded to some degree within Darwinian gendered and racialized time-scapes of progress and backwardness, in binary oppositions between postmodern versus the modern, where the modern or the liberal now stands in for the intellectually and culturally primitive, whose origin in faux theories of racial primitivity is minimized if even referenced. One of the reasons I wrote *Chicana Art: The Politics of Spiritual and Aesthetic Altarities* (2007a) was because of an anecdote related by a 1960s-generation female artist that a Chicano male artist ten years her junior had publicly disparaged references to indigeneity in Chicano work in general as passé and naive, a sure sign of backwardness, nostalgia, nationalist romanticism, and idealism. He and another male Chicano member of the art panel they were all sitting on presented themselves as new, hip to poststructuralist theory, new in their disavowal of stereotypes of what Chicana/o art might be. Given that her work is well known for engaging the indigenous, she was without question being thrown under the bus in public, as Exhibit A: Dinosaur. Not only was the male artist rude and self-serving; he was wrong, unable to understand the decolonial character of her work. His assumption, derived from unexamined neocolonial logic, though parroted increasingly by people of color anxious to appear nonessentializing, was that by virtue of passage of time, first-generation 1960s and 1970s thought and art must be less sophisticated, unwittingly "primitive" in its naïveté, no longer relevant to postmodern sensibilities, if not realities.

There is much that can be analyzed here, around racialized gender and economic differences between the pair in question, and thereby the greater ease of passing into dominant cultural art worlds of the one over the other, but suffice it to focus on the inability of the post-Chicano self-styled antihero to allow the possibility of decolonial aesthetic politics at work in referencing the indigenous and to see that such citations are not folkloric but rather highly philosophical and ideologically critical. This, however, cannot be read from Eurocentric art historical and philosophical registers. It requires knowledge of what are in fact living indigenous worldviews about art, artist, perspective, knowledge, truth, and being that are about the present and the future, and not simply artifacts of a lost past. When engaged seriously, strategies of indigenous and African diasporic art historical hybridity create third spaces that refuse either/or binary thought and oppositions such as the unexamined assumption that the past is dead and reference to it romantic, ahistorical, and useless for the complexity of our moment.

Reading more recent writings, including the foreword to *Phantom Sightings: Art after the Chicano Movement*, an exhibition catalog by the CEO and director of the Los Angeles County Museum of Art (LACMA), Michael Govan, I have also been struck by the anxiety that renders inclusion into the historically mainstream art museum, via what is, on some level, an apologia for Chicana/o art.

The artists in this show consciously position themselves within the broadest development of contemporary art. Several of them have international careers.

While their art reflects the Chicano experience in a variety of locales, from San Francisco and Los Angeles to San Antonio and New York, these artists do not identify themselves as Chicanos first. They have assimilated mainstream American culture as much as mainstream American culture has assimilated its diverse and divergent demographic. If they are grouped together here as Chicano artists after the Chicano movement, it is not by their own volition or consensus; it is a curatorial artifact, a device to reflect and speculate on the interests and issues facing Chicano artists today. (Gonzalez, Fox, and Noriega 2008, 11)

Apart from the utopian assertion about mutual assimilation that ignores the widespread racialized inequity that is obvious walking throughout the Los Angeles metropolitan area, particularly in its major museums, and that is also a theme in some works in the exhibition, the assertion that these artists do not identify as Chicanos first when many have only been able to advance their careers through that still politically significant self-denomination, this argument is again, at best, naive. The point that as artists they do not identify as Chicana/os first does not constitute an innovation; to assume that it does is Eurocentric and condescending. For some art writers, whether in art reviews, curatorial essays, or scholarly presentations about Chicana/o art after the mid-1980s, there is an uneasy tension among all the contributing writers, rooted in the assumption that more recent work is okay because it is so different from most earlier Chicana/o movement art, and there is the undebated, incorrect, and caricaturizing assumption that the self-identified Chicana/o cultural politics and notions of identity of the previous era were simplistic, one-dimensional, and now mercifully surpassed by more universal, or at least local, concerns. The solution to this intellectual impasse is to identify two lineages, one represented by artists such as the multimedia performance group Asco, characterized as conceptual, and the other characterized as naive, essentialist, nationalist art.

Ongoing concerns within the larger Mexican American community and its plight are, in fact, the abiding backbone of Chicana/o, U.S. Puerto Rican, and other U.S. Latinx cultural politics of various ideological hues. It is an unsubstantiated premise that Chicana/o artists born in the mid-1950s, 1960s, and 1970s rather than the 1930s through early 1950s are more at ease with the idea and practice of identity as nonessential, fluid, changeable, ambiguous.

Noting that Chicana Gloria Anzaldúa, a foremost theorist of the hybridity and queerness of identity as constantly changing, was born in 1942 should perhaps suggest the naïveté of such a view. Key French poststructuralist philosophers were born much earlier: Gilles Deleuze, theorist of rhizomal politics and assemblage theory in 1925, and Félix Guattari, psychoanalyst and coauthor with Deleuze of foundational works, in 1930; Michel Foucault, theorist of epistemes, genealogical alternative historicizing, the panopticon, discipinarity, and biopolitics, in 1926; Jacques Derrida, theorist of difference in discourse through ideologically significant slippage and the undecidability of meaning, in 1930; Giorgio Agamben, theorist of the "bare, naked life," of domination versus the disruptive life of the living, and thereby also of assemblage theory, in 1942; Bruno Latour, another theorist of assemblage beyond binaries, in 1947. Most of these European men were older than those who came of age in the late 1960s. Chronology is hardly a reliable indicator of progress, particularly if the seeming newness is due only to the lag in translation from the original French publications. Nor is the intellectual capital in dominant cultural academia of assimilating French philosophical discourses a guarantor that this thought is of necessity superior, that is, more complex, subtle, deep, or refined, than U.S. women of color's thought, which emanates organically from the significantly different locations of still oppressed populations, still oppressed bodies.

As if they are infectious, we are now careful to avoid cultural celebration or affirmation of Mexican American cultural difference, unlike the historic CARA (*Chicano Art: Resistance and Affirmation*) show, which surveyed work from the mid-1960s through the mid-1980s. What we are ostensibly to celebrate, strangely enough, is the absence of aesthetic antidotes to the internalized racism and essentializing myths regarding Mexican cultural and biological inferiority and the supposed superiority of the European and the Euro-American. We are to translate as legible to Euro-American dominant cultural art the work of Chicana/o artists "now," as if the latter had advanced within an undisputed notion of progress and backwardness around identity, as if a new generation of artists finally got what European poststructuralists a generation older than the first generation of Chicana/o movement intellectuals understood. Thus, Chicana/o cutting-edge "postidentitarian," postmodern, post-Chicano, post-*algo* (post-something) in effect means finally

all caught up, almost, with the tired contradictions of imperialist, neocolonizing modernisms.

Here is the thing: The unread, not undead, the insufficiently read, the
widely misread archives from the 1960s, 1970s, and early 1980s of intellectual and artistic work of U.S. women of color have not been surpassed in the
complexity of notions of identity as changing, fluid, compromised, negotiating, problematically imposed, continually transformed, that is, in current
terminology, identity as performative, neocolonizing or decolonizing, and
as both essential and nonessential, and as constantly shifting, transforming
"assemblages" in terms of being-as-a-becoming and in terms of the effect of
different locations on being and action.

U.S. women of color feminist thought from Frances Beal, Audre Lorde,
Anna Nieto Gómez, Elizabeth "Betita" Martínez, Marta Cotera, the Combahee
River Collective, and Carol Lee Sanchez articulated "double," "triple," "multiple," and "simultaneous oppressions" as the intellectual, decolonizing analytical tools for deconstructing dominant cultural ideologies masquerading as
universal truths, and they analyzed their racialized and gendered conditions
within the politics and economics of patriarchal, heteronormative, ethnocentric (Eurocentric) racializing imperialism and colonialism.[2] Puar sketches
a straw-man caricature of WOC thought through one of its articulations, "intersectionality," a concept she neglects to contextualize in its development in
critical legal studies as a tool in courtroom practice. Puar appears unaware
of the complex notions of being and existence that women of color in the
U.S. articulated nearly two decades before this term (which in 2016 electoral
politics even Hillary Clinton appropriated). In Puar's erroneous renditions,
"intersectionality" is the product of unsophisticated, unwittingly obedient
notions of identity, being, and existence, and is based on some rigid geometric
model of discrete "coordinates" (2007, 195) that work "synthetic[ally]" and
"[bind] [dominant cultural] identity politics" (202). This misrepresentation
of intersectionality and of the more complex notion of simultaneity of oppressions and multiple identities from which the former is derived serves as a
foil against which to contrast the European assemblage theory that she now
adopts for thinking various kinds of queer and terrorist bodies, as instead
being "in concert . . . as interfacing matrices" (197), as fluid, changeable processes rather than static, locationally fixed identities. The critique of falsely

essentializing, falsely discrete identities that reproduce the master's tools, as Lorde puts it, by reproducing the logic of divide and conquer as truth-based, is by necessity first made in U.S. feminism *of* white middle-class women *by* African American and Chicana feminists and other women of color and not the other way around. Even Giorgio Agamben points to the necessity of differently located, differently produced voices around being and existence as crucial to what he calls a coming politics, one that from a person of color perspective must operate in a decolonizing way, more fully outside the colonizing and the neocolonizing (Kishik 2012).

We are post-something, but post-what? We are understandably having a very difficult time analyzing the economic and political realities of the last forty years and connecting them to our theorizations, curation, and scholarship. We are challenged to see how the last twenty years of dominant culture have reckoned with the 1960s' and 1970s' powerful, destabilizing critiques and the shifts in social reality. With respect to Latina/o culture, nowhere is the problem of difference under prevailing power relations that create subjected individuals and communities illuminated and analyzed than in U.S. Latina feminist and queer thought, and in serious engagements with non-Western, indigenous, African diasporic, and other notions of being and their explorations of thought beyond binaries and categories within the logic of Eurocentric thought. This thought is in dialogue and nurtured in coalition with U.S. women of color thinkers, including artists, quite often outside the gatekeeping strictures of academia. U.S. WOC thought does not arise from armchair theorizing but rather surreptitiously feeds it. Borrowing language from European philosophers as old or older than U.S. WOC thinkers of the 1960s and 1970s to describe social and political relations in their spheres of experience and knowledge is useful. But it is not automatically a better way to describe the social reality, being, and experience that arise from careful reflection on the locations, histories, and strategies for survival that U.S. women of color experience as well as study — quite the contrary, I think anyone would argue. How to survive on this continent and planet promises to be more clearly illuminated by the indigenous elders, who not only carry knowledge that has survived and helped them survive more than five hundred years of genocidal cultural repression and other forms of violence and warfare but also transmit millennia of specific knowledge about life in this part of the planet alongside scientific and philosophical knowledge about humanity in general.

European leftist or progressive thought regarding the possibilities of knowledge and social justice is a welcome voice in what should be a global body of knowledge, and one that preserves the ancient wisdom of all peoples, alongside the ancient Greeks. I am eager to also read the women of color of France and the rest of Europe. But I am at pains to understand the logic of how a nation, the United States — which has been characterized since its inception by the struggle for survival against colonization, colonial settlerism, anti-indigenous physical and cultural genocide, African slavery, anti-Mexicanism due to imperialist war against Mexico, and anti-Asian discrimination — is to be lectured on multiculturality and the complexities of survival tactics and strategies or berated into another Darwinian lecture on the superiority of European and Euro-American thought. Dominant culture imposes its narrative of intellectual value on the dominated, but the result is a double consciousness in the dominated, a cultural hybridity, a knowledge that there are at least two cultures, and more than this, two philosophies or worldviews at play, albeit one that is largely invisible to the dominant culture, which has fallen for its own mythology of superiority and universality and therefore lacks respect and curiosity for the rest of humanity's answers to questions that are today most urgent for humanity as a whole, and not just one ethnic group or a cluster of peoples, whether "white" or "people of color."

Gatos-por-liebres, cats passing as hares: not quite the same meat to chew in your taco. Patriarchy passing as not-patriarchy in postfeminism. Racism and Eurocentrism passing as postidentitarian ideologies and practices. The neocolonial passing as the postcolonial. The postindustrial passing as post-*maquila*, postsweatshop, postfactory economies. Global domination passing as the postnational. *Gatos por liebres*. Cats passing as hares.

FAULT LINES IN LATINA/O ART WORLD DISCOURSES

Undead Darwinism and its posts create some of the fault lines that we must navigate in the U.S. Latina/o art world. There is no question that there is a difference between the early Chicana/o and other U.S. Latina/o boomers born in the 1940s and early 1950s and those born in the 1960s and 1970s who benefited and who may have been raised from childhood in more decolonial ways with respect to racialization, gender, and sexuality. This is no doubt also true for mixed-race and younger Euro-Americans. But women of color in the late 1960s and throughout the 1970s who analyzed and theorized the simultaneity of racialized, gendered, sexed, and class oppression elaborated a basic premise of the complexity and contradictions of subjectivity of the human, exacerbated by colonial and neocolonial shifting, changing, imbricated oppressions. People of color in the Americas have analyzed, negotiated, and, to the degree possible under conditions of varying duress, opposed their physical, psychological, spiritual, and social dehumanization. Biological or cultural essentialism is not an easy intellectual pill to swallow for people who daily navigate stereotype, cultural oppression and silencing, and the fatal effects of racist and colonial Eurocentrism, although it has been imposed on the colonized and the negatively racialized, gendered, and sexed as truth.

The capacity to perceive complexity does not belong solely to dominant cultural philosophy and its derivatives. In fact, it could be argued with little difficulty that where relations of intellectual, cultural, social, political, and economic power are at play, the opposite has proven true. Contrary to Eurocentric Darwinian declarations of the destruction of ancient indigenous American philosophies, the turning of perception to the non-Western that 1960s and 1970s people of color intellectuals embarked upon, which in many cases involved oral transmission in unbroken lineages, began to circulate far more complex, rigorous, and ambitious ways of understanding being and natural reality. There are numerous works now published by PhDs, MDs, RNs, and other people highly accomplished by Western standards, who are also high initiates in the numerous, culturally different traditions of the Native American and African American peoples (e.g., Avila 1999; Vega 2000; Torres 2005; Gonzales 2012; Román 2012). The Mayan elder don Miguel Chiquín, who traveled to speak publicly in the San Francisco Bay Area in April 2011, by authorization of the Council of Mayan Elders of his village, conveyed to me at that time that the lineage of Mayan thought is direct and unbroken, belongs to humanity, and does not function through the logic of Western either/or dualism. But it does preserve thinking and practices that help pierce the ideological illusions we have lived with for more than five hundred years.

Who authorizes our notions of being, identity, and the meaning of art and artist and its social function? Wherein lies the decolonial? Certainly it cannot lie in that which dehumanizes and reproduces social inequity, as a product of binary paradigms that falsely describe reality, obscuring our view of truth and integrity.

14

THE INVIOLATE EROTIC IN THE PAINTINGS OF LILIANA WILSON

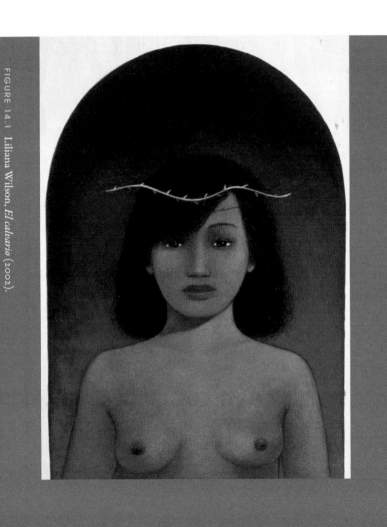

FIGURE 14.1 *Liliana Wilson, El calvario* (2002).

THE RECURRING, CENTRAL SUBJECT OF much of Liliana Wilson's work of the mid- to late 1990s and beginning of the twenty-first century is survival of the inviolate beauty and eros of the human spirit amid trauma (see Herman 1992). Her paintings and drawings of this era feature somber, self-contained youths, luminous and beautiful, tensely holding their own within threatening environments, in contrast to works following this period, such as *La diosa del amor* (2002), *Las amantes* (2002), or *La espera* (2007), where peaceful figures are at one with each other or the surrounding natural environments.[1]

The resolute self-containment of her subjects, their youth and strikingly androgynous beauty, stand in sharp relief to the suggestion of danger, strangeness, loneliness, imprisonment, and psychic fragmentation conveyed by the surrounding space. Wilson's subjects are captured in the middle of some dehumanizing narrative, or in its shadow, yet embody resistance as innocence and integrity with respect to the evil of violence's wounding, fragmenting effects. Spectral, omnipresent danger is insistently met by inviolate eros, the life energy of love and interdependence: the human spirit's endurance, vitality, and beauty in the face of the suppression of empathy, love, and care for the other. Androgyny, the coexistence of so-called feminine and masculine attributes here, in classic and cross-cultural tradition, are symbolic of human and psychic wholeness. Given the persistence of patriarchal heteronormativity, gender androgyny figures in Wilson's work not only as symbolic of a more humane condition but as a way of being that persists and resists psychosocial violence against gender and sexual identities not in conformity with gender stereotypes that reproduce patriarchal heteronormative gender roles. Androgyny in Wilson's work, pictured as youths resisting menacing backdrops, also calls attention to violence as gendered and eroticized, that is, those perceived as feminine or queer are targets of dominant cultural violence, so violence is overdetermined in this way. However, Wilson's hero/ines simultaneously embody the refusal to perform gender splitting precisely because we cannot easily say this is a female or male figure, and in doing so, they also perform a space of being that is resistant to internalization of external, social (i.e., human) forms of violence. Wilson's youth under duress thus represent the inviolate power of the erotic, understanding the erotic in the sense that Audre Lorde elaborated as the life force that is vital to women of color, expressed not only through the goodness of sexual love and romantic intimacy but also as joy, as the human right to happiness, self-love, and love, and through these, wholeness.[2]

Amid troubling narratives, the young bodies pictured are impassive, serious, with full red lips unsmiling. *"¡No pasarán!"* — You shall not pass! — they seem to cry from the core of their being. I am reminded of the Argentine-born Latina philosopher María Lugones's (2003, 10–11) affirmation of the almost imperceptible psychological and physical acts of resistance in extremely oppressive, momentarily inescapable situations that crucially allow the preservation and strengthening of wounded subjectivities and eventual escape from these. Wilson, self-exiled to the United States during the brutal years of Chilean military dictatorship, seems to illustrate this philosophy of the importance of everyday practices of resistance, at the level of consciousness, to both extremely violent periods of oppression and the everyday violence of normative culture exercised within domestic and social spheres. Wilson's work often pictures domestic interiors as scenes of impending violence, recalling Chicana painter Patssi Valdez's early paintings, which similarly gave way to exuberant natural elements and harmonious exteriors in her later oeuvre.

Wilson's portraits also immediately bring to mind those of other painters similarly concerned with capturing unseen presences of the seemingly unreal, such as Remedios Varo, Leonora Carrington, Leonor Fini, Kay Sage, Yves Tanguy, and Salvador Dalí. But Wilson's work differs markedly from that of European artists who came of age in the 1920s through the 1940s. It is not psychic perception and spiritual realities or oneiric visions and fantastic imaginings or the unexpected truths of the insane or the possible fluidity of time-space that are pictured as a kind of antithesis to bourgeois instrumental rationality. Here the language of the spectral or the fantastic suggests the irreality of normative violations that strain the mind and the body and defy what we believe humans capable of. What Wilson bears mute witness to is the repression itself of such violences, through mapping their haunting effects on shuttered flesh that reflects wary minds on guard against depredation — and

FIGURE 14.2 Liliana Wilson, *Bearing Witness* (2002).

what survives it (Stein 1995).[3] Something is amiss in the remarkably respect-able and orderly domestic, middle-class interiors and subjects that Wilson depicts (see, for example, *The Successful Family* [1999]). And something deep emerges to counter and protect against these forces.

Thus, if color bleeds in many of Wilson's paintings, particularly the reds, as soaking through clothing and a canvas now symbolic of the human frame, it is also true that it becomes a burnished, polished, ultimately jewel-like trans-mutation, a diffusion, as if emanating from within a victim, for example, the white-shirted young man in *El inmigrante* (1982) or the bare-chested young woman in *El calvario* (2002; figure 14.1) or the youth in *La caída de un ángel* (2004). This work is a journey toward the indestructible, toward illuminat-ing *lo que perdura*, what perdures unbreakably, like a precious gem within.

Wilson's painting *Bearing Witness*, part of her 2002 exhibition *Erosio-nes internas* (*Internal Erosions*): *Bear Witness to the Experiences of Nuestra Gente* (*Our People*), conveys the fearful sense of being watched (figure 14.2).

Whether by one's own split sense of self or by an informer or a disciplinary social force, we know not, but we are led to *compartir*, to sense the heightened awareness that results from such surveillance. The disembodied, threatening ability of that eye within an amorphous red wash of a wall threatens to grow, perhaps having already engulfed what lies beyond in the shadows. Its own penetrating formlessness helps illuminate the necessity of the compact, self-contained *nitidez* (clarity) in the corporality of the young woman portrayed—and in other figures in Wilson paintings from this era.

Wilson paints people who are watched, menaced, or live haunted by harm done and the fear of being wounded or entrapped again. They too are watchful: their eyes show quiet alertness and their bodies convey tense attentiveness. These bodies stand and sit amid invasive exteriors and crumbling interiors, alone in barren lands, mute and containing the unspeakable. What is familiar to them has been taken away — they have suffered physical, psychological, and social losses — and now their lives are full of estranging intrusions (fish- and bird-headed men), yet they emit a steady glow. They are persons. They have histories. They have feelings. They have hope even as they bear the closed faces of grief, sadness, and deep resolve. They resist and survive dehumanization even while walking on its very brink.

Wilson's sobriety in depicting the unspeakable follows an ethics of respect for the wounded other, whether victim of political repression, as in her native Chile of the 1970s and 1980s (*War* [2001]), or of so many other countries during that time and into our present, or of homophobic culture (*La caída del ángel* [2004]), or of violence and violation within intimate social spaces, or of some other unspecified suffering that demands repression to the point of split consciousness (*Mujer dividida* [2001]; *Deterioros* [2002]). How do we denounce and speak about violence without unwittingly causing new injury? It seems that this is the tremendously delicate, vital task that Wilson has set herself: creating images in solidarity with those who have suffered violence but taking care not to further traumatize, humiliate, or incapacitate by inadvertently reproducing the ultimate lie rationalizing their dehumanizing experiences. Thus her work forgoes depictions that suggest the object-like insignificance and submissiveness of those violenced psychologically or physically by family, foe, or government.

Her response in the groups of works I have mentioned, only a portion of her oeuvre, is astounding. It is as if by her painting she could reanimate and

FIGURE 14.3 Liliana Wilson, *Las amantes* (2002).

substantiate or ground the body in danger of physical, mental, and spiritual disintegration. For her eye does not dwell on the body in pain, in torture, undergoing physical, sexual, or psychological violence and violation or repression, but rather on it yet or still or once again intact, albeit surrounded by undeniable, pressing, and still present, if momentarily unseen, menacing forces.

To see Wilson's larger body of work together, now including images of people in soothingly erotic atmospheres — such as *Cisne* (2005), *La diosa del amor* (2002), *Las amantes* (2002; figure 14.3), *Mi reina* (2003), *La bella durmiente* (2004), and *La espera* (2007) — reveals strong lines of continuity between the earlier, painful works and the subsequent joyful ones. That point of continuity is in the depiction of the beings themselves, now, however, fully restored to an Edenic, natural, harmonic environment, one in which the integrity of these beings is rooted in that self-same well of nature that is now fully accessed, no longer *acosados*, hunted by hostile, estranging forces.

In all of Wilson's work, what is sited, mapped, affirmed as present is a full, rich interiority, an inviolate being rooted in eros, being as love. What is recorded is the capacity to love, the healing font not only of self-love, and love of and respectful relation with the other, but of beauty, harmony, goodness, and peace.

THE PERFORMANCE OF SPIRITUALITY AND VISIONARY POLITICS IN THE WORK OF GLORIA ANZALDÚA

FIGURE 15.1 Celia Herrera Rodríguez, *Ojo de sabiduría* (2006).

I HAVE COME A LONG WAY with Gloria, elated as a sister Chicana and radical woman of color when I read *This Bridge Called My Back* (Moraga and Anzaldúa 1981) in the mid-1980s, and then giving away my copy of *Borderlands* (1987) like a disease, after erasing my mad pencil markings against the author throughout the book's margins. I was a grad student; half of me about order and footnotes and foolproof arguments; the other half about radical politics and, at least theoretically, about experimental poetics. And here was this flaw of a book that was about a different kind of knowing, a knowledge we could only access by seeing how fallen apart we actually were, how colonized our wholeness, a book too much a solo flight into the unknown, the instinctual, and the scary-as-hell *"facultad."*

To embrace *Borderlands* then would have been to pay to be jumped: an unadvised *revolcada* from head to toe that promised worse than nothing, to the taunting tune of "I know more than Freud." In 1987 Anzaldúa's book was an invitation into the deeper recesses of margins I already inhabited, not the exodus promised by a grad school where I only ever came across two other Chicana/os in the entire humanities and social sciences, one of whom did not want to come out and play.

But by 1990, not only had I bought a new copy; I was teaching it, as I have continued to do, two to four times a year. It has been a steady, twenty-five-year intravenous drip of the Anzalduan way. The transfusion was complete in the early 1990s, in one of the first papers I ever presented, in high *macha* mode, at a philosophy conference. There I argued that Anzaldúa's *Borderlands* presented us with a new philosophical framework outside of Western binary thought, a different way to think and conceive of the making of meaning, a way beyond the hegemonic, a multiply queer way of knowing.[1]

In the spring of 1998, I published an essay discussing the centrality of the spiritual and the psychic, or *la facultad*, as other ways of knowing in

Borderlands. That essay, "Spirit Glyphs: Reimagining Art and Artist in the Work of Chicana *Tlamatinime*," argued that a decolonizing politics of spirituality was at work, alongside gender, race, class, and sexual critiques in the work of Gloria Anzaldúa, Cherríe Moraga, Ana Castillo, and Cisneros; in visual artists Yolanda López, Yreina Cervántez, and Ester Hernández, and in filmmaker Frances Salomé España, alongside many others. That essay became the cornerstone of a book that grew up around it, a book I conceived as an altar, and that focused on the spiritual and aesthetic hybridities of over forty artists in various media, published in 2007 as *Chicana Art: The Politics of Spiritual and Aesthetic Altarities.*

In the opening paragraphs of *Altarities*, as I have always called my book, I recounted that my journey to spirituality in the work of Chicana art began reluctantly, in the early 1990s, after reading a white feminist theorist who exhorted feminists to take up science and defy their gendered lot in the touchy feely, unscientific realms of goddess and other unscientifically grounded realms. But what was disturbing to me was that in a chapter recounting the history and development of the concept of gender in the U.S., when summarizing the contributions of Anzaldúa, she silenced the centrality of spirituality in her work and failed to engage her critically for it, as we would have expected. I felt that this was, at best, a condescending act of solidarity with a woman of color feminist. And I said so to a friend, who said that I should write about it.

But there was no way that I was going to commit intellectual suicide in the basic black, piranha world of fashionably atheist, leftoid academics for whom religion and spirituality on the personal level were good for snide appetizers.

At that time, outside of anthropology, sociology, and theology, neither literature nor art history, Chicano nor Ethnic Studies, feminist nor queer studies, poststructuralist nor postcolonial theory could conceive of spirituality as a terrain of political struggle, let alone as a site of consciously decolonizing ideology, alongside gender, sexuality, class, and racialization, as Anzaldúa, and so many U.S. women of color in her generation and those following, did in their literary essays, poetry, stories, novels, and visual art.

It is very likely due to *Borderlands* that in the fall of 1990, like the tarot deck's fool, I embarked on a private return to spirituality, devouring along the way a mad mix of spiritual writings in my shadow life. Coupled with the legit readings of my professional life, my mind survived the numbing rot of ego-drenched, spirit-strangling critical theory. In this way, I jumped a kind of double-dutch in my spirit-mind, and in so doing salvaged my mind, my spirit, my creativity, and set upon a path of greater intellectual, emotional, and spiritual wholeness, following the compass of my own heart and body.

Without knowing it then, I realize now that with Anzaldúa as the psychopomp, I was led through an underworld, into a different politics of lived being, one seeking anchor in a more real, complex, and, most importantly, integral conception of subjectivity as multiple and changing, and of coexistence as interdependent, simultaneous, and in which difference is valuable and necessary to the whole. This was a perennial philosophy found across the globe's ancient peoples of individual and social being as a path of continual growth and transformation, and of human and social health through integration and empowerment, rather than social marginalization, psychic fragmentation, and disempowerment.

Anzaldúa's way spoke powerfully to me as a person to whom the visual was very important. In *Altarities*, as I had argued in an earlier essay called "*El desorden*" (1999), I wanted to make a feminist and interdisciplinary argument: that Chicana feminism was the product of many languages, including those of visual and performance art, and of literary art, and not only of feminist journalism or scholarly articles. I wanted to argue that the arts, through their own languages, were a way of making meaning, of thinking, indeed of cutting-edge insights and theories. It was lifeblood to me that the arts spoke other than linguistically or that when they were word based, they spoke through poetic suggestion and fiction rather than through a belief in definition and denotation.

I also knew that I wanted *Altarities* to be formally and conceptually experimental, that I did not want it to look or be shaped like dominant cultural academic studies. I wanted it to be poetic and creative and subversive. I do not know that I accomplished that, but it was soul food to work on the book in this way, working on its key parts through creative journaling and grounding myself in nonacademic sources, especially those related to spirituality.

Throughout the decade when I worked on my book, I was mindful of the company I kept in my head and heart once I realized that I wanted *Altarities* not only to map the politics of the spiritual in Chicana art but to be spiritual as well, to discuss spirituality from the inside, and not only as a disinterested pseudo-objective observer. The politics of the spiritual eventually became the guiding thread of the book, as its title suggests, symbolized in the word *altarities*, a hybrid of the words *altar* (both English and Spanish) and *alteridad*, alterity.

And so in spite of my "No way" to writing about spirituality in *Borderlands*, I found myself, both in my personal life and in my research and teaching, continually accompanied by Gloria and the psychological and spiritual mythological roadmap of multiple and simultaneous planes of existence that she created to navigate these times: bridges and borderlands; the Coatlicue State; *nepantla*; the practice of making face, making soul, and later, *conocimientos y desconocimientos*.

I want to honor Gloria Anzaldúa as a tremendous thinker, artist, activist, as a tremendous spirit who wrote of the necessity and rewards of transformation, of creating other ways beyond the binary logic of the various dominations we have been shaped within, beyond the dominating logic that is the foundation of colonialism and of the patriarchy, heternormativity, religious intolerance, and unjust social orders that followed the invasion of the Americas and have persisted through five hundred years of inhumanity against a majority of this continent and the planet.

From *This Bridge Called My Back* to *Borderlands / La Frontera*, and up through *Making Face, Making Soul* (1990), into *This Bridge We Call Home* (Anzaldúa and Keating 2002), in her deeply compassionate essay within it, "and now let us shift," and now, still, through her posthumously published writings, Gloria broke ground for the rest of us. She showed us pathways beyond the internalization of hatreds that render us various shades of living death. Because this was not about writing, about metaphors, but about real survivals, real transformations, toward real better presents and futures, she was careful to not hide the dangers and fearsomeness that lay ahead.

I do not know that I have ever read a writer, not even Anaïs Nin, so committed to exposing herself, to patrolling her own duplicity and fear, as Gloria Anzaldúa. Writing was a spiritual path for her, a spiritual practice among other spiritual practices. Through it, she engaged in meditation, reflection, and self-scrutiny, and this in turn allowed her to gaze at the social world made by humans more clearly and to scry a vision of a different, better way of being.

Gloria's writing was her embodied thinking and, I dare say, her prayer or incantation, her words of power, delivered with intentionality, as acts. As she pointed out in *Borderlands*, she understood writing as image-making, a calling forth from the imagination that at its core was performative, and powerfully so.

> My "stories" are acts encapsulated in time, "enacted" every time they are spoken aloud or read silently. I like to think of them as performances and not as inert and "dead" objects (as the aesthetic of Western culture think of art works). Instead, the work has an identity; it is a "who" or a "what" and contains the presences of persons, that is, incarnations of gods or ancestors or natural and cosmic powers. The work manifests the same needs as a person, it needs to be "fed," *la tengo que bañar y vestir.* (*Borderlands*, 67)

Thus she spoke of her book as alive, as needing to be bathed and combed, even as a kind of "precocious girl-child" (*Borderlands*, 66). She distinguished her aesthetics from the formal virtuosity of modern decades, increasingly emptied of any kind of social or visionary power, and gradually reduced to mute decoration. Instead, she sought to resuscitate the *tlacuilo-tlamatinime's* performative path of the red and the black inks, one among many ancient and cross-cultural, intentional, and sacred ways of object making, not necessarily called "art." "Picture language precedes thinking in words; the metaphorical mind precedes analytical consciousness," she wrote (*Borderlands*, 69). Thus, she strove to return to art making as an image-producing activity an awareness of its actual, literal power in this time when even the thought of art as powerful is laughable, or perhaps limited to a moment of insight that might move us emotionally or intellectually.

Her project was more ambitious than formal virtuosity, in fact, not possible through it, really. She sought to restore to consciousness the awareness of psychic power itself as the seedbed of image making and therefore of thought itself and its omnipresent embeddedness in material reality, beginning with our own bodies: our guts, our genitals, the flickering thoughts escaped from our unconscious recesses. For her, the flesh was also the dwelling place of the unfleshed; the body itself, a borderlands and a nepantla.

The *Interviews* (2000) and the 2009 publication of *The Gloria Anzaldúa Reader*, a selection of decades of her writings, edited by AnaLouise Keating, show how hard and continuously Gloria worked on harnessing the performative power of the imaginal. It is no coincidence that *Borderlands*, for example, is a multigeneric or hybrid text, as has been pointed out many times. The multiple and simultaneous registers on which it performs together enact a way of being and consciousness that sees much, at once. Its language is the language of conocimiento, drawing its strength on the fuller truths of what we actually are as humans, that is, spiritual and psychic, and what is happening on these levels, as indicated by heart, gut, and desire as sites of spiritual or psychic speech, as it were, and not only by what has been programmed into our brains by culture and through *familia* as truth or permissible.

Anzaldúa wrote that she hated institutionalized religiosity (*Interviews*). Instead, she spent her life as an artist intellectual spiritual guide, a tlacuila-tlamatinime, uncovering spiritual power and disempowerment that go by other names. She sought to decolonize, that is, to extricate spirituality from its institutionalized control at the hands of dogmatic churches, and its debasement by dominant intelligentsia. She sought to deghettoize a more complex notion of spirituality, and a more empowering one, one that is anchored in the mind and body, as embodied, and therefore necessarily enacted in the flesh and in thought. She studied world spirituality, psychology, philosophy, and the arts, searching for knowledge beyond those which reproduce the present orders.

Like the philosophers of old and their continuum in the cross-cultural spiritual teachers of the present, she sought wisdom. And like them, she sought not only for herself. She was therefore a seeker and an activist, and somewhat like Gandhi and Martin Luther King Jr., she sought, in the universals of ancient spiritual truths from all quarters of the globe, a way for humans to live better, to live more fully, more justly, more honorably. Like many spiritual teachers, she was a gender bender, seeing no solace in the structures of gender and in *metiche* (busybody) prohibitions labeling how love and desire must or must not flow, in disregard of how, in nature, love and desire actually exist.

Anzaldúa wished to perform the path of integrity, the struggle for wholeness, the acceptance of all the Glorias, as she put it, of all the selves, that in moments like sexual and spiritual ecstasy, in particular, coexisted consciously, harmoniously, no longer fragmented off as a habit of social rejection and self-loathing. She conceived of being and existence as spiritual and thus of everything natural as interrelated. She wrote of feeling great connection with plants, animals, the ocean, the sky, even inanimate objects like corral posts and windmills. In her short stories, she sought to fictionalize the experience of characters stretching beyond their conceptual and physical borders to pass through or unify with other beings and objects.

She was able to write of the spiritual as a borderlands, alongside the geopolitical U.S.-Mexico border and cultural, psychological, and sexual borderlands, because she had lived her interest in the paranormal and in noninstitutionalized world spiritualities as a taboo. She is remarkable for having set out to weave together the many innovative and visionary strands of the 1960s and 1970s as a form of political activist social action theory. Born in 1942, she lived these decades with open eyes: for in 1960 she was eighteen, and by the still-happening mid-1970s, in her midthirties.

The 1960s and 1970s were not only a cultural and political renaissance in this country; they were also a spiritual revival and break with a past of institutionalized religiosity. If Black and Chicana/o Power were freshly minted and spread like wildfire among massive numbers, along with the gay and lesbian and feminist liberation movements, so did Eastern spiritualities, the resurgence of Native American and African diasporic spiritualities, and the mushrooming of new religious movements, neo-pagan magic, and goddess rituals. Indeed, Gloria trod the risky path of immersing herself into New Age spirituality, into UFO literature, astrology, and other forms of the occult. I wonder if this fearlessness of hers was because she nearly died four or five times and because of this, like other psychics, this human capacity became pronounced in her, a door, as it were, left thereafter ajar.

After the publication of the *Interviews/Entrevistas* in 2000, I dare say that the women will be separated from the girls, or, more precisely, the daring from the timid. The gauntlet that Anzaldúa threw down there, refusing us a dull moment in our companionship with her, was to more fully elaborate on often-glossed snapshots in *Borderlands*: possession, merging, and outright sexual trysts with spirit beings and aliens. What can be done with that? There is really no way to make nice with that against her many critics, among these Chicanas and Native American women who view her as little more than a Latina New Ager. What will philosophers and theorists now wanting to write from nepantla as a freshly discovered so-called decolonial space do with this, if they do not politely ignore it or drop her like a hot potato?[2]

And I have to smile, because I realize that Anzaldúa's body of work as a whole has made it difficult to vampirize its power, ripped off and unacknowledged as her complex concepts of borderlands and queerness continue to be, worldwide. Anzaldúa was really talking about gnosis, literally, not metaphorically. She did not only mean that the oppressed experience cultural and social reality differently and therefore have a different point of view from which to tell reality, in the style of Akira Kurosawa's *Rashomon*, for example. What will political science look like if it locates power within the psyche, as Anzaldúa did, and not only in its external management via the state or social blocs?

Anzaldúa is not the first to suggest that revolution as social transformation cannot happen in any lasting way without inner transformation. Marxists and Socialists argued the point a hundred years ago, face-to-face with Marx and his followers. The bearers of a directly transmitted spirituality and philosophy thousands of years old, the Hindu social activist yogi Gandhi, whom I mentioned earlier, the late Tibetan Buddhist Chogyam Trungpa, and the Vietnamese monk Thich Nhat Hanh have also explained that inner transformation affects our bodies and society, simultaneously, causally, and thus that social revolution cannot be just or lasting without first having inner revolution.

Spiritual masters of traditions across the globe and across time make clear that spirituality and religiosity are about power. But greater power for the greater good, they have told us, is earned and developed through self-discipline and unwavering commitment to the right use of power in service of the greater good, over self-aggrandizement and enrichment. Chogyam Trungpa (2009 [1984]) said the spiritual path is a warrior's way, for it takes a warrior to not close one's heart in the face of so much suffering and to remain in love with the world and to be a beacon of healing love within it. Gandhi, a yogi whose path was through social action, who developed a powerful form of nonviolent spiritual activism, said it was not for the faint of heart but rather a path of courageous self-sacrifice for a world we might not live to see. Martin Luther King Jr. learned this way from black religious social activist elders who had sought Gandhi out in India and, like Gandhi, did not live to see the way he peacefully led through a spiritual politics of love.[3]

At her core, Gloria Anzaldúa was also a spiritual activist. And I want to frame her study and practice of many different spiritualities not as a shallow New Ageism but rather as an excavation and a *rescate*, a rescuing of universal and enduring truths in this time of what I consider a neocolonizing secularism that privatizes spirituality to cage it and denies spirituality or the scope of its nature. This is an investigation that she undertook in the face of the irony of poststructuralist atheism and the stubbornness of Western scientific atheism, both, in my view, herdlike postures that attempt to pacify us with the fiction of intellectual superiority over our ancestors and almost the entire population of the country and the planet.

For Gandhi, truth, God, and love were one. For Anzaldúa, the truth of being was our oneness and interdependence, founded in a common nature that is spiritual.[4] Anzaldúa sought to translate the meaning and function of the spiritual through comparative study of the religions and spiritual practices of many peoples. A kind of decolonizing Joseph Campbell, she looked for coincidences and commonalities beyond imperialist and Eurocentric Darwinian catalogs of primitive religiosities. And from this perspective, she was not afraid of speaking of essences in the face of the rise of extreme social constructivism in academia, an extreme of the argument that how we think and are is due to how the societies we are born into shape us.

Anzaldúa was a spiritual teacher, though she did not call herself that. I think that instead she understood her responsibility as a public figure in the "making face and soul" of those who heard and read her. She navigated the New Age, astrology, Don Juan, Seth, magic ritual, meditation, paranormal exercises, contact with UFOs, and I believe prophetic vision not to conduct weekend vision quests for $500, or to gather groupies to vampirize psychically and do her *mandados*. Throughout her work, I see the surviving words of the Nahua and Maya ancients guiding her ethics of self-knowledge and service to others, guiding her journey through the bric-a-brac of the spiritual marketplace of the last four decades. "Not this, not that," I imagine her saying to herself, as she separated treasure from junk.

Anzaldúa's rediscovery in the areas of spirituality and politics was that spirituality was political activism. It could be passive, or called by another name, such as political ideology, or willpower, and reproduce reality as the status quo, or it could be active, consciously deployed as a performance, an action creating effects that matter politically.

Anzaldúa dedicated herself to thinking about consciousness as a very real, spiritual, and productive site which, if invisible, is visible in its effects.[5] And so I want to argue that if Frantz Fanon has been invaluable in helping us to think about the internalization of colonial thought in, for example, discussing how self-loathing colonized peoples have been force-fed by racist regimes of power, and if Foucault has helped us to think better about the way in which we internalize power in general and at large in policing ourselves for the state by wanting to be good citizens, party to hegemony in whatever measure possible, Anzaldúa goes even further. For discourse and ideology are not just powerful intellectual phenomena with effects that are materialized on the social, cultural, economic, and political planes. Discourse and ideology are themselves the effects of spiritual awareness or ignorance, of conocimiento and desconocimiento. We are not merely subjected to and produced by the politically, socially, economically, and culturally empowered of our times. We are not merely a walking net of interpellations, soft clay misshapen by the constant *manoseadas* or manhandlings of mass media, law, and education.

At our core, within Anzalduan thought, we are all by nature powerful beings, and "being-becoming" is the reclamation of the right use of that power. Unlike the invitation to the cloisters, the monastery, the yogi's cave, or discipleship, Anzaldúa's message and methodology is radically simple and cross-culturally classic: know thy self and to thine own self be true, as Shakespeare's Polonius advised.[6] We are the compass on the road that she told us was made as we journeyed it. *"Caminante, el camino se hace al caminar,"* she wrote, remembering Antonio Machado's verses (Anzaldúa 2002 [1983], 352). If a mystic, as she identified herself several times, it was, like a big sister, to come back and tell us about it in order to get us to move and do something to empower ourselves in the world.

In direct opposition to the path of ascetics, however, for Anzaldúa, the path of spiritual awareness for herself and others in some way like her, born into negatively racialized, gendered, and sexed bodies, must first embrace and heal, *desembrujar*, as it were, unbewitch the despised, gendered body of color, traumatized further as a *mita' y mita'*, a gender half and half. Chogyam Trungpa, I believe, once noted that exercises immolating the ego were not appropriate for U.S. beginners because their egos were not healthy.[7] How much more true is this for people of color women and queers, generally from poor social backgrounds to boot? The sad statistics of suicide, disproportionate physical and mental illnesses, and dropping out among our ranks top to bottom say it all.

In Anzaldúa's worldview, the body is a wretched cage against which the spirit flails only to the extent to which we have been taught to desacralize our bodies, our authentic feelings, thoughts, and desires as suspect, unworthy, or evil.

We have to recognize the total self. . . . And we have to work with the body. To not say "Oh, the body is dirty and vile and we should escape it because it's a prison. The flesh is a prison, and the spirit is all important; we should discard the body and let it rot." No. It's the other way around. Matter is divine also. (*Interviews*, 103)

Borderlands has not turned out to be a vehicle of demonic possession, as a young undergraduate warned me the very first semester I taught it the fall of 1990: it was the beginning of an exorcism, an exorcism that continues to be guided by a litany of readings of the work of this very brave and generous woman, a woman not afraid to be called crazy or New Age or lightweight, because what was at stake was more important than her reputation among the intelligentsia of the day. In this sense, Gloria Anzaldúa knew that she was sacrificing herself as she wrote, in her very beautiful, punctuation-free poem of 1977, and to which she returned in a later essay.[8] I quote that poem in full here.

THE COMING OF EL MUNDO SURDO
(For Joya Santanlla)

> "This is not Pharoah's Egypt and we are not his slaves."
> — THE PASSOVER PLOT

I walk among you
I see sad things in my head
not being free is being dead

This is the year
the people of peace
break out of bondage

Together we walk
through walls   by the lunar
light see our
left-handedness
with our third eye

I am the temple

I am the unmoving center
Within my skin all races
sexes   all trees   grasses
cows and snails   implode

spirals   lining   thought
to feeling

The day of I am is   now
I discard the wings
and claws I wear to
disguise my humanness
A collector of wo/men
and androgynes will proclaim   me
One will prepare their way
Love is the doctrine

I am becoming-being
the questor   the questing   the quest
You and I have already met
We are meeting we will meet

The real unknown is feeling
The real unknown is love
do not be afraid
to touch each other
We go naked here.

This is not the year of revenge
Give it up   give up that hatred
of yourself rise   up   reach
Come to me my sister-brother
We will share the moment

We are the awakening feminine presence

We are the earth

> We are the second coming

GLORIA ANZALDÚA,

The Gloria Anzaldúa Reader (2009)

I want to end by saying that I am very grateful to Gloria Anzaldúa for naming the place that by necessity we must occupy, nepantla, as the place of visionary politics for "unrequited social justice lovers," as George Lipsitz once put it.[9] In that place, the social world is thankfully disturbed, its logic upended. Here we together begin to imagine and thus call into being a visionary, political eros that is simultaneously individual and social, spiritual and political. Here, it is true that we are different and same, we the many, the unknown, the welcome, where self is also somehow other, *donde tú eres mi otro yo, según los maestros maya*, where you are my other me: *In Lak'ech*.

16

DAUGHTERS SHAKING EARTH

FIGURE 16.1 Juana Alicia, *Cool Plants, Hot Planet* (2010).

Daughters Shaking Earth: Earth Shaking Daughters
Daughters
shaking Earth
(trembling Earth).
Earth in mayúscula
then, colon:
Bridge.
Link.
Passageway.
Fiber.
Hilo.
Tejido.

Artistas latinas,
hijas de la shaking earth,
la Tierra,
this place,
this continent,
this planet,
this time,

this moment shot through not only with energías vitales that help us see perceive
    feel know more sharply, more plainly, more truthfully, but also las energías
    sociopolíticas, económicas, that cause mighty creator-destroyer goddess Mother
    Earth to shake, shake, shake us into awakeness

for the Earth is alive.
It breathes, it sighs, it groans, it burps, it shouts, it calls, it moves.

The Earth moves
continuously
movimiento
movimiento.
Es vida,
es muerte,
regeneración,
constante circulación de energía,
de movimientos.
And we, tiny creatures, swarming the Earth.

Our ancestors, many ancestors
Spoke of energies crisscrossing, weaving this planet,
Coursing through us, broken into and reshaped into all manner of beings.
Us too, energies in movimiento

Aligned, misaligned, realigned, once, again, more, again, looping, scooping,
    diving, dancing, breaking, dashing, fusing, fleeing, merging, making,
    new beginnings, new dyings, loosening losses, then recuperations,
    amalgamations, concatenations, aglutamientos, pensamientos,
    sentimientos, proyecciones, esperanzas, sueños e invocaciones,
    energías,
luz,
conciencia,
ser,
be-ing
aquí,
con,
with,
on,
as
Madre Tierra, Mother, Earth,
matrix, Earth, matriz
you
me.

Vida-Energía-Luz-Espíritu

sagrada, sagrado,

life-giving throughout our lives,

throughout Life on the Planet,

throughout all of Time and Space

on this vibrating,

shaking,

moving

Tierra-Earth.

Life-giving, Life-taking, Planet Earth.

The place, our place, of life, of dying, perhaps too of perviviendo, of still living,
    fleshlessly. Perhaps. No sé. (And does it matter?)

Where are you, ¿dónde están,

Ancestors of mine,

marrow of my bones,

heart of my blood,

sight of my soul,

pulse of my entrails,

compass of my breath?

Hello, hello,

Buenos días, buenas tardes, buenas noches,

Ancestors of mine, of yours,

you,

me,

Hello, hello

¿Dónde están?

¿Dónde   están?

¿Me oyen abuelitos, abuelitas?

¿Tatitos y tatitas?

¿Dónde están, dónde están?

Bienvenidos, bienvenidas,

Abuelitos, abuelitas.

Gracias, gracias

¿Dónde están?
¿Dónde están?

¿Dónde estás?

Where are they,
Ancestors of mine,
Ancestors of yours?
Where are they,
where are they?
Do you hear me?
Do you hear me?

Where are *you*?

(The wind whispers, a woman says, a man murmurs: they are here, now, reborn,
    rechanneled, remade, rethinking, returning and turning us, the great turn, the
    turn, nuestro, nuestra turno, nuestro cambio, nuestro estar al revés, nuestro upside
    down, nuestro rightside, leftside, squint-eyed, no-eyed, heart-seen, gut-felt recon-
    nection, re-enchufe, super-rechargation into a new onda, a new energetic wave, a
    new mandate, an old call, an old way, a way, from away to the way, camino, Path,
    vision, profecía, speaking with tongues of light, hands with hearts, third eyes,
    facultades en motilidad, captando móvidas, hechando maromas, recosiendo,
    retejiendo, caminando, caminando camino vital nunca pisado twice because we
    never tread the same way twice, even when we think we do; time, if not space,
    is movimiento, electric stairway, digital freeway, faster than the speed of light of
    living itself, of Spirit.)

Spirit time, flesh time, y descarnado time, my carnalas y carnalos, flesh of each
    other's flesh, you, me, him, her, us, we, they, in-between, endless being sin o con
    entrometidos.

And so I ask again, are the antepasados really reborn? And is it now?
Would it matter?
Does it matter si In Lak'ech, if You are my Other Me, and I yours?
If we were them, you, me, those to come?

Not as karma but as fulfillment, as the hope,
We, you-me, the caretakers, of this space this time
For you, for me, for descendants, as ancestors,
in the end, our own gurus?

The Earth is shaken:
we are shaken
because the Earth, our Mother, is shaking.

Arrebatos, posesiones, powerful transfers of energy from, to, and through us;
shaken by anger, shaking with anger,
trembling with fear, trembling in anticipation,
shuddering in pleasure, delight, joy, too.

Kinds of movimientos, kinds of shaking
(milkshakes, shaken not stirred, shaking hips, y así . . .)
Powerful movimientos through us
(and not only through La Madre Tierra).

Oh, what happens to the Earth is happening to us!

Ay, hijas, ay, hermanas, you well know that
in this incarnated dream which is this social structure in dissolution:
what happens to us as femaled folk of all the colors, those meant to be subjugated
    in male-centered mind-set bad news enredos:
militaries, like Cronos, consuming their own children, imperialist rapes of cultures,
    peoples, women, children, men;
capitalist vampirizations upon the bosques, animales, minerales, aguas, soils, en un
    desenfrenado feeding frenzy as if, as if, as if, there isn't, won't be enough, enough,
    enough for you, for me, for us, and so and so and so
buy sell buy sell buy sell
but it is yourself greedy brother, greedy sister, greedy selves
sold down that river, yourself, yourself, your own arm, your own leg,
your heart, your liver, me, me, me,
that is, your other yo, your other you, y así, así, like that.

And so too, it is, the ancestors say, it is ourselves, me too, ourselves, we sell down
 the river.

No you, no me, no separate selves that time and space and spirit haven't shaped
 from self same energía.

Daughters and their mamas, mamas and their hijas.
In the hands of the soul-blinded, spirit-starved, we are all vulnerably innocent hijas,
 all discarded,
aged mamas
And so and so
What happens to us hijas, whether so-called boy, so-called girl, all daughters of the
 shaking earth is like what happened, what happens, what is projected to still
 happen upon Earth, Life Itself, treated as worthless, aged, old mother: "ya no
 sirve, ya no sirve," dicen los mal agradecido ungrateful ones, ungrateful ones.

The planet in its rich, thick, fragrant, humid embodiment is femaled,
 she-d — because patriarchal imperialist man attempts to shackle and violence
 and waste the soil, the air, the water, the energy of life itself, our mindsets, our
 capacity to dream, to envision, to be happy, at peace, at will.

Pero lo que es madre, lo que es tierra, lo que es hija, lo femenizado y mujer, sí sirve,
 what is mother, what is daughter, what is feminized and female, is good, does
 serve, and we, daughters of the shaking earth, serve only Life Her-Itself, that is
 ourselves, that is you.

Artistas, pensadoras, hermanas of mine, teachers of mine, fellow time travelers,
 sister warriors of love, enamored guerrillas, how Time braids his-her hair with
 you, with me, with the neighbor, and the one who thinks us enemy!

Life runs through forms like forms through thoughts.

The sands of time empty quickly, more quickly, so live we must, and say we must,
 and make, and do, and breathe and stand against a different screen, a different
 canvas, a different page, a different vision, a different knowing, a different living.

Each one of you: a beautiful warrior queen, a splendid picture- and mark-making scribe, Ustedes recuerdan, you remember, mujeres, why we have come like flowers speaking through beauty and fragrance, ephemerally, of our short transit through this plane of peopled planet.

Madre
Tierra
Tú
Yo
We are all each other's other self,
daughters
shaking
Earth
Earth
shaking
daughters.
We are all earth.
We are all shaking.
We are all daughters.
Shaking it all up
the earth moves
the spirit quickens
the heart blossoms
again, again, and again.

FASHIONING DECOLONIAL OPTICS

Days of the Dead Walking Altars and

Calavera Fashion Shows in Latina/o Los Angeles

FIGURE 17.1 Rigo Maldonado, *Callas* (2006, detail).

FROM 2003 TO 2006, and again from 2008 to 2010, Tropico de Nopal Gallery Art-Space, in Los Angeles, produced a yearly Calavera Fashion Show, featuring what by 2006 were called "walking altars," as part of its month-long Days of the Dead art exhibition and events.[1] The Calavera Fashion Shows and Walking Altars formed a new chapter of Days of the Dead celebrations in Los Angeles and the United States. They are vibrant new art forms that draw on mixed-media altar installation, performance art, and are a unique contribution to the Los Angeles phenomenon of dress-based installation and performance art, alongside the "paper fashions" pioneered there.[2] By coining the "walking altar" concept in their 2006 artist's call, Tropico refocused the production of this hybrid performance installation art form, beyond literal fashion shows and Halloween costumes. This new media performing altar-installation-as-dress became for many artists a device for exploring the core idea that on Days of the Dead, November 1 and 2, the living visit with their dead, according to Mesoamerican indigenous worldviews.[3]

Like other Days of the Dead artwork, walking altars commemorate deceased family members and friends, cultural hero/ines, and the unknown whose deaths trouble the living. At Tropico, walking altars have honored and made socially visible the "disappeared" young women of Juárez, casualties of the U.S.-Iraq War, the homeless, and victims of domestic abuse and rape. They also remember undocumented migrants who have died crossing the border, and the lethal toll on the environment due to the methods of the Immigration Naturalization Service (INS). Walking altars have paid homage to artists, singers, dancers, and poets, both the well known and the lesser known, and to inspiring figures such as Sor Juana Inés de la Cruz and John Waters's transvestite star, Divine.[4] But above all, the walking altars have provided a communal space for the artists to mourn for relatives and friends, and to lovingly remember them during this season.

Some of the walking altars broached death philosophically, in particular the Mesoamerican indigenous concept of the duality of life and death, a worldview seeing the continuity of life in the beyond, and thus the presence in our own lives of our ancestral dead. Many of the walking altars worked against erasure caused by racism and marginalization of the historical contributions of Latin American female, U.S. Latina/o, and queer artists. As live events, the Calavera Fashion Shows and walking altars created a space for communal, interactive celebration of the life of the dead, and a public space for acknowledging and mourning both physical deaths and social losses. In creating such a space through community art, Calavera Fashion Shows and walking altars worked toward restoring an individually and socially healthier way of dealing with physical death, social marginalization, and psychological or emotional losses.[5] In this, Calavera Fashion Shows and walking altars, like other Days of the Dead art and religious practices, enact a social critique of the denial and repression of death in dominant cultures. They speak to recognizing death in its many guises (trauma, violence, loss, extinction) and the human necessity of survivors to do something about it, both for themselves and for the dead.[6] In effect, the walking altars of the Calavera Fashion Shows worked to transform discourses of life and death in the mainstream of U.S. culture, circulating ancient and persistent ideas about the coexistence of the living and the dead, and the necessity of mourning and commemoration, for both the living and those who have passed on.

To the extent that they articulate themselves through respectful reclamation of Mesoamerican worldviews about the spiritual nature of being and reality, recirculating and reinterpreting aspects of these philosophies for the betterment of our communities in the here and now, the Calavera Fashion Shows and walking altars operated in ideologically decolonizing ways. Even where not culturally intact, and given that they are not religious ritual but rather spiritual art practices to some degree, such engagements form part of five hundred years of resistance against the historical repression of Mesoamerican indigenous spiritual practices and their folklorization in the service of Eurocentric, Latin American elite nation-building.[7] Such Chicana/o and Latina/o Days of the Dead practices consciously self-authorize themselves against (neo)colonizing censure and prohibitions that charge that non-Anglo, Hispanic "mixed-bloods" have no right to claim indigeneity or that the indigenous is irrecuperable, and therefore that attempts to identify with indigenous identities and practices are expressions of intellectually and spiritually naïve nostalgia, politically ineffectual, ostensibly idealizing the past rather than addressing the present and future.[8]

As performance events, the Calavera Fashion Shows produced a way of seeing and understanding that consciously fashions an optics beyond the blinders of centuries of widely popularized pseudoscientific racializing mythologies claiming that non-Europeans are biologically, intellectually, and culturally inferior: that is, that they are somehow less fully human, and therefore less deserving of respect, rights, and services, and in short, unworthy of full social existence. The colonial, and its persistence in contemporary neocolonial logic, consigns the indigenous, the indigenous-identified "mixed," and even at times the completely "deracinated" to socially liminal presence, to de facto segregation, to ghettoization in underserved yet tax-paying neighborhoods, to stereotyped, projected criminalization and disproportionate incarceration, that is, to various forms of social death-in-life.[9] In the face of this, the Calavera Fashion Shows and walking altars are also a performance of the survival and the vitality of the supposedly better-left-as-dead. They point the way to philosophies of how to live and social visions of successful communal life that do not depend on the domination-unto-death of others.

The first decade of the new millennium was a time, as continues to be, of the historic concentration of wealth into the hands of a different kind of minority: the numerically tiny, extremely wealthy, disproportionately "white" and male. Correspondingly, the number of poor has grown, with the majority of the impoverished in many parts of the world, including the U.S., continuing to be women of color, female-headed households, and their children. A callous, extreme profit-driven logic continues to rationalize and sharpen economic and social inequities. Regardless of claims that the U.S. is now "postracial" and "postfeminist," the most "modern" economic policies and the radically materialist values they spawn and circulate through mass media re-marginalize, re-gender, and re-racialize the indigenous and Third World poor and impoverish the lower middle classes.[10] Within this context, the production of art performance "fashion shows" might seem frivolous, and in any case, an ineffectual ideological response to the powerful advances of domination in this phase of postmodern "phantom capital" globalization, as economist David Korten (2010) has called it. I am arguing, however, that communal Days of the Dead practices in the U.S. "revivify" still negatively racialized Chicana/o and other Latina/o artists and their communities precisely against the forms of psychological, social, political, economic, and physical deaths that such marginalization, exploitation, and criminalization bring. Days of the Dead practices, even those that are artistic rather than religious ritual proper, allow for greater individual and communal integration with the community of our dead, as well as with personal, intra-psychic losses or "deaths."[11] The Calavera Fashion Shows and walking altars are particularly apt and new expressions of integrative bridge building to the disincarnate within the self, to each other, and to the physically deceased that somehow also function as our larger community, according to the living traditions of ancient beliefs in the Americas.

Articulated conceptually and formally through Mesoamerican philosophies of humanity's responsibility to maintain harmonious relationship within one's body (which includes "mind" and "spirit"), with each other, and with the rest of the natural world, including the world beyond physical life, the Calavera Fashion Shows as a whole, and certain walking altars in particular, also shed light on what is life- and death-giving in terms of the economic, the social, the political, the cultural, the psychological, and the spiritual, as well as the physical. Building on four decades of community-based Days of the Dead celebrations and events in the Chicana/o-Latina/o United States, by performing as the dead the walking altars "tell it like it is," from the socially and materially disinterested perspective of death as the place where "you can't take it with you."

The Calavera Fashion Shows gather walking altars that are witty, humorous, satiric, joyful, educational, sad, religious, predictable, or completely unexpected. As a whole, they are beautiful and startlingly creative, so many evidently crafted with great care as part of the homage, akin in this way to religious art. In ranging across a wide spectrum of figures and themes, they are like Mexican popular folk craft figurines that humorously depict the worlds of the living and the dead as mirror images of each other come to life, with *calavera* (skull face and exposed body part) mariachi bands, skeletons in curlers at the beauty salon, and newlyweds in coffins. In some respects, they are like José Guadalupe Posada's "calaveras," satiric skeleton drawings lambasting political corruption and social folly of the late eighteenth and early nineteenth centuries. But in making use of performance, in mobilizing the altar installation via the body, walking altars and the Calavera Fashion Shows go one step further in literally animating the ideas that the dead are alive and that the living are dead. The "models" perform the body as altar. The "dress" is the installation of various objects. And while all the dress installations are exquisite, complex, or wonderfully creative, mastery of media is not the central point, nor is exploration of this new media. Performance and commemoration is what takes center stage: the play of the living and the dead celebrating coexistence.

RENEWAL WITH A LITTLE HELP
FROM OUR DEAD

Marialice Jacob and Reyes Rodriguez opened Tropico de Nopal in 2000 with a Days of the Dead exhibition of altar installations. Following artist Yreina D. Cervántez's suggestion, they called these installations "*ofrendas*," in order to center the ancestral, indigenous spiritual tradition of remembering, honoring, and caring for one's dead on November 1 and 2 through rituals, offerings of food and flowers, and other memorial acts. This foundational emphasis on the spiritual also served to interrupt the tendency to appropriate Days of the Dead in culturally decontextualizing ways as nothing more than a Mexican-style Halloween party.[12] Tropico, that is, Jacob and Rodriguez, in dialogue with a circle of friends and seasoned artists, thereby chose to continue a tradition within Chicana/o art and cultural politics of recentering indigenous worldviews.[13] As it is so often misread, it must be said that this conscious effort to reincorporate or reanimate the indigenous within Chicana/o and U.S. Latina/o cultures, a cultural and spiritual politics dating to the 1960s, is a path markedly different from that of Mexico and Latin America's Eurocentric "mestizo" discourses that "celebrate" the achievements of the indigenous civilizations of the Aztec, Maya, and Inca but are contemptuous of living indigenous peoples and their supposedly degraded cultures.[14] Pioneering Los Angeles–based Chicana art historian Sybil Venegas, creator of a walking altar herself, observed of the indigenous relationship for Chicana/os that

it is the return to the ceremonies, practices, and ways of their ancestors and the revival of these practices in complex, oppositional contexts that give Chicanos strength, healing, direction and empowerment. This can be seen as a central and

key element in the evolution of Chicano political struggle and artistic development in the past twenty years. The Day of the Dead in Aztlán is one of the most
significant contemporary expressions of this sacred act of self preservation and
empowerment. (2000, 53)

Venegas thoughtfully theorizes "the overwhelming community-based response" to Days of the Dead in the U.S. as

a reflection of the postmodern condition of demographic change, uncer-
tainty, and an absence of meaning, spirituality, and spontaneous creativity
in contemporary, established social ritual. It is also a phenomenon rooted in
Mexican/Chicano history and grounded in . . . the conquest of the Americas by
European colonizers. For it is only against a backdrop of crisis, trauma, dramatic
loss of life and economic exploitation that we encounter the tremendous human
capacity for survival, adaption, and reinvention, which can be identified as
"sacred acts of self-preservation." (2000, 53)

Four decades of the enthusiastic popularization inside and outside the
Chicana/o-Latina/o communities of Days of the Dead spiritual and religious practices speak to their usefulness in creatively and meaningfully engaging social, economic, political, and cultural realities while functioning as
vehicles of spiritual expression and connection, of a healing and empowering
perspective about death, whether physical, social, or cultural.[15]

MAKING ALTARS WALK

The Calavera Fashion Shows would seem to have drawn on the post-1970
Chicana/o art tradition of calavera makeup for Days of the Dead and on the
Los Angeles phenomenon of "paper fashions" that Patssi Valdez and Diane
Gamboa came to develop as signature art forms. But if this is so, it appears
only indirectly. Gamboa, in particular, would deploy paper fashions as worn,
sculptural, and mobile "hit and run" performance art pieces that escape and
exceed the limits of curatorial acknowledgment and inclusion/exclusion by
essentially crashing exhibitions that the artist was excluded from, oftentimes
stealing the show.[16] In response to my queries about the possible influence of
early Asco-circle and other paper fashion shows, and in particular of Diane
Gamboa's paper fashion work with Asco and after,[17] Rodriguez clarified that

though he had never been to a paper fashion show, he had seen Diane Gamboa's "hit and run" pieces over the years. He conceived the idea of a calavera fashion show as a Tropico Days of the Dead event and discussed it with Gamboa, who, with Marialice Jacob, Yreina D. Cervántez, and Consuelo Norte (who were influential in the development of the Calavera Fashion Show's spiritual component) influenced its signature Chicana/o-Latina/o urban aesthetic. Rodriguez captured the influence of Gamboa's punk aesthetic in an anecdote, recalling Self Help Graphics's Days of the Dead procession to Evergreen Cemetery, where Diane Gamboa showed up dressed as a cowgirl with calavera make up. "Who does that?!" he asked, laughing. "The whole city is her stage, her 'calavera walk.' It's that spirit that underlies the whole thing [the Calavera Fashion Show]."[18]

As Rodriguez observed in the opening text of the video he made of the Calavera Fashion Show in 2005, "Friends and fellow artists have all inspired Tropico de Nopal's Calavera Fashion Show. For over twenty-five years the Chicano art community has refined and celebrated the calavera look in Los Angeles. The event is a natural evolution of the process."[19] Indeed, the walking part of the Calavera Fashion Shows and the walking altars can also be seen as natural outgrowths of Self-Help Graphics' artist-led Days of the Dead processions from 1972 to 1979 in East Los Angeles, and of the Galería de la Raza's San Francisco Mission District neighborhood Days of the Dead processions from 1981 to 1986, and subsequent Days of the Dead processions that continued under the direction of different organizations.[20]

As to the roots of Days of the Dead altar making and altar installation in the Bay Area, Tere Romo, curator and historian of some of the earliest Chicana/o art exhibitions, recounted that artist Yolanda Garfias Woo taught altar making for Days of the Dead, which she learned from her Oaxacan father, in the early 1960s. An artist herself, Garfias Woo introduced other Chicana/o and Latina/o San Francisco Bay Area artists to altar making, including Amalia Mesa-Bains, whose powerful installations have brought the medium the most attention in the dominant cultural art world. Garfias Woo also introduced altar making to the collective of artists that cofounded the Galería de la Raza.

The success of Days of the Dead in both California epicenters of Chicana/o and Latina/o arts, Los Angeles and San Francisco, would lead to annual events that eventually attracted thousands of people, including the media, and outsiders in Halloween costumes looking for "the parade" (Romo 2000,

34–37).[21] Lourdes Portillo's and Susana Muñoz's film *La Ofrenda: The Days of the Dead* (1988) sheds light on the popularity of Days of the Dead among both Latina/os and non-Latina/os, particularly during the 1980s. Using interviews, the film suggests that Days of the Dead provided a necessary language for people to begin to honor their dead against not only homophobic repression of the HIV and AIDS crisis but also more generally in mainstream culture where death may be repressed as embarrassing, as something that is best forgotten and thus becomes doubly wounding.

MORE CALAVERA FASHION SHOW BONES

The Calavera Fashion Shows and walking altars in Los Angeles also emerge from the sensibilities, aesthetics, and politics of Chicana/o 1970s underground rock and urban punk culture, infused with intergenerational aftereffects of 1940s and 1950s pachuca/o culture.[22] They are immersed in Hollywood film and popular media culture. But these cultures in turn have been influenced by Chicana/o and East Los Angeles artistic and street cultures, as Tim Burton's *The Nightmare before Christmas* and Disney/Pixar's unsuccessful 2013 bid to copyright the words "dia de los muertos" show.[23] While many of the walking altars share the wit and raw talents of a Tim Burton film production, the occult world of the spirits is not domesticated as the unreal. Like the religious altars they pay homage to and elaborate on as art, the Calavera Fashion Shows and many, perhaps most, Walking altars seem to take the life-death, human-spirits liminal threshold seriously.

On one level, the space of the Calavera Fashion Show has real elements of the memorial and of Days of the Dead religious rituals: of recalling the dead, grieving their loss, celebrating their lives, and dwelling with them through the creation of altars holding favorite foods, beverages, candies, and other objects. In Juana Flores's *Pachuca Educada*, this is seen in how the artist's mother, a stylish young pachuca in her youth who later became a teacher, is recalled. The "model" performs her in skull body makeup, fine pachuca clothing, hairstyle, stylishly matching baby stroller carrying baby and books, dancing her way up and down the calavera catwalk to the music of the "Pachuco Boogie."[24] In walking altars such as this one, the dead really are being lovingly remembered, their presence somehow felt in their re-creation through the human-as-medium that embodies the spirit of the honored.

For other walking altar artists, the reality factor behind their performance of the body-as-art-installation may involve more direct identification with religious Native American, "folk Catholic," or other beliefs that the dead continue to live, but differently. Orquidia Violeta's *Angel*, for example, suggests this. Her "Artist Dedication" states: "The boundaries which divide Life from Death are at best shadowy and vague. Who shall say where the one ends and the other begins? The Premature Burial. 1844. To all the Poets and Writers whom [*sic*] affected our lives" (Calavera Fashion Show 2008, program). This dedication points to a "real" something that survives in artwork itself, and that survives in us, shapes us, and in some literal way does dwell in us, sometimes feeling more real and affecting than many of those living around us. There are many walking altars dedicated to artists that suggest such feeling. In the 2008 Calavera Fashion Show, these included *Homage to J. G. Posada* by Guadalupe Rodriguez and Sandy Rodriguez, *Viva la Vida* to Diego Rivera and Frida Kahlo by Rosanna Ahrens, *Homenaje a Nahui Olin: A Woman of Eternal Cosmic Movement* by Lara Medina, and *Homenaje a Rosa Covarrubias: The Chicana as Tehuana* by Sybil Venegas. In all but the Posada piece, where the Mexican printer's iconic image of Death as an elegant lady in a hot pink slinky dress is courted by one of his frolicking signature devils, these walking altars pay homage to the artist by performing her or him. Thus, though walking altars are an art form that fictionalizes embodiment of a dead or fleshless other (e.g., a spirit, deity, or archetype), the human performer is a "carrier," a "channel" of the invoked spirit. In Spiritism, and in the temporary ritual spirit possession of individuals in Santería, for example, what is plain is that living bodies are the places, the altars, where divine and human, living and dead cross.[25] Walking altar performances of the dead as the living enact this logic.

UNDEAD STILL LIVES

In the Calavera Fashion Shows, walking altars are living bodies performing memory. They are altar installations in motion, performing the reanimation of the dead and the reality of spirits and deities. They perform the dead as part of a living spirit world, and the living, as the dead. Walking altars also enact or activate the crossing of various "languages" through the performance of body as altar, dress as altar installation, and fashion show as the world, the stage of life and death, human and spirit worlds. They operate through synesthesia, addressing multiple senses simultaneously through the choreography of discourses of dress, movement, and music, and crossing performance and multimedia installation such that the performing body is both stage and protagonist. In being set to music, with dance, swaying, or synchronized movement, walking altars literalize the idea of the dance of life and death.[26]

The performers give body to what memory returns through its various "archives": music, style, objects, a feeling or a mood. Walking altars embody the idea of memory as a persistence, a paradoxical *pervivencia*, a kind of living, within the mind and feelings of the undeceased, or in museums, books, and other forms recording social memory more generally. In the altar dresses, memory of loss is a kind of hologram, a three-dimensional reconstitution of the apparently invisible, momentarily garbed in the flesh of the actor and model, a stand-in for the dead. This symbolic coexistence of living and dead, of the tangible and the intangible, a literal coexistence in the religious altar, signifies the identification of the living and the dead, the fleshed and the disincarnate, not just in terms of the spirits of the dead but also in the unseen dimensions of corporality or the body: thoughts, emotions, desires, fantasies, and visions.

In skeletal makeup covering exposed body parts, what such performances of the dead-as-living and the living-as-dead materialize is, of course, that not all is as it appears, and that being is not simply appearance, easily accessible through visuality. The body as skeleton is the body inside out. It externalizes the internal, makes visible that which is invisible, because it is shrouded behind flesh and the tissues of muscles and organs. What is contained is released, dissolved even, to the bare bone, symbolizing the imbrication of life and death, and the cyclic nature of this embrace.

LARGER THAN LIFE

It is hard to describe the great energy, the enthusiasm and appreciation for the Calavera Fashion Shows' wonderfully creative takes on the idea of the walking altar, or the centrality of the communal in their production and, reception. Walking altars became a venue for exploring a new, performance- and installation-based hybrid medium. Few of the mainly visual artists had experience with performance.[27] According to Rodriguez, Cervántez, and

Rigo Maldonado, the collaborative nature of creating walking altar pieces and of producing the Calavera Fashion Shows was particularly welcome, given the typically solitary nature of making artwork.[28] That the exploration of this new hybrid medium offered fresh, genuinely original possibilities for rethinking the meaning of Days of the Dead and memorials more generally is strikingly evident, even in documentary photos and films. Perhaps the stimulating new possibilities offered by walking altars and the warm support and festive spirit of Calavera Fashion Show events explain why many of the artists have participated in the Calavera Fashion Shows more than once: Consuelo Flores, Rigo Maldonado, Orquid Velazquez (aka Orquidia Violeta), Araceli Silva, Sandy Rodriguez, Guadalupe Rodriguez, Robert Quijada, Margaret Guzman, Zoe Aguirre, Poli Marichal, CiCi Segura, Carolyn Castaño, Ofelia Esparza, Abel Alejandre, Rosanna Ahrens, Maria Elena Castro, Daniel Gonzalez, Katiria Gomez, Juana Flores, and Edith Abeyta.

While it is difficult to single out a few from the dozens of walking altars that have appeared since 2003, I will briefly describe some in order to give a sense of the range of these works, and where possible, their reception. Poli Marichal is a Puerto Rican printer and painter, now a part of the Chicana/o-Latina/o arts community of Los Angeles. In 2008 she performed a moving tribute to her deceased father, silently narrating her parent's love story, *The Dance of Love and Death* (figure 17.2), to operatic music, "Felice," by Nicola Piovani.

El [altar ambulante] del 2008 es el que dediqué a mi padre, el artista canario, Carlos Marichal. Mis padres vivieron un gran amor que mi madre, Flavia Lugo, ha mantenido vivo a través de los años. Yo quise honrarlo con este altar ambulante. En él, mi madre va a visitar [sic] la tumba de mi padre y él se le aparece. Ella se sobrecoge asustada pero, cuando se da cuenta que es él, le toca la cara y después lo abraza. Juntos en ese abrazo, los dos amantes bailan y, luego crean un corazón con las mitades que cada [sic] uno tiene en su mano al unirlas.[29]

The character of "Death," both puppet master and stage, was dressed in a long, silver-gray skirt and matching overalls-style bib that, with a large cross on it, had the effect of a tombstone. The face of the model (as Death, the Puppet Master, and Stage) was covered in a silver mask, the Moon, with a circular perimeter extending some six inches or so all around the face, and a long gray veil trailing from it to the floor. From the arms of the figure's black, close-fitting sweater, two hand puppets emerged, representing the artist's

FIGURE 17.2 Poli Marichal, *The Dance of Love and Death* (2008).

father and mother, and worn like gloves but projecting about a foot and a half beyond the hands. The impression of the walking altar, performed by the artist, was of death as the looming stage against which the dance of court-ship and life occurred, a dance of stage and puppets paced to complex and dramatic operatic music. Marichal also created *Tanta Vanidad: So Much Vanity* . . . (2006), dedicated to her grandmother, and in 2009 performed as La Muerte / Blue Death with a puppet, Los Ojos, "un niño indigente," in *La Muerte de los Niños de la Calle / The Death of Homeless Children*. Her 2010 walking altar, *Soul Catcher*, was based on Remedios Varo's "Star Catcher," she explained, "a sort of merciful death" (program notes), and dedicated to her recently deceased aunt (figure 17.3).

Rigo Maldonado created three walking altars in 2005 whose construc-tion details are useful to understanding the significance of walking altars to

FIGURE 17.3 Poli Marichal, *Soul Catcher* (2010).

some of the artists. He explained that he had never sewn before the Calavera Fashion Shows but had grown up watching his mother construct wedding and *quinceañera* (sweet fifteen) dresses, though he did remember drawing dresses as a child.[30] *La Divina . . . A Tribute to Gia* (2004) was constructed of drawings and other things that the artist found when helping to clean out the apartment of his friend, a young female fashion illustrator and designer who committed suicide. Maldonado later installed this dress in Tropico de Nopal's gallery, with other longer-term *Ofrenda* installations. *Callas* (2005), used on the Calavera Fashion Show invitation for 2006, featured a beautiful diva in a copper wire mesh skirt cage decorated with flowers and photos of the opera singer (figure 17.1). Other materials beside textile included pearls, silk, feathers, and birds. The artist's statement explained, "The guilded bird-case skirt is left open, offering an alternative to life in the public eye amidst powerful men and morally flexible jetsetters. Through it all the fighting spirit of Callas lives on . . . Vine [*sic*], Vidi, Vici!" In Tropico video documentation of this piece, the performer stepped delicately and slowly to one of Maria Callas's tragic arias. *Basquiat* (2005) honored Haitian Puerto Rican New York painter Jean-Michel Basquiat and incorporated his New York City tag, "SAMO" (same ol' shit), into the design. *Chávez, Cruz, and Warhol* (2005) played upon a Kellogg's Corn Flakes promotion that strangely lumped together the Cuban salsa chanteuse and a very serious-looking César Chávez, head of the United Farm Workers. Maldonado created a dress and matching purse made of corn flake boxes.

Maldonado's *Too Much Is Never Enough* celebrated John Waters's transvestite film star, Divine, and the actor and drag queen Harris Glenn Milstead (1945–88), who performed her. The artist described the music, the name of the piece, and the spirit of its design in his artist's statement:

Fashion Name: Too much is never enough. Music: Little Richard — Girl Can't Help It. Model Name: Shakina Nayfack. *Statement* — In celebration of one of the most important figures in too-wrong fashion, glamour and glitz, this walking altar is dedicated to "the most beautiful woman in the world," Divine! Even today we can still look to her, the originator and reigning queen of camp, trash and sass, for the inspiration and courage to be shamelessly excessive, ruthlessly indulgent and in all ways larger than life![31]

In an interview with me, Maldonado further explained that the dress was inspired by the tradition of quinceañeras, Latina/o coming-of-age celebrations. The bustier was composed of the traditional Days of the Dead flower, marigolds, and the skirt from a vintage green lace tablecloth. The corsage and the headdress were made from flowers and images of Divine from Waters's films, framed in little hearts.

In Sandy Rodriguez and Guadalupe Rodriguez's *Una Ofrenda a los Santos Inocentes* (Calavera Fashion Show 2006), death-masked Frida Kahlo and Diego Rivera danced around a buxom Death dressed in white bustier-topped, wide-skirt diaphanous dress and shawl, imploring her to deliver the

FIGURE 17.4 Rigo Maldonado, *Too Much Is Never Enough* (2004).

FIGURE 17.5 Rigo Maldonado, *Too Much Is Never Enough* (2004, detail).

FIGURE 17.6 Rigo Maldonado, *Too Much Is Never Enough* (2004, detail).

three baby *calaveritas* crawling at her feet, barely visible beneath the long hem of her skirt. Death is the last to exit, triumphantly holding up one of the skeleton babies. The effect is not gruesome, however. Based on Kahlo's biographical miscarriages and medically mandated abortion, the scene appears philosophical: memorializing the Mexican artists' lost children and their grief as a couple.

Maldonado's and Sandy and Guadalupe Rodriguez's pieces also convey two other elements central to many walking altars, whether through the "dress," the music, or the movement of the models: the manifestations of desire and of humor. Death is often represented as sexy, a desirable seductress or seductor, draped in the U.S. flag while dancing with a soldier, for example, or slow dancing while surrounded by daggers, or as an updated *Catrina* (following Diego Rivera's *Dream of a Sunday Afternoon in Alameda Park* [1947–48]), serenaded by a lascivious leaping red devil that mugs to the audience. Whether dancing seductively to salsa or rock music, or cavorting humorously, the audience sways, claps, or laughs appreciatively and is often engaged directly, through eye contact by the performers. This is as close to a Latin American holy day procession and festival, with its mixture of serious spiritual ritual and earthy human feasting, as some will ever get north of the U.S.-Mexico border.[32]

FASHIONING A DECOLONIZING OPTICS

According to specialists in trauma and nonviolence, enacting and surviving violence requires psychologically distancing mechanisms.[33] This observation can be applied to visuality as well. When violent, our gaze can be penetrating, hostile, and objectifying, and yet we typically do not let our vision dwell on what we are violencing or what has been violenced by others. Discourses of dehumanization function similarly. We consign to the margins of social visibility and ethical accountability (i.e., intellectual or spiritual awareness) what is ideologically minimized as inferior, uninteresting, dispensable, or despicable. Similarly, what we oppress culturally is what we endeavor not just to refute or to minimize but to obliterate from the shared worldview, the cultural imaginary, social perception, and psychological awareness. This shuttered view produces erasures within the social imaginary, a "narrow-mindedness" that reproduces the violence of colonialism and neocolonialism, of patriarchy, homophobia, and classism, on the cognitive level and the visual, as hardly visible, if not unreal or nonexistent. Violence then becomes masked as something other than what it is, something normalized within dominant cultural logics, a nonissue to all but the survivors of such dismissals, reductions, denials, oppressions, erasures.

The uncolonized or the less colonized, however, exist apart from the narratives that dominant culture fabricates, which labor to limit our capacity to perceive more fully, more universally, rather than in very culturally and ideologically bound ways. Thus, while dominant cultures do not wish to see what they consign to the shadows, this does not mean that these other spheres do not exist, and with optics of their own, obeying different logics. And while colonial domination involved physical and cultural genocide of millions of Native Americans throughout the Americas and the Caribbean islands, it did not exterminate their core philosophies based on spiritual and scientific knowledge about the natural world in its human and nonhuman dimensions. Human beings are not the masters of the natural or spiritual worlds, nor of each other. And those who resort to violence to uphold such fantasies are not even masters of themselves, according to spiritual adepts cross-culturally.

Chicana/o and, more broadly, Latina/o art practices around Days of the Dead such as the Calavera Fashion Shows and walking altars are one set of practices among many that people "of color" in the U.S. and indigenous peoples of the Americas have discovered, re-created, or received and by which they survive and strengthen themselves in the face of centuries of violence. In the Calavera Fashion Shows and walking altars, racist, classist, sexist, and homophobic dehumanizations are counteracted, reminding us of the profoundly political, democratizing, and ecological view from which Days of the Dead celebrations arise: that life and death exist in a continuum, and are part of the interdependence of all being, the visible and the invisible, the human and the nonhuman.

The Calavera Fashion Shows and the walking altars create a crossroads where dominant culture meets supposedly dead cultures, dead people, and dead ideas. As Marjorie Garber observes in her book *Vested Interests* (1997), crossing is crisis-inducing when the space of crossing is revealed as such, as a space beyond, as a borderlands (to invoke Gloria Anzaldúa), a third space outside binary logic, a zone operating by multiple codes, and not just those of dominant cultures. In the Calavera Fashion Shows and walking altars, the twilight citizenships and undocumented lives of the negatively racialized Chicana/o and Latina/o communities of Los Angeles are brought into view. But the objectified are now subjects with stories to tell, insights to share, pictures to show, energies to transmit.

Ideologically, intellectually, spiritually, and visually, the Calavera Fashion Shows operate from a different dimension, a culturally real way station of hybrids, righteous misfits, inevitable rebels, and brainiacs. The audience claps enthusiastically at the beauty, the imagination, the creative brilliance, the loveliness of the affection, the beauty of the respect, the incomprehensible rightness of remembering our dead, our losses. What has gone missing in our hearts, our heads, and our lives is collectively found in these sold-out gatherings of initiates and sympathizers, of Chicana/o and Latina/o artists, family, friends, and fans. A Calavera Fashion Show is an event to fill the eye and feed the soul. Neither a marketplace for the selling of fashion or art nor a museum or pretentious gallery event, the Calavera Fashion Shows are a display of an unruly cultural logic. Taking Death as advisor, they parade for inspection that which gives life, nourishes, ministers to the losses of our loved ones, showing us that they can and must be incorporated into our lives, as must the many other forms of death we suffer while in the flesh. Calling for a little help from our dead, as my mother says, things will get better, you will see. *Ya verás*.

18

ON JEAN PIERRE LAROCHETTE
AND YAEL LURIE'S *WATER SONGS*

FIGURES 18.1–18.9 Jean Pierre Larochette and Yael Lurie, *Water Songs* series (1999–2007). FIGURE 18.1 (left) *A Well of Living Waters.* FIGURE 18.2 (right) *The River in One.*

ONLY SONG CAN RESPOND to the call that are the nine tapestries that together form the *Water Songs* of the artists Jean Pierre Larochette and Yael Lurie. The heart recognizes its own mute but pulsating language in the visions, dilated in meditation, of the natural world.

Water Songs (2008) is a book in the way that our ancestors taught that nature was a sacred writ. For some, it will appear an epic of the esoteric, of that which lies beneath the surface, captured in details that are, perforce, symbols of the archetypal story of being and becoming, of the identity of the individualized

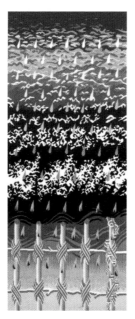

FIGURE 18.3 *Seminal.*   FIGURE 18.4 *Returning.*   FIGURE 18.5 *Quietude.*

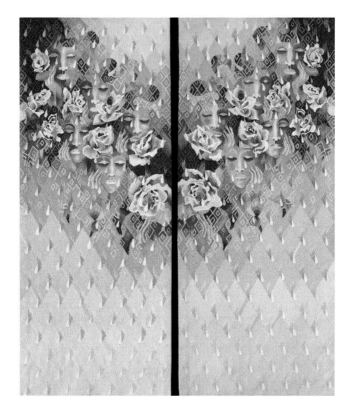

FIGURE 18.6 *The Ancestor's Garment* (previously *Seven Generations*, as one panel).

and the all-encompassing whole. And it is a song of joy, of awe, of praise and celebration, of the human soul in sweet embrace with the spirit of all creation.

From the divinely vibrating nothingness, starbursts of energy. Here, sky, there nighttime reflection upon the sea. Waterdrops collecting as fountain, matter blooming into garden. All script in the Book of Life.

The palette grows: lavender, magenta, pink-reds, and orange-browns. Across the moonlit mist a rainbow braids the lion-maned waves.

From deepest blue to a wash so light, the pattern beneath, within, fades from view. Yet, at that moment, like a fist piercing paper: a stand of roses. The fire and water of six-pointed stars now, here, green leaves. Bud to bloom, again and again. Time-bound if patterned.

FIGURE 18.7 *Waterfall.*   FIGURE 18.8 *Yosemite.*   FIGURE 18.9 *Watershed.*

A churning ocean, sun sets on the foam. In brief space, the eventide shall sweep away a shallow barricade. A snake, entwined on a bamboo stake, invites a change of skin.

Creation thickened amid the densely gathered wet. A toad crisscrosses the forest floor, its croaking, a lover's canticle. Greens and blues and lavenders in steady, joyful presence.

The weaving yields, weft pulled apart that we might peer at traces of each other in the now, before, and after. All ancestors, all progeny, we are bound one to the other as to ourselves by threads of soil and of silver.

The weaver unleashes, in horizontal strokes, meandering torrents of shape and color. The glimmering rush rounds in time the massive rocks and greens gone brown, ground blue waters.

Golden rain falls in gentle, steady murmur on primordial walls. All is movement and alive. Rain's become the tongue of stones and chant is heard that has no words.

Browns are quickened in lifeblood and woven is the ebb and flow. The loom is singing the One Song. All is One, then not, then is again.

PRAYERS FOR THE PLANET

Reweaving the Natural and the Social:

Consuelo Jimenez Underwood's

Welcome to Flower-Landia

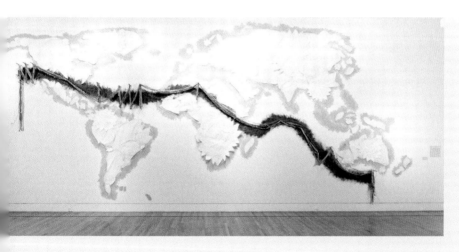

FIGURE 19.1 Consuelo Jimenez Underwood, *Flowers, Borders, and Threads, Oh My!* (2013).

CONSUELO JIMENEZ UNDERWOOD'S RICH, thirty-year career is characterized by a passionate call to what lies beyond the conventional, whether in terms of artistic media or, more importantly, in terms of the cultural imaginary that limits our perception of the normal and even of the possible. This is no flight from reality but, rather, forays from which to remedy the social and environmental wounds of our time and place. The urgency and the promise of this call to more clearly perceive the social worlds we have fabricated and to more deeply feel our relation to nature is perhaps nowhere more evident than in her fall 2013 exhibition, *Welcome to Flower-Landia*, although it marks her oeuvre as a whole.

Jimenez Underwood leapt beyond the gendered and racialized demarcation between craft and fine art early on, creating work that mixed weaving, painting, print, embroidery, found objects, and multimedia installation: no small feat. To her art world contemporaries and teachers, the medium of weaving seemed part of Europe's art historical past, and in the present, more suitable as a feminine, Native American, or "Third World" craft. Regardless of skill in execution, loom and needlework seemed practical or decorative, not the matter of serious art, of ambitious aesthetic, philosophical, and social considerations.

We now begin to know from traditional indigenous weavers of this continent that weaving has been both a historical archive of cultural knowledge and a record of the heightened awareness of its practitioners — literally a social text. Jimenez Underwood is positioned at the crossroads between this ancient art form and those of the Westernized present. First introduced to the loom in her childhood by her father, a man of Huichol ancestry, during her graduate art school days she discovered in the loom, thread, textile, and needle particularly effective media by which to focus on seemingly removed, marginal aspects of reality.

In the 1990s, a renewed anti-immigrant, anti-Mexican, and post-9/11 anti-terrorist sentiment gave rise to the construction of a multibillion-dollar concrete and steel wall, with high-tech surveillance equipment positioned at check points along the United States' 1,933 mile southern border. Thus far, only some 700 miles of wall have been completed, largely due to the massive expense of what has turned out to be a highly ineffective means of barring undocumented immigration. Instead, it has driven border crossers to more remote mountainous and desert crossings, resulting in many more deaths, numbering in the thousands, through exposure to extreme temperatures with access to little water and food.[1]

Through her loom- and needle-based mixed media, Jimenez Underwood has consistently drawn parallels between near-extinct, overhunted wildlife, such as the buffalo and the salmon, and the dehumanizing and dangerous pursuit of undocumented immigrants (e.g., *Buffalo Shroud*: *Almost 1,000 Left* [1995]; *Sacred Jump* [1994]; *Rebozos de la Frontera: Día/Noche* [2001]). In the artist's work, xenophobic nationalism is of a piece with alienation from and callous disregard for the environment as an ecosystem. Physical senses and awareness dulled to the instinct for survival itself in our corporate-driven consumer culture of insatiable acquisition are not only using up the planet and laborers through excessive extraction and insufficient replenishment of resources. They are consuming us all.

Jimenez Underwood's work — apace with the funereal roll call of extinctions, alarming global warming weather pattern changes, the rise of cancers linked to the synthetic chemicals that gratuitously lace the processed foods lining grocery store shelves, and the spread of air, water, and soil pollution to all corners of the Earth — returns us to an acute awareness of the short- and long-term necessity to care for the natural world that feeds, clothes, and heals us. And if we are moved to care about our environment because we ourselves are literally a part of the environment, then perhaps we can care about the dehumanizing treatment of our southern border's human migrants.

Welcome to Flower-Landia is an invitation to glimpse beyond the norms and givens that have brought us to the precipice of irreversible ecological damage and human insensitivity, to a life-giving perspective, a more expansive, ambitious, and yet completely natural intelligence grounded in the natural world and the preservation of the beautiful within it — and within us. Given that this exhibition was a retrospective, what follows is a review of some of Jimenez Underwood's prior work concerning itself with the environment, extinction, and immigration, before returning to *Flower-Landia*.

One of the most powerful and now signature elements of Jimenez Underwood's mixed-media work is the use of barbed wire. Over time, the artist has repurposed this and other wire — some of it precious copper, silver, and even gold — and recycled it from industrial waste into the ink of her handwoven and stitched, mixed-media texts. Writs of our time, in early pieces she hand wove grids that functioned like fences or nets over paintings or textiles. One of her earliest flag-based mixed-media pieces, *Frontera Flag #1 Revolution* (1993, 4' × 6' × 3"), featured the overlapping and rotated flags of the United States and Mexico. In one corner, as if beneath and beyond these flags, she stamped images of the Virgin of Guadalupe, Coatlicue, and Mictecacihuatl (the last two, Mesoamerican goddesses of creation and the underworld, respectively). Woven, painted, and stitched, the piece was girded with a wire grid and crisscrossed by sharp barbed wire.

In *Deer Crossing* (1997, 9' × 15'), painted white barbed wire was laid over the length of a woven and dyed ghostly strip of the four border state flowers, topped by the yellow highway caution image of a family crossing. The piece anticipates the rendition in the present exhibition of the four border flowers in *Las 4 Xewam* (i.e., "flowers" in Yaqui). While each flower is still visibly crossed with barbed wire, they nonetheless pulse with vibrant, joyful golden orange, bright grass green, lapis lazuli, papaya pink, and warm vanilla white. The top of this tapestry seethes with multicolored energetic forms. In the set of four palm-size (3.5" × 3") *Sun, Set: Rise CA* linen and cotton weavings, the scar-like seams of barbed wire have disappeared altogether, and instead, the life-giving star of our planet is pictured as a California poppy, its fissures only those that shape its petals.

The use of rich color strikingly characterizes earlier work, such as two sumptuous pieces from 1999, *American Dress: Chocoatl* and *American Dress: [Chile] Tepin* (59" × 39"). Dark burgundy silk robes were stitched with metallic threads in a grid-line pattern, "representing the colonial mindset," and bearing in the folds of the first, barbed wire.[2] Handwoven, wide grids were reshaped in *Alba*, a 30' × 6' × 6' installation from 1997, into a conical stairway to heaven, honoring the spring ritual of spiritual ascent to the moon of the Yaqui, a culturally autonomous indigenous people from both sides of the U.S.-Mexico border, to whom the artist is related through marriage.

Weaving itself is transformed in this and other sculptural work, as it is in the artist's *Rebozos de la frontera* (2001), where barbed wire served to suspend each of two *rebozos* (shawls) constructed not as the durable, strong fabric the loom produces but instead something held together by ordinary safety pins.[3] At first glance, these beautiful pieces suggest glamor and wealth, but on closer inspection the garments are patched together from bits of fabric stamped with the highway family crossing caution signage that for the artist recalls the remains of those who met their deaths migrating in search of silver and gold, the colors of the flimsy pins binding each shawl.[4]

In the 8' × 12' × 12' installation of 2003 at the San Jose Museum of Art, *Diaspora*, the artist installed a two-dimensional rendition of the globe on a slightly raised platform off the floor. Set against different blue fabrics, a landmass of pale pink fabric was configured or bordered through flower appliqués and strewn with flower petals and corn kernels. A red barbed-wire grid covered the entire planet. Over a fourth of this flattened sphere, the artist positioned a mist-like white gauze fabric. Hovering above all of this were three hoops, each increasingly smaller than the other, and rising up and away into the ceiling. Made of barbed wire, these hoops were carefully covered in multicolored, rubber-coated wire.

The circular as a sign of the planet, unity, and integrity and the spatial dimension of *Diaspora* was further worked in 2005 and 2006, in food-centered sculptures of tortillas, peppers, and cooking implements made from corn husks, fabric, reeds, barbed wire, and other wire.[5] Responding to the multibillion-dollar, high-tech, heavily militarized fence that extended into the ocean at the San Diego–Tijuana border, in a 2005 performance under the watch of Border Patrol agents, Jimenez Underwood set free a corn-husk tortilla as large as herself into the ocean, the ironically titled *Kaut Tortilla*, to see if it would cross the border. The following year, she made a six-foot reed basket and an organza, petal-lined cloth to cover more of the human-sized cornhusk pieces. She then went on to make two six-foot-wide barbed wire, chicken wire, and plain wire *molcajetes*, evoking the traditional mortar and pestle made of polished lava stone still ubiquitous in Mexican kitchens. She also added proportionally oversized barbed wire hot peppers.

This *Tortilla* series marked the persistence of ancient indigenous foods and their preparation, much as she had called attention to the remarkable, tenacious survival of American animals and plants in *Buffalo Shroud — Almost 1,000 Left* (1995), mixed-media pieces featuring salmon (known for their return against the current to their ancestral spawning grounds), *Deer*

Crossing, and *Zewa Sisters* (2000), which embroidered the flowers of American squash rather than roses over the Virgin of Guadalupe. The life-size scale of the more recent traditional food-based work, constructed with countless, full-sized corn husks, suggests an identity between these foods and migrants, who, though hounded as illegal, are like the flora and fauna of the continent. As she suggests in the earlier piece, *Sacred Jump*, undocumented workers are like salmon, returning against all odds, natural and man-made, to their homelands. In this sense, the artist's increasingly humorous work opposed immigration law and xenophobic nationalism with the proven might of the humble yet persistent and increasingly cross-cultural tortilla — and its makers.

A 2009 installation, *Undocumented Tortilla Happening*, featured three "undocumented tortillas" of white silk organza entrapped within a painted red chicken wire enclosure. Installed on an oilcloth-covered table, an "undocumented border cloth" and a silver barbed wire "undocumented border basket" made of barbed wire sat poised to receive—or had lost—three runaway tortillas suspended from the ceiling as if magically flying. The translucent organza fabrication of the oversized tortillas, their whimsical adornment with flower petals, and the white-on-white stitching of Virgin de Guadalupe imagery suggested that spiritual and cultural nourishment were simultaneously at play as basic foodstuffs, and at risk.[6]

In this same, recent period, Jimenez Underwood began her *Flags* series, many of which she showed in 2010 at the Gualala Arts Center, in California, in an installation that "rained" from red banners across the ceiling of the gallery hangings made of flowers; images of maize; recycled Target, the *New York Times*, and Trader Joe's plastic bags; small patches of the family border-crossing signage she had used in her safety-pin shawls; beads; and other recycled bits. Several of the small flags she mounted on the wall functioned as prototypes of *Welcome to Flower-Landia*'s two large flags, *One Nation Underground Flag* and *Home of the Brave Flag*.

A composite flag made of portions of the U.S. and Mexican flags and an intermediary space between or beyond had already appeared in some of her earliest work, as I have mentioned. In the 2010 exhibition, an intermediary white zone featured images of a hoe, a laboring worker, and a Libby's can, or a small circle. Other flags appeared to be slices from presumably full-sized flags, and replaced stars with guns (*Guns and Stripes* [2008]) or with abstract geometric renderings of flowers (*Roses and Stripes* [2008]; *Flag with Flowers* [2009]). The triangular *Election Flag* (2009, 56" × 23"), made of dyed and embroidered fabric, featured flowers throughout, and returned to the four border state flowers used in earlier works, in place of the stars.

Home of the Brave Flag (2013, 72" × 99") and *One Nation Underground* (2013, 56" × 90") both return to the three-part composite structure of the Mexican and U.S. flags and a blank white intermediary space. The first flag has a very raw texture and construction, using large safety pins to "quilt" (that is, bind) the flag's façade to the bottom layer, a traditional Guatemalan textile hanging several inches below the hemline. The safety-pin method of binding, in place of sewing, recalls the use of this technique in her *Mendocino Rebozo* (2004) and the silver and gold *Rebozos de la Frontera: Día/Noche*, a method she has explained as reflecting the lack of time to sew of working and migrant women. In this piece, the Guatemalan weaving below the top layer represents the ancient, unbroken lineage of indigenous weaving in the Americas. The safety pin construction of the piece here doesn't so much mark precarity as the flimsiness of the façade of more recent national flags, or the cultures they represent, which have not succeeded in three (U.S.) or five (Latin America) centuries of unraveling or fully hiding the more ancient mother cultures. The second flag also uses the three-part composite structure but now also superimposes the two national flags, producing an effect of double vision. The visual-conceptual palimpsest is further layered with four oversized border flowers embroidered over the entire flag and the snaking diagonal borderline of blue barbed wire.

I Pledge Allegiance, I and *I Pledge Allegiance, II*, also completed in 2013 but palm-sized in scale (3" × 1.5"), zoom into the microscopic and out astronomically. Across the fields of blue, even more abstract or elemental renditions of the star portion of the canton of the U.S. flag now appear as floating units of quantum and cosmic energy. The artist's tapestries now thematize a materiality that is inclusive of the animating physical energy that weaves visible materiality and the less visible auric.

This binding life force is counterposed in much of Jimenez Underwood's work to the fencing of barbed border fences and mental or ideological closed-mindedness. This, for example, was visible in one of her earliest pieces featuring the four border flowers. The fiber, mixed-media wall installation *Border X-Lings* (2004, 8' × 6' × 3") featured the magnified silhouettes of the California poppy, the Arizona saguaro, the New Mexico yucca, and the Texas bluebonnet, covering the focal border area. Shown with *Diaspora*, discussed above, red barbed wire also lay like a grid over the entire piece.

"Border wands" — made of beads, miniature images of the *Frontera Flag #1 Revolution*, and the names of the checkpoints at the ten border towns on either side of the new border wall that was under construction at the time — suggested that the works were performative, or actively, consciously marked by the practices of "prayer," that is, of focused, intentional, directed, and energetically concentrated awareness.

The artist's immense 20′ × 60′ wall installation *Undocumented Border Flowers* (2010, Triton Museum) and the even larger fiber-based installation of the same name at the Conley Art Gallery at California State University in 2011 both placed the man-made, national borderline center stage within giant maps of the U.S.-Mexico borderlands. The 2010 installation featured red barbed wire around large nails at the ten checkpoints, a kind of gash, tearing open the unified field of blue pigment on either side of it. The 2011 brown-red borderlands map also visualized the border as a sharp cut in the cloth. However, the entangled mess of barbed and other wire also appeared fraying in both pieces. And in both cases, huge images of poppies, bluebonnets, saguaros, and yucca floated above, beyond, and below the proportionately shrunken line representing the nearly two-thousand-mile border. In both cases, "border wands" also appear, bearing the names of ten twin border city checkpoints.

Flowers, Borders, and Threads, Oh My!, the 17′ × 45′ installation in *Welcome to Flower-Landia*, features a very different, soft whites–based palette and represents the two-dimensional silhouette of the planet entirely covered in three-dimensional border flowers (figure 19.1). The thick, messy barbed wire borderline, though also a knotted entanglement, perhaps is on its own way to extinction, even as it crosses the globe. The focus is no longer only the specific binational tensions of the U.S.-Mexico border but more fully a planetary and environmental crisis.

The matter is simultaneously frightening, a kind of Dickensian ghostly image of Christmas past, and yet perhaps it is also a vision of hope, of the earth thickly repopulated by plant life, visible in their spiritual structure as a unified, barely material field of energy. The abundance of flowers in this piece, and its unabashed embrace of flowers in their lovely materiality, surely signals, as few things can, the intrinsic, seemingly gratuitous and yet essential and healing beauty and power of the Earth. This ephemeral beauty of nature is evoked

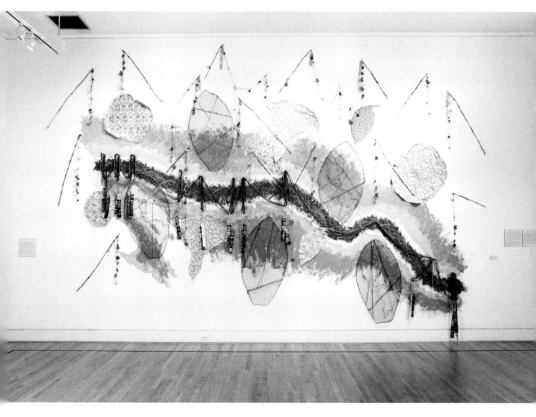

FIGURE 19.2 Consuelo Jimenez Underwood, *Welcome to Borderlandia* (2013).

in *Tenured Petals*, ten 36" × 30" pieces, originally to be scattered across the 45-foot length of *Flowers, Borders, and Threads, Oh My!*, on pedestals of various heights from the floor, corresponding to global "border checkpoints," but finally on only one.

Scale and reversal are likewise central to *Welcome to Borderlandia*, five metal cactus paddles, one of which is "embroidered" with the image of the American continent crossed by barbed wire but also crossed with rays of light shining from the highly reflective metallic wire, as are two others (figure 19.2). Here too, prayer ties, power wands, or blessings (as the artist has variously called them) hang in space around this ancestral, highly nutritive and healing food plant that along with maize is an essential part of the continent and its oldest inhabitants. Awareness and gratitude for the sustenance the Earth provides and the shelter it gives humans characterizes the

FIGURE 19.3   Consuelo Jimenez Underwood, *5 Mothers / Rebozos* (2010–13).

traditional guiding philosophy of this continent, a nature-based worldview grounded in the care and maintenance of respectful relationship to environment and other beings. This is a pragmatic "spirituality" and, more to the point, an ethos of everyday social, cultural practices aimed at maintaining the reciprocity basic to the well-being of an energetically, and therefore materially, interconnected reality.

I next want to turn to Jimenez Underwood's *Rebozo* series (figure 19.3). Although five were hung in the exhibition, when complete, the artist explained to me, she projects four per season in honor of each of the following "mothers": "Malinche/Mundane Mother," "Earth Mother," "Mother Ocean," "Moon Mother," the "Virgin of Guadalupe," and "Mendocino," the beautiful northern coast of California where the artist lives part time. All these pieces move, it seems to me, even more fully into the realm of art as intentional act of spiritual awareness, an awareness that contributes to harmonization of the energetic life force that undergirds visible, ordinary perception and the order that escapes material and conceptual grids, enclosures, and traps.

Shown in the *Flower-Landia* exhibition together for the first time, the shawl series was initiated in 2010. These exquisite rebozos, made of fine metal wire warp (the vertical threads) and other natural and synthetic fibers, turn the mind's eye away from centuries of imperialist carving of the continents, globally unequal power relations between peoples of different "nations," and disregard of the planet and its natural "resources" to the lasting power, strength, wealth, beauty, and endurance suggested by the metals from which they are fabricated. They also suggest that these are "feminine" qualities, notwithstanding patriarchy, and even more to the point, qualities of those living with awareness of nature as our sheltering rebozo and nurturing "mother."

The rebozos speak to what protects and abides: the ground, the warp and weft of human and other life on the planet, the Earth's animating forces themselves, and to the mundane, everyday woman, the backbone of life on the planet, whether as gender-assigned or self-identifying caregiver. The beauty and strength of these rebozos, woven with precious metal threads, powerfully render homage to everyday women, to the so-called Malinche, the fabled "first" indigenous mother of the "new" colonized, mixed peoples after invasion of Mesoamerica. Tellingly, in modern-day parlance, a *malinchista* is a *vende-patrias*, one who betrays the nation or community. Here, the mundane woman "Malinche" is honored as an Every Woman, a protector of life and therefore of nature, who works to realign the man-made social to the natural order. She therefore is a certain danger to patriarchal and neo-colonial nationalist orders from which have sprung the selfsame logic that rapes nature and women, that wrings dry the planet's and humanity's life forces in the name of the individual pursuit of wealth and power.

Welcome to Flower-Landia works to shift viewers' awareness to natural reality, the ultimate test case against the denials of multinational corporate spokesmen and the evaporating front line of scientists aligned with them that insist that no significant danger is posed to humans or the environment from unnecessary (and ineffective) pesticides, animal growth hormones, synthetic pharmaceuticals, genetically altered seeds, chemical toxic waste, nonbiodegradable garbage, excessive animal sewage runoff into water tables, global warming, and so on.

The artist returns to our awareness a perspective that is beyond political ideologies of modern human craft, whether of the right or left, to the undeniable fact that we are literally made of the same stuff as the planet. Beyond feminism and patriarchy, like the near-extinct animals and plants, we too are of this planet, natural to it, part of it. Therefore, quite literally what happens to "nature" happens to "us." We are far beyond being able to continue using the planet as a garbage bin, beyond thinking that the Earth is so vast that no matter what we trash, it will not show or really matter.

Welcome to Flower-Landia, a gallery installation of giant fabric- and metal wire–centered murals, flags, and rebozos, aligns itself with the planet and via scale, repeatedly calling our attention back to a nature that has been para-doxically and perilously minimized, not least within our own rib cages.

In some spiritual traditions, prayer is, above all else, intention. It is the directing of attention, of energy, toward a particular outcome, often toward loving union with whatever name and idea we have of the Creator(s), the creative energy that constitutes. But whether religious or secular willpower, prayer is an invisible yet energetically real act of alignment. It is a kind of weaving of our intent toward a particular outcome, whether this be replenish-ment of our own flagging forces, the regular maintenance of our well-being and that of others, or the powerful plea for change to remedy situations of crisis. Prayer is an act of harmonization, the sewing up of tears in the fabric of being, the reweaving of new patterns for better futures, a protective rebozo.

Weaving is an ancient, cross-cultural spiritual and practical art form. For the ancient Greeks, the art of weaving served as a metaphor of both nature's creation and of healthy human social relations, including those of good gov-ernment. Power was thus acknowledged, according to ancient Greek texts, through practices of "investment," of dressing statues of the Gods or of human rulers in ceremoniously presented, intricately embroidered woven robes and cloths (Scheid and Svenbro 2001). The so-called Huichol, who call them-selves the Wixárika, and the Colombian Kogi are among today's traditional peoples for whom weaving remains a sacred activity, one undertaken mind-fully, through physical and spiritual preparation, sacrifice, and offerings.[7] At heart, it is simultaneously a practical art and a path of spiritual growth or wisdom, akin, I take it, to icon painting in Orthodox Christian traditions.

I cannot help but to feel and think that across time and space, to create with the intention of the Greater Good is "prayer" by whatever name, if by this we mean a profoundly ethical act of care and a harnessing of power, act-ing with an awareness that all acts, including those of art, can be acts of power, rather than mere metaphors. Having discovered and loved Consuelo Jimenez Underwood's work since the mid-1990s, I can say she continues to cultur-ally hybridize art forms that meaningfully bring together the arts, media, and aesthetic and spiritual philosophies of different cultures, thus contributing toward truly more universal art histories and, beyond this, human knowledges.

With aspirations of spirituality and social purpose in art still dismissed as naïve, wishful, or delusional, or dismissed as merely politically moti-vated rather than "real," ostensibly ideologically disinterested art, Consuelo

Jimenez Underwood's work, making use of whatever materials and media serve her purpose, continues to enact social awareness as art's inevitable intellectual, historically grounding reason for being. It continues to affirm the reality of "the spiritual," the energetic, as a practical matter. And it continues to act like an acupuncture needle, unblocking flows of awareness necessary to well-being.

In *Welcome to Flower-Landia*, she has moved the practice of art more fully into the zone of power-filled, intentional prayer, directed toward remedy of the effects of a toxic century of massive pollution and equally massive human injustice, violence, and cruelty that the legacy of the unbridled pursuit of wealth, land, and power has transformed into the highest aspirations of humanity. Consuelo Jimenez Underwood's work jumps off the loom and canvas to invite us to reweave ourselves into the fabric of a more real reality, that of nature, of which we are each vital strands of living, intelligent energy. We can recycle the waste of this era that we have inherited and learned to reproduce ourselves, into new social fabrics in harmony with ecological well-being. In this beautiful show, Jimenez Underwood's work suggests that we can reweave *ourselves* with fibers of deeper perception, greater care, and much-needed creativity for the greater good.

20

"UNDOCUNATION,"
CREATIVITY, INTEGRITY

FIGURE 20.1 Yreina D. Cervántez, *Mujer de mucha enagua: PA' TI, XICANA* (1999).

WE ARE WITNESSES TO and cocreators of a powerful, creative historical moment, one much like the birth of the ideas-become-actions called Black Nation, Chicana/o Nation, and Queer Nation.

It is an act of creative social imagination to name on one's own terms what has been named by status quo others as not there, or as rightly marginal, rightly in the shadows, rightly without full rights.

Undocumented youth and allies seizing visibility and demanding full social and cultural inclusion is, in fact, an act of personal and social healing and transformation, and a powerfully political act. As the late Grace Lee Boggs (1915–2015), the brilliant social activist, theorist, and philosopher, reminds us (2011), the revolution begins now, here, in us, for power resides within us, and therefore we literally ARE the change we have been waiting for. And spirit, as the Mayan elder don Miguel Chiquin Yak pointed out to me, is faster than the speed of light.

Before continuing, I want to especially thank Marco Antonio Flores and Kevin Escudero for their vision, creativity, and commitment to making visible the presence, the experiences, the needs, and the desires of undocumented youth. Escudero's commitment to illuminating the experiences of Asian and other undocumented youth, alongside Latina/os, and of mixed cultural heritage, and Flores's insistence that dreamers not shove back into the closet the queer among them are both important, deeply humanizing interventions that enact a politics of compassion and social justice for all beyond stereotype and beyond status quos.[1] It is human to want to belong, but it is deadening when the price of that belonging is acquiescence to homogenizing, neocolonizing samenesses, patterned after models that recolonize us in other ways: Where full belonging means not being able to be us, or to identify positively with our working-class and peasant, immigrant, refugee families and our non-European or rural cultures. Where the price of belonging means shame, erasure, suppression of parts of our own being.

I TEACH ABOUT THE LARGEST so-called minority in this country, Latina/os, and explore what they and other U.S. women of color show us through creative literature, the visual arts, and performance arts. I especially focus on what women, queer and straight, speak through their artwork, whether these are creative autobiographical essays, poems, plays, performance scripts, installation arts, paintings, comics, or films.

The arts are a form of thought, through their own media. Often that thought is far ahead of philosophy and other academic disciplines; rightly so, for the arts are barometers of useful thought on the ground and laboratories of necessary visions for the future. Art thinks with the heart, calling on the eyes, the hands, the body itself as a moving paintbrush, a fleshy pen, another site of intelligence.

This MO, this method of operating, this way of thinking with and through the body is not only about the identity of being an artist and of making objects or events called "poetry" or "art." More profoundly, art points us all toward creativity as a methodology of integrity, of greater wholeness, and thereby greater ability to discover who we really are and to deliver whatever gifts we have been given for our benefit and that of our larger communities.

Wholeness and integrity are characteristics of health and well-being. We do well to deeply question that which represses our way of being, in the sense of both our ancestral cultures and our uniquely personal desires.

Wholeness and integrity are the enactment of an empowerment that is first and foremost a self-empowerment: the claiming of the power to be as one wishes, as one longs to be. The queer Chicana writer and thinker Gloria Anzaldúa called this a new kind of *mestizaje* or mixing, reminding us that self is a becoming, an inescapably Do-It-Yourself (DIY) operation. And while not without its risks and ups and downs, she further observed that this life project of integrity, of aligning our innermost desires, our heart and our soul, with our faces is a necessary act, and a courageous one.

To be outwardly who we are inwardly, to align face and soul, is an ethical concept from the Native American Mexica peoples, otherwise known as the Aztecs, but also, unsurprisingly, it is an ethical precept of ancient Greek, Buddhist, and Hindu thought. It is a concept that Anzaldúa also studied in the work of the psychologist James Hillman, who writes of creativity and imagination as the royal road of soul making, soul, psyche in Greek, being the reclaimed realm of Jungian-shaped psychologists like Hillman ([1975] 1976).

Aligning heart and face is a human longing, whether we are guided to it through religion, through nonreligious principled ethics, through psychology and the roadmap of our wounds and addictions, or through art and creativity. Our efforts to resuture ourselves into a greater wholeness of our own making are literally healing acts. They are also creative acts with each of us as the hand-made, inspired subject and object of our own life art.

The struggle to discover and be ourselves more genuinely is a path, an ongoing journey. The highly influential DIY scholar of mythology Joseph Campbell, who compared world religions and myths his entire adult life, called the life of integrity the hero or heroine's journey and the artist one of the most visible enactors of social and psychological heroism (1990).

Our innermost, heartfelt, haunting desires that do not go away show us the way, in the mapmaking that is our unique individual path, and whose map therefore only exists in our making of it. "*Caminante, el camino se hace al caminar*," in Antonio Machado's verse. Traveler, the road is made trodding it.

Spiritual activists engage in social change activism by bringing spirituality back into the discussions of social change as arguments for material social well-being. From a spiritual activist perspective, our truths, our desires, and our spirit are linked to the great creative force that is a common denominator of all that is alive: people, birds, sky, and the soil itself, rich in microorganisms and other creatures.

Integrity from a spiritual activist perspective is the mind-body-spirit as infused, the one within the other. Therefore erasure or suppression of body, or spirit (by whatever name we call spirit), creates imbalance in both private and social life. Even more specifically, it creates disempowerment in us as socially responsible beings with a voice and a vision that are important to the whole, and to our own lives. It is knowing and therefore using our fullest resources to make things happen, to envision and create them into being.

Yet we live in a place and time where talking about spirituality is viewed as being "too dangerous," impossibly biased, or privately thought of as being superstitious and naïve, a vestige of more primitive times and peoples, something to outgrow once we get more education. But there are living elders, "spiritual athletes," as one book aptly calls them (Berry 2000), who have received and disseminate teachings that are thousands of years old about science, medicine, psychology, the earth, the cosmos, and social as well as personal well-being who tell us that the opposite is vital to harmonious personal and social existence and that of the planet.

Likewise, unless we are dancers and athletes, the numerous ways in which the body knows are denied, as if nonexistent, and perhaps chalked up to intuition or lucky hunches, but not open to a real way of knowing that is inarticulate because it speaks and knows without words, and is much faster than the brain's translation into words that are culled from languages that shape what we know and how much we know. That is, verbal, written, and visual languages teach us what to see and think and say and what not to see and think and say by what they name or do not name. Thus whole other culturally different worldviews and possibilities are preempted, shut off from the start.

Poetic and nonverbal arts are therefore byways, highways, underground tunnels throwing up and out into social awareness what also exists but that has gone unnamed, misnamed, repressed from consciousness, though somehow, sometimes, surely felt. Thus at both the personal and the social levels — and these are connected though not the same — the creative impulse facilitates integration of realities, the unseen or marginalized and those of the status quo, and in so doing, allows for fuller knowledges, and this in turn allows for more effective personal and social projects, because more fully based on reality as a more complex whole.

The mystery of the muse, of our inspiration, is driven by our innermost desires and our capacity to "know" or sense before and beyond what we have been taught to see or not see, to think or not think, to feel or to not feel, to know or to not know.

Our heartfelt desires, those felt and impulsed from our hearts and our guts, and expressed many ways beyond neat, nice, logical statements — these desires are creative. Indeed, our deeply felt, socially ignored, marginalized or repressed desires cannot avoid being creative. The effort to express what we are uncertain of because untutored or repressed or denied in us must forge for itself a path, create it, and must fashion for itself a media, a language, a form. This effort calls on all our resources: an enlivened spirit, an enlivened body, and a mind told to cooperate with and learn from and thus share the knowing with the rest of the body.

I want to link expression of heart-impulsed desire with decolonization, with the transformation of the legacy of colonialism in the Americas, with transformation of the patriarchal or male-centered and homophobic racist and socially unequal social orders that colonialism imposed on the Americas, the Caribbean, and the Pacific Islands. European and then Euro-American and creole colonialism and cultural neocolonialism imposed, through violent domination, the self-serving belief that European, especially Northern European, cultures are best, that they are the model of intellectual, political, social, cultural, artistic, and even spiritual superiority. In a word, as a childhood racist saying used to go, that "white is right."

I want to link a well-oiled mind-body-spirit as an anticolonial antidote to the mind-body-spirit split that European colonizing post-Enlightenment thought has circulated widely throughout much of the globe. If it is true that we do not want religious dogmatists and fanatics interpreting spirituality narrowly for all of us, let alone running governments, it is nonetheless still not true that all spiritual or religious thought is bad news. Elders from many cultural traditions, many parts of the globe, plunge deeper, because they are more authoritative in their lived knowledge and lack of bias toward materialism, on many philosophical questions, than some of the most schooled contemporary philosophers.

Precisely because of the legacy of colonialism in the U.S., which is directly responsible for our very small numbers as faculty in colleges and universities, our elders, our wise, and not just our educated people of color and numerous Native American peoples are largely absent from the dominant cultural educational system. Like artists, the languages they use, the approaches they take, are not beholden to the props that dominant culture will give them or us for being intelligible to them and performing well by their neocolonizing standards. Many of our elders teach in our communities, in their own languages, whether English or not, in languages that are not fancy, are not studded with the latest fashion in footnotes. And it is telling that when educated at the college level, they often choose a creative, artistic voice, a choice that is precise, tactical — necessary, in fact.

Many of our elders and our heart+mind+spirit smart young ones speak through the various arts, to the degree that different media are available to them. Thus, the brilliant social theory and philosophical insights of U.S. women of color in the 1960s, 1970s, and 1980s, many of them queer, and since then, of our queer young men of color too, are found within the creative pages or images they crafted.

Contrary to the pressure in academia to caricaturize these intellectual and spiritual activist foremothers as "old," as "passé," as embarrassingly unsophisticated, a careful, serious study of their writing and art forms shows creative, complex, and genuinely useful and deeply decolonizing thought — so much so that they have been repeatedly appropriated from with little, if any, credit, and their critique of middle-class white feminism and gay and lesbian politics has been turned back onto them, reversing who the critic was, who the essentialist. *¡Ojo!*

Chela Sandoval (2000), incisive queer Chicana scholar and theorist, has read the nonacademic essays and creative writings of these women alongside some of the most influential European and Euro-American philosophers of the 1960s through the 1980s to show the indebtedness of European philosophy to anticolonial Third World people's movements. Her work shows current progressive thinkers what surviving racism, sexism, classism, and homophobia in the U.S. has taught women of color about how to survive and retain one's humanity as intact as possible in the face of its denial as subhuman, because not white upper-class male-ish, or straight.

I would like to leave you with some image-thoughts from Chicana visual artists Yreina D. Cervántez, Consuelo Jimenez Underwood, and Diane Gamboa.

Yreina D. Cervántez's *Ruta turquesa*, created during the era of the Proposition 187 initiative to prohibit "illegal aliens" from using health care, public education, and other social services (1994), reminds us that people moved and traded freely across what only recently — that is, since 1848 — is called the U.S.-Mexico border. Anthropologists and linguists have long noted that people from preinvasion tribes traveled across the Americas, trading coastal shells or turquoise for rare feathers and obsidian, for example, and that some settled, leaving greater or lesser traces of their mother languages and cultures in their new communities.

Belonging to the largest population group of the largest ethnic minority of the United States, Chicana/o or Mexican American artists like Cervántez have much to say about an issue that directly affects their families, their communities, and their own lives. For Consuelo Jimenez Underwood, the eighteenth- and nineteenth-century history of the U.S. imperialist expansion from the thirteen colonies across the Midwest, Southwest, and West is captured in her 1992 mixed-media installation of weavings titled *Land Grabs*.

Some of her most recent weavings, paintings, and installations powerfully consider national border policies in light of the ecological communities of natural wildlife that know no such borders. Her 2011 exhibition *Undocumented Borderlands* captured this in painted and woven maps sprinkled with flowers characteristic of the U.S.-Mexico borderlands that are endangered by the ecological effects of border walls and patrols, as well as in a series of U.S. flags where stars have been replaced by native flowers and, in some versions, move across the stripes. In various pieces, Jimenez-Underwood's "undocumented border flowers" are placed as they are in nature, on both sides of the border.[2]

Meanwhile, Los Angeles–based Diane Gamboa's six-year *Alien Invasion: Queendom Come* series (2006–12) started with her asking, "Why do they call Mexicans aliens and all others immigrants?" In drawings and paintings of turquoise-fleshed, powerful women, and in related paper fashion installations and performances, Gamboa links the fear of women, fear of 2012 (produced by interpreters of the Mayan calendars unauthorized by Mayan spiritual elders),[3] and fear of extraterrestrials. Her question stands. We do not often think of Canadians, Irish, and other Europeans who are here without proper papers as "aliens" (figure 10.2).[4]

Highly conflictive views of immigration that are rooted in wars of imperialist expansion and their attendant fears do not serve those of us born and raised during or after the civil rights movements who experience mixed-race and cultural difference as something much more familiar and natural than it was to the slave-holding, anti-Indian Eurocentric Founding Fathers. A study reported that the then-youngest members of the U.S. workforce, those born in the early 1990s, are highly comfortable with peoples of different cultures both at home and globally, in contrast to older members of the workforce who confessed personal discomfort with multiculturality (Hewlett, Sherbin, and Sumberg 2009).

For half a century in the United States, and increasingly so, self, family, and friends are people whose ancestral roots cross various continents. Humanity appears more interrelated because we are more so, quite literally. When immigration is not a euphemism for colonization, nor for slavery, nor for the attempt to invalidate Native American reclamation to the Americas as homeland, but rather when immigration refers to the peaceful movement and resettlement of people, we can feel appreciation for those who come in search of economic, social, and political well-being, and compassion for those who leave home and hearth to protect life itself against starvation, civil wars, and patriarchal or homophobic violence.

In light of ethnic and religious intolerance, and in light of the global environmental crisis, immigration policy and discussion around legality and documentation can shift to reflect a humane ethics of respect rather than fear, of recognized interrelationship rather than false belief in essential difference, and of creative aperture rather than ethnocentric and nationalist closure. Let immigration policy move into the future that is also now, and reflect the personal, cultural, and global well-being that arises when peoples of different cultures share their ancestral knowledges of this continent and the rest of the planet in order for us to coexist in sustainable fashion with each other and the larger natural world, of which we form a vital part.

WRITING WITH CROOKED LINES

Dedicated to my father, David "Miguel" Pérez Ordaz
(February 7, 1931–April 20, 2010)

My friend Fr. Eddie Fernandez, a Jesuit doctor of theology, once said to me, in response to my worries about the possible errors and confusion that writing about hybrid spiritualities could cause, "God writes with crooked lines." This is so, Fr. Eddie explained, because "*Dios es bueno*," God is good. If you Google the phrase, what turns up most often is the phrase "God writes straight with crooked lines." But it occurs to me that it is not just that God fixes our mistakes. God writes crookedly. The natural world and human nature as a part of it are neither really straight nor straightforward. The natural world is in constant motion — fluid, porous, changeable, inexhaustibly enigmatic.[1] And our handiwork, the social worlds and all the cultural objects humans create within these, including our individual and collective ways of being through the cultural, are likewise continually improvised, never fully decipherable, contours.

SPIRIT WRITING

Split as we are into various shades of unhappiness by the tension between undomesticated being and desire, and how we have been socialized to be and want, we are taught to embody, to produce reality as binary.[2] We live on the crumbling faith act, the historically specific aftereffect of colonization of the

Americas and the rationalization of racialized, gendered, and sexed hierarchical orders in post-Enlightenment thought that we are unrelated, gulfs apart from nature, from other people, even from parts of our own selves, as if our interdependence on all these levels were fantasy, delusion, superstition, or the demonic.[3] And so, swept away is the ancient, cross-cultural imperative to know ourselves, to be true to ourselves, and to care for others as our own self.[4] Discovering ourselves, nonjudgmentally, is dismissed as useless navel gazing rather than the indispensable road to respectful coexistence with others.[5]

Perhaps, therefore, the crooked lines of our living are a spirit writing, traces that life forces some of us call spirit(s) and/or Spirit(s) leave, testifying to that which is disincarnate in us, not quite killed yet not fully born in us, yet the marrow of our being.[6] Traced in us and by us is a different alphabet, markings between and beyond the social text of dominant, dominating orders: a spirit writing. Winding, returning, spiraling, and seemingly dead-ended jagged paths characterize the pilgrimage toward understanding that the (re)harmonization of the mind-body-spirit and the synchronizing of humanity to the rest of the natural world is sane, healthy, necessary, a craftwork that is not solely personal but perhaps the most pressing ideological and political work, the heart of the "decolonial."[7]

Working to undo or shift to a different form of consciousness beyond the racializing, patriarchal, homophobic, and classist ordering of social reality and being in the Westernized world is, by necessity, a journey through the dark forest of human power gone awry. The hypnotic suasion of ideological discourses of supposed superiority that have rationalized power over and exploitation of one kind of human over another, and of human over other beings in nature, dehumanizes us; that is, we are desensitized and alienated from what is natural within and to us. Social disempowerment occurs in tandem with disempowerment at the level of individuality, within our psyches, and more generally within our entire being's multiple sources of intelligence and our capacity to "know" through our contact with human and nonhuman life-forms. Gloria Anzaldúa (1987, 2002) called this extrarational knowing "*la facultad*" and "*conocimiento*," the faculty and cognizance, but numerous writers alongside her speak of intuitive awareness and the multiple, simultaneous, complex forms of knowing that our different senses produce beyond the more obvious capacity to consciously reason through the intellect (e.g., Gardner 2006).

Art, spirituality, and traditional popular wisdom rooted in timeless truths remind us that love is the source of all life, and its lack, the source of error and psychological, somatic, and social suffering and illness. The intention and practice of loving care seems to be a fundamental, harmonizing expression of the natural, perduring, and enigmatic reality of which we form part,[8] signified cross-culturally as energy, the vital life force, *ashé, qi/chi, shakti, khora,* s/Spirit(s), and by the names of numerous deities and natural entities in ancient and surviving "mythologies" and theo-philosophies.

Elders from different cultural traditions, including scientists, have long cautioned that to the degree that we collude in disrespect, exploitation, and oppression of others, humanity destroys itself and our planetary habitat.[9] Such collusion depends on our own fragmentation, which is another way of thinking about our "interpellation" (Althusser [1971] 2001) as subject(ed)s within modern Western(ized) culture that consents in various degrees to the interests of dominating economic, political, and social classes rather than to our personal, humanity's, and the planet's greater good.[10] We are inculcated with the historically recent credo that there are no essences, let alone a "quintessence" connecting all life-forms, and that the only "real" forms of power are guaranteed by the threat or enactment of violence and the amassing of economic, social, and cultural powers. A "successful" life is therefore the succumbing of our will, the "consent" to perform socially prescribed roles and in other ways coproduce the "world" that domination over others has imagined and continually re-utters like a mantra through the dominating circulation of its imaginary as the blueprint of social and psychic reality. In this psychic landscape,[11] out of which political ideologies of the Left and the Right alike are fabricated, we are alive, as if alive. *We* are the simulacrum,[12] walking billboards of unreal reals; the vitality, creativity, resiliency of genuinely meaningful existence dwindle, as if these natural impulses were mere fancies and delusions.

I gather that the task of thinkers, artists, storytellers, spiritual students and elders, curanderas/os and all manner of healers, by whatever names and functions these are defined in different cultures, involves perceiving through, sensing beyond, understanding in spite of culturally and historically specific veils, and acting within and upon the social body to ensure harmonious

relations based on enduring realities and truths derived from the careful observation of human and nonhuman nature, notwithstanding the ultimately
enigmatic nature of nature.[13] From this perspective, the cross-cultural injunction of wisdom traditions to know one's self results in both psychological
healing and ideological and political empowerment, for the practice of integrating a psyche that has been splintered as a consequence of the psychological
and social violence of racializing, classist, patriarchal, and heteronormative
socializing processes, for example, returns power to us as individuals and
thereby as active, meaningfully engaged members of the human ecosystem as
well as the planetary ecosystem.[14]

For Audre Lorde, the erotic, arising from our authentic and deepest nature and expressed as love of self and other and the joy and knowledge these
bring, is both regenerative and liberatory.

> For as we begin to recognize our deepest feelings, we begin to give up, of
> necessity, being satisfied with suffering and self-negation, and with the numb-
> ness which so often seems like their only alternative in our society. Our acts
> against oppression become integral with self, motivated and empowered from
> within. . . . In touch with the erotic, I become less willing to accept powerless-
> ness, or those other supplied states of being which are not native to me, such as
> resignation, despair, self-effacement, depression, self-denial. (Lorde 1984b, 58)

DECOLONIZING HEART AND HEARTH

My own journey toward decolonized and decolonizing consciousness ger-
minated in a childhood and youth during the 1960s and 1970s of much
spiritual, intellectual, and social diversity, cross-pollination, and openness to
change. I was raised in a Catholic, Spanish-speaking Mexican home in Chicago in which my mother respected the pantheons of different religions and
spiritualities as she became aware of these. In her childhood mestiza home in
Mexico, she learned indigenous worldviews and healing practices, which she
conveyed within our home. Part of this philosophy is an openness to truth
and knowledge in different traditions, in her case, particularly regarding
healing and spiritual assistance. In time, her pantheon included the Buddha
and a Hindu guru, the last of whom she invoked successfully for healing purposes. My mother's principal practice, however, has been prayer, the power-

ful and intelligent use of intention as directed, positive energy to help herself and others. This aperture in my mother to universal truths in culturally different spiritual traditions was modeled by my father with respect to thought more generally. From him I learned to think critically about social and political realities in different parts of the world. I was taught that learning is a continual process, one that involves discussion, reflection, and revision of one's opinions, aimed most importantly toward the transformation of individual practices. I learned that intelligence is reflected in the prudence of how well we live in relation to our families, our relatives, our communities, and in the personal tranquility with which we live our daily lives.

I have also been nourished by feminist and queer thought (especially women of color's), and the theo-philosophies of diverse Native American (especially Nahua and Maya), African diasporic (especially Santería and African American women's spirituality), Hindu (especially through Gandhi), and Buddhist (especially Tibetan and Zen Buddhist) systems of thought, and by European esoteric holistic writings of the "perennial philosophy" (particularly as relates to the teachings of Pythagoras) and those of early Christian desert Church fathers and mothers and other Christian mystics, including modern ones such as Thomas Merton. I have greatly benefited from reading the poetry of Sufi mystic Rumi and of poets of every culture and tradition. I have been particularly attentive to the role and function of creativity in spiritual-intellectual personal and social transformation.

From childhood, I have been increasingly surrounded by cultural difference, and not only mine, vis-à-vis Euro-American culture. The lived experience of on-the-ground, coinhabited cultural diversity has functioned as a fluid, omnipresent, alternative, and global social imaginary always-in-the-making. This is different from cultural appropriation; this is multicultural coformation, cross-cultural synchronization, sympathetic attraction to the humane, against the dehumanization of beliefs and practices from dominant cultures. It has been the affinity for truth and meaning.[15]

In my experience, I observe that spiritual awareness works like a muscle, growing clearer and stronger with attentive use. I work to realign my overworked brain and my underworked muscles with the heart, as vehicles of spiritualized consciousness. I also observe that the body regenerates through the circulation and exchange of spiritual or vital life force energy within itself and between itself and other life-forms; otherwise it is increasingly depleted on every level.

I find myself in an ongoing process that is decolonizing within me, detecting and releasing binary habits of thought and inflexibility, of rebuilding psychological-spiritual boundaries, of recuperating my energy from self-deprecating, other-centered ideologies still occupying and colonizing me, and of increasingly trusting my intuition and creative impulses. I have felt internal tectonic plates shifting within, as old thoughts are released, and others remembered, as in Irene Pérez's image of the once-dismembered Coyolxauhqui healed (see chapter 11), with the piecing back together of my own severed psychic members. This has happened every time I have gone back to important places where I have lived, with the express intention of psychically calling myself back, through gratefully recollecting how I grew and received gifts there, rather than focusing on losses sustained in these places. I have gone back for the "good," leaving behind the "bad," as a Diné elder once advised a small group of us, to count my blessings, as my father urged in the face of sadness, depression, and the feeling of being overburdened. Instead of my old habit of racing forward to the future, without grieving for what is left behind, and without fully gathering all my pieces to take with me on my journey, I have found that it is good to reclaim my scattered being and, with it, my life energy as my inner hearth.

"INTERBEING," "SPIRITUAL WARRIORSHIP," AND "IN LAK'ECH"

"Making face, making soul," Gloria Anzaldúa's (1990) version of the Nahua concept of personhood and integrity (*in ixtli in yollotl*; face, heart = person), speaks to aligning one's spirit-directed heart to the countenance by which the world is faced and engaged.[16] The antidote to the *susto* (i.e., spirit fright / psychic loss) of culturally induced mind-body-spirit fragmentation is in the pilgrimage to the Self within self, to Nature within one's own unique nature. It is in the reclamation of one's social shadow, in Jungian terms, of one's cultural, gender, sexual desire for expression of s/Self, and any other aspects of being that have been shamed, repressed, misunderstood, or punished. It is reassembling the essential tool kit natural and unique to us, the gifts necessary to realizing our fullest potential.

Integrity is tied to interdependence in the writing of Zen Buddhist monk Thich Nhat Hanh, who expresses this relationality as "interbeing."

It is difficult to find English or French words which convey the same meaning as Tiep Hien. There is a term from the Avatamsaka Sutra, "interbeing" that conveys the spirit, so we have translated Tiep Hien as interbeing. In the sutra it is a compound term which means "mutual" and "to be." Interbeing is a new word in English, and I hope it will be accepted. We have talked about the many in the one, and the one containing the many. In one sheet of paper, we see everything else, the cloud, the forest, the logger. I am, therefore you are. You are, therefore I am. That is the meaning of the word "interbeing." We "interare." (Hanh 2005, 88)

Similarly, Chogyam Trungpa writes that "inner authentic presence comes from exchanging yourself with others, from being able to regard other people as yourself" (2009, 160). Tibetan Buddhism emphasizes compassion (Latin: *com "together"* + *pati* "to suffer"), care for the psychological, physical, and social well-being of others, and understanding that we are all interrelated and therefore interdependent. For me, the Sacred Hearts of Jesus and Mary convey this teaching as well. From hearts pierced with compassion and crowned with the thorns of suffering, roses bloom, and the flames of spiritual awareness and power blaze.

Chogyam Trungpa's "spiritual warrior," Mahatma Gandhi's morally powerful, politically victorious anticolonial activism, and the lunch counter sit-ins, Freedom Rides, and other disciplined acts of noncooperation with Southern racism by James M. Lawson Jr.'s carefully trained Student Nonviolent Coordinating Committee (SNCC) are all characterized by a paradoxical, highly active and effective "meekness," a nonviolent ethics and politics that is nonetheless steadfastly committed to socially transformative action.[17] The nonviolent activism of the spiritually disciplined occupies another, a different, a "third," an "x" space beyond good-evil and other dichotomized perceptions of reality that call for reactive solutions that are ultimately within the logic of dominant paradigms. Nonviolent spiritual activism performs a shift of consciousness, enacting differently imagined social realities and ecological relationships actualizing into being a different worldview and logic, one based on harmonious, respectful relationships of diversity-within-unity.[18]

Based on the spiritually discerned understanding of the nature of the interrelationship of all planetary life-forms, nonviolent being performs not as repetition of the status quo, nor only as disidentification with dominant, oppressive orders, but to identify, to reharmonize with respect to a different, wilder, undomesticated, natural, lush, rich, plural, multiple, transformative, continually hybridizing, and interconnected reality.[19]

This gentleness, this acceptance of a natural drifting toward each other, called sympathy, attraction, affinity, and love, is founded on the knowledge that we are made of the same stuff, resonant in the beautiful and powerful Mayan concept of *In Lak'ech*: *tú eres mi otro yo*, you are my other me.[20] Writing in the shadow of the atomic bomb, Maya linguist and scholar of Amerindian languages Domingo Martínez Parédez (1904–84) dedicated his scholarly efforts to the circulation of this concept, in the hope that humanity could learn to peacefully coexist. He observed:

Esa manera de concebir al Ser Absoluto y su manifestación matemática, como el Ser de todos y no ser de nadie, evitó esas odiosas divisiones raciales y trajó como consecuencia admirable el que el pensador maya llegase a la genial conclusión de que EL TU es mi OTRO YO, con la expresión IN LAK'-ECH, ERES MI OTRO YO. (Martínez Parédez 1973, 19; see also 129, 141, and 153)

(That manner of conceiving Absolute Being and its mathematical manifestation, as the Being of all and of not belonging to any, avoided those odious racial divisions and had the admirable consequence that the Maya thinker arrived at the genial conclusion that the you is my other me, in the expression In Lak'ech, you are my other me.)

WE ARE POWER

Elder, philosopher, and activist Grace Lee Boggs, born in 1915, witness to and participant in more than half a century of social change movements, speaks of the necessity of seizing our own power *now* and alongside growing numbers of people across the nation and globe, meaningfully re-creating devastated communities *ourselves*, reinventing work, education, and culture *ourselves*. Rebuilding community and the self as a communal being in ways that make sense for our varying local conditions, she urges us to be the change we wish to see. She writes:

At this point in the continuing evolution of our country and of the human race, we urgently need to stop thinking of ourselves as victims and to recognize that we must each become a part of the solution because we are each a part of the problem. . . . Each of us needs to undergo a tremendous philosophical and spiritual transformation. Each of us needs to be awakened to a personal and compassionate recognition of the inseparable interconnection between our minds, hearts, and bodies; between our physical and psychical well-being; and between our selves and all the other selves in our country and in the world. Each of us needs to stop being a passive observer of the suffering that we know is going on in the world and start identifying with the sufferers. Each of us needs to take a leap that is both practical and philosophical, beyond determinism to self-determinism.

. . . . Despite the powers and principles that are bent on objectifying and commodifying us and all our human relationships, the interlocking crises of our time require that we exercise the power within us to make principled choices in our ongoing daily and political lives — choices that will eventually although not inevitably (since there are no guarantees) make a difference. (Boggs 2011, 29, 33–34)

SERPENTINE WRITING

Writing with the crooked lines of our lives against the grain of dominating cultures is a serpentine journey of embodied, increasingly aware, spiritualized being. It is a multiply sourced feeling-sensing-thinking-being of constant growth and fluidity that seeks to make harmonious connections across time and space, across cultures and geographies, across the span of the living and the disincarnate, in search of deeper truths: the kinds of truths that will allow us to recapture the power and energy necessary to transform self, humanity, and society for the greater good.[21] Shedding the old skins of profoundly wounded and wounding excessively profit-driven and materialist culture, s/ Spirit that is l/Life escapes moribund ideologies, with the heart as a compass, shifting in transformation, enacting the yes that lies within our powers.

NOTES

Preface

1. See, for example, the work of French intellectual historian Didier Eribon (*Michel Foucault* [1991]), and Richard King's *The Party of Eros: Radical Social Thought and the Realm of Freedom* (1972). King also provides an insightful intellectual history of Norman O. Brown's work, including his *Love's Body* (1966).

2. Promising as the title of French philosopher Luc Ferry's *On Love: A Philosophy for the Twenty-First Century* (2013) seems, I find his arguments that "European civilization can and must deepen its quest for autonomy" "culminat[ing] in [a] revolution of love" (30), as the product of a "second humanism," problematic in many ways. This cannot be the place for a detailed treatment of Ferry's book, but his focus on the human (excluding other life-forms) and his conception of love as imagined through a parents' feelings for one's child and thereby future generations, remain human-centric and fail to acknowledge and engage traditional indigenous/Native American philosophical and ethical discourses of acting in the present with "seven generations," human and nonhuman (the rest of nature), in mind. Even if his concerns are explicitly Eurocentric, a position he wishes to depoliticize as simply a question of preserving a great tradition, he erroneously universalizes in many ways from his parochial position, for example: "For the first time in history, we are witnessing the emergence of a principle of meaning that, even though it justifies a long-term action and sacrifices, is not in itself a sacrificial ideology destined to kill huge numbers of people. The only sacrifices for which it calls are those carried out by human beings on behalf of human beings — not for great causes that have always led to the extermination of vast swathes of mankind" (95). For Ferry, "there is one collectively

and sociologically new passion, namely love, which is found in different types of feeling, including sympathy. To repeat my previous point: love has always existed but, before the triumph of marriage for love, it did not have the now central role it plays as the major bond within the family and society" (101). "The fundamental political question is that of the future of Europe, in so far as Europe is the bearer of a civilization — a singular and precious civilization — of autonomy. It's not just political autonomy that I have in mind, not just the invention of democracy and human rights. It is also the civilization in which art and culture have emancipated themselves from the authority of religion: this can be seen in the fabulous revolution represented by Dutch seventeenth-century painting, which, for the first time in the history of mankind, produced pictures that were emancipated from any religious or cosmological subject and could devote themselves to the depiction of daily life, of the human as such. This staging of daily life, of human life as such, is the prime example of the ideal of autonomy that has increasingly characterized Europe throughout its history" (102–3). Why autonomy from Christian culture should be a great achievement for the (non-Christian) world at large, depends on the generalization that all religions and cosmologies function in presumably restrictive, unfree, irrational ways. There are too many points in passages such as these tautologically claiming universal achievements. In addition, the anti-poststructuralist position of the author renders the political cultural project of Derrida, Bourdieu, and Foucault (30) a caricature of their important and highly democratic critiques.

Alain Badiou, in *In Praise of Love*, a published interview with Nicolas Truong ([2009] 2012), writes, "My own philosophical view is attempting to say that love . . . is a quest for truth. What kind of truth you will ask. I mean truth in relation to something quite precise: what kind of world does one see when one experiences it from the point of view of two and not one? What is the world like when it is experienced, developed and lived from the pont of view of difference and not identity? This is what I believe love to be" (22). "Love doesn't take me 'above' or indeed 'below'. It is an existential project: to construct a world from a decentred point of view other than that of my mere impulse to survive or re-affirm my own identity" (25). "I don't think that you can mix up love and politics. In my opinion, the 'politics of love' is a meaningless expression. I think that when you begin to say 'Love one another,' that can lead to a kind of ethics, but not to any kind of politics. Principally because there are people in politics one doesn't love. . . . That's undeniable. Nobody can expect us to love them" (58). Interesting as this short publication is, as my own book will make clear, the binary either/or thinking of affirmations such as "In politics, the struggle against the enemy constitutes the action. The enemy forms part of the essence of politics. Genuine politics identifies its real enemy. However, the rival remains absolutely external, he isn't part of the definition of love" (59) does not persuade me that it offers something hopeful and new. Badiou states the "reinvent[ion of] love" finds new possibilities in "a resurrection, a re-affirmation, of the Communist idea, the idea of a world that isn't given over to the avarice of private property, a world of free association and equality" (72–73). As I argue, the either-orism of ideologies of left and right are cut from the same historical and cultural cloth; both fail to overcome a sense of fundamental difference and disinterest in some as absolute others, such as the ideological "enemy" of the other side of the political spectrum. Jung's critiques of the failure to see the enemy as our own unintegrated projections is well placed in this respect. As I argue, a philosophy such as the Mayan "In Lak'ech," you are my other me, departs from the literal understanding of the relationship between all, including the seeming foe.

Martin Luther King Jr.'s thoughts on this are remarkably similar to those of the Maya, and other traditional non-Western philosophies: "A vigorous enforcement of civil rights laws will bring an end to segregated public facilities which are barriers to a truly desegregated society, but it cannot bring an end to fears, prejudice, pride, and irrationality, which are the barriers to a truly integrated society. These dark and demonic responses will be removed only as men are possessed by the invisible, inner law which etches on their hearts the conviction that all men are brothers and that love is mankind's most potent weapon for personal and social transformation." And "I must not ignore the wounded man on life's Jericho Road, because he is a part of me and I am a part of him. His agony diminishes me, and his salvation enlarges me" (King [1963] 1981, 38).

3. Mahatma Gandhi, "Truth Is God," Bombay Sarvodaya Mandal & Gandhi Research Foundation, accessed June 28, 2018, http://www.mkgandhi.org/momgandhi /chap10.htmm.

1 The Social Body of Love

1. I want to make clear that the argument for joy as a peaceful, healthy human state is found in mystical Christianity as well as in Buddhism. Audre Lorde (1984b) makes the important argument that joy, through the erotic, is an important compass regarding freedom and what it means to be living more fully as a human, particularly from the point of view of women of color who have been made to feel unattractive, undesirable, and that sexual and emotional intimacy of their own choosing is not a right or a reasonable expectation. Sara Ahmed, in *The Promise of Happiness* (2010),

rightly critiques the injunction of dominant cultures, particularly the Eurocentric heteronormative, to be happy and the assumption that if we are not, it is because there is something wrong with us. Being unhappy in the impossible conditions of denial of part or all of self for the queer person of color, for example, Ahmed argues, is an appropriate response and one that can lead, finally, to the possibility of actual happiness. I am, therefore, talking of the deeper, more genuine form of being in which the marginalized practice their own notions of freedom, joy, and happiness as a form of self-affirmation, of inner, and socially transformative freedom, against the denial of these states of being to them as dominated, erased, closeted, violenced, even killed.

2. See Jane Bennett's *Vibrant Matter* (2010), a philosophical "manifesto" that repeatedly identifies itself as atheist and shies away from any nonmaterialist talk of spirituality, and therefore does not cite in any way the long and widely circulating thought of different Native American (African diasporic and so on) peoples on the topic, nor any but European and Euro-American thinkers. This interesting (for many reasons) work uses recent science to speak of the "vibrancy" and relationality between all life-forms.

3. See Anzaldúa's introductory essay in *Making Face, Making Soul / Haciendo Caras: Creative and Critical Perspectives by Feminists of Color* (1990).

4. On neurosis in modern Western people, see "The Stages of Life," in *Modern Man in Search of a Soul* (Jung [1933] 1965, 95–114). Jung also writes: "If we are still caught by the old antithesis between mind and matter, the present state of affairs means an unbearable contradiction; it may even divide us against ourselves. But if we can reconcile ourselves with the mysterious truth that spirit is the living body seen from within, we shall also see the belief in the body cannot tolerate an outlook that denies the body in the name of the spirit" ([1933] 1965, 219–20). And in *The Undiscovered Self*, Jung explains: "But fear of the evil which one does not see in one's own bosom but always in somebody else's checks reason every time. . . . If only a worldwide consciousness could arise that all division and all fission are due to the splitting of opposites in the psyche, then we would know where to begin" (1990, 55).

5. For Jungian studies assessing Jung's thought on queer sexualities and gender, and creative development of Jungian thought in this regard, see Robert H. Hopcke's *Jung, Jungians, and Homosexuality* (1989) and Claudette Kulkarni's *Lesbians and Lesbianisms: A Post-Jungian Perspective* (1997).

6. Note that Anna Nieto-Gómez's "La Chicana — Legacy of Suffering and Self-Denial," originally published in *Scene* 8, no. 1, and reproduced in García 1997, was originally published in 1975, not 1995. Thanks to Lillian Castillo-Speed for verifying this with Alma M. García, editor of *Chicana Feminist Thought* (1997).

7. *Ideology* has been defined probably most famously by Louis Althusser ([1971] 2001) but also by other poststructuralist French philosophers, including Jean-François Lyotard, Foucault, and Derrida. But a more complex notion of ideology as not residing solely in those who control the means of intellectual and other cultural means of circulating the values and worldviews of people has been most richly developed by U.S. "ethnic studies" thinkers. See, among these, Sandoval's *Methodology of the Oppressed* (2000) for an account of how people of color, and women foremost, preserve and survive by other means of reading reality, navigating it, and preserving alternative, life-giving values and perspectives.

2 *Methodology of the Oppressed*

This chapter was originally presented at a panel on Chela Sandoval's *Methodology of the Oppressed* (2000) at the "Mapping the Decolonial Turn: Post/Trans-Continental Interventions in Philosophy, Theory, and Critique" conference, on April 22, 2005, organized by Nelsón Maldonado-Torres and others in the Department of Ethnic Studies, University of California, Berkeley. This piece sought to dialogue with and further explore some of Sandoval's ideas on the "social physics of love" in particular, and its possibilities in the era of "liberal exhaustion" among even progressive intellectuals and anti-PC (Political Correctness), anti-Mexican, and anti-immigrant sentiment more widely in California and other parts of the U.S.

1. What has no name.

2. See Plato: "Wherefore, the mother and receptacle of all created and visible and in any way sensible things is not to be termed earth or air or fire or water, or any of their compounds, or any of the elements from which these are derived, but is an invisible and formless being which receives all things and in some mysterious way partakes of the intelligible, and is most incomprehensible. . . . Wherefore, also we must acknowledge that one kind of being is the form which is always the same, uncreated and indestructible, never receiving anything into itself from without, nor itself going out to any other, but invisible and imperceptible by any sense, and of which the contemplation is granted to intelligence only. And there is another nature of the same name with it, and like to it, perceived by sense, created, always in motion, becoming in place and again vanishing out of place, which is apprehended by opinion jointly with sense. And there is a third nature, which is space and is eternal, and admits not of destruction and provides a home for all created things, and is apprehended, when all sense is absent, by a kind of spurious reason, and is hardly real — which we, beholding as in a dream, say of all existence that it must of necessity be in some place and occupy a space, but that what is neither in heaven nor in earth has no existence.

Of these and other things of the same kind, relating to the true and waking reality of nature, we have only this dreamlike sense, and we are unable to cast off sleep and determine the truth about them" (*Timaeus* [1982], 1178–79).

See Jacques Derrida: "*Khora* reaches us, and as the name. And when a name comes, it immediately says more than the name: the other of the name and quite simply the other, whose irruption the name announces. . . . The difficulty declared by *Timaeus* . . . at times the *khora* appears to be neither this nor that, at times both this and that, but this alternation between the logic of exclusion and that of participation . . . stems perhaps only from a provisional appearance and from the constraints of rhetoric, even from some incapacity for naming" (1995, 89). Julia Kristeva, drawing on psychoanalysis and linguistics, theorizes that "discrete quantities of energy move through the body of the subject who is not yet constituted as such and, in the course of his development, they are arranged according to the various constraints imposed on this body — always already involved in a semiotic process — by family and social structures. In this way the drives, which are 'energy' charges as well as 'psychical' marks, articulate what we call a *chora*: a nonexpressive totality formed by the drives and their stases in a motility that is as full of movement as it is regulated. // We borrow the term *chora* from Plato's *Timaeus* to denote an essentially mobile and extremely provisional articulation constituted by movements and their ephemeral stases" (1984, 25).

3. Sandoval (2000) describes the "methodology of the oppressed" as the continually creative, tactical, and often "meta-ideological" (capable of critiquing and maneuvering around dominant cultural ideologies and practices) actions that negotiate various degrees and forms of oppression, marginalization, and other forms of violence, developed in order to survive. The thinking and other practices of oppressed and socially marginalized people, such as those developed by U.S. women of color, give rise to a "differential consciousness," an ability to think from and with a variety of differences of position and ideology, including those with respect to dominant cultures.

4. As Sandoval explains, "Differential consciousness is described as the zero degree of meaning, counternarrative, utopia/no-place, the abyss, *amor en Aztlán*, soul. It is accessed through varying passages that can include the differential form of social movement, the methodology of the oppressed, poetry, the transitive proverb, oppositional pastiche, *coatlicue*, the middle voice. These puncta release consciousness from its grounding in dominant languages and narrative to experience the meanings that lie in the zero degree of power — of differential consciousness" (2000, 147). In *Methodology*, Sandoval dialogues, as does the present piece, with the conclusion of my 1999 essay: "We occupy a nation that does and doesn't exist. We practice a nationalism that we do and don't believe in. We produce art and thought from useful

scraps and norms we mock. We can converse in English Only to say: 'Opposition is not necessarily the negative of the Master's positive dyad.' 'The Father's presence is not necessarily ubiquitous.' 'There are uncolonized spaces within the imposed symbolic orders where the imagination can transform meaning.' *I/We remember.* Our social psychological, and spiritual well-being continues to depend upon the discursive disordering of 'power's' collectively imposed imaginings. The kinds of cultural practices I have discussed follow discursively and visually insane logics, with respect to various dominant cultures' 'orders.' . . . To reoccupy Aztlán, the oppressed hallucinate — and that practice has no borders" (Pérez 1999, 39).

3   Long Nguyen

This chapter was originally published in *Fresh Talk, Daring Gazes: Conversations on Asian American Art*, ed. Elaine H. Kim, Margo Machida, and Sharon Mizota (Berkeley: University of California Press, 2003), and in the catalog to the exhibition curated by JoAnne Northrup, *Tales of Yellow Skin: The Art of Long Nguyen* (San Jose, CA: San Jose Museum of Art, 2003).

4   Hidden Avant-Gardes

1. The "historical" avant-garde has been defined as the decades just before, during, and just after the world wars. See the work of scholars such as Peter Bürger, *Theory of the Avant-Garde* (1984), among countless others studies of the period.

2. As previously cited in *Chicana Art*, "Spirits, Glyphs": On the Toltec/artist, see León-Portilla (1980, 208; 1988, 160–71); on the tlamatinime, see León-Portilla (1988, 62, 123–26; 1980, 200).

5   Ester Hernández's *Libertad*

Originally published in *Born of Resistance:* Cara a Cara *Encounters with Chicana/o Visual Culture*, edited by Scott L. Baugh and Victor A. Sorell (Tucson: University of Arizona Press, 2015).

1. Interview of Ester Hernández at her home in San Francisco, California, on June 26, 2009. My thanks to Sara Ramírez for accompanying me and for adding her own questions.

2. Today *Libertad* circulates internationally in silkscreen prints, reproductions in exhibition catalogs, art books, journal and newspaper articles, book covers, postcards and greeting cards, websites, and even T-shirts.

3. Please note the correction to the original publication of this essay (Pérez 2015).

4. Details regarding Emma Lazarus's poem and its placement at the Statue of Liberty can be found in Bette Roth Young's biography *Emma Lazarus in Her World* (1995) and facts about the statue at https://en.wikipedia.org/wiki/Statue_of_Liberty.

5. My thanks to Professor Gerardo Aldana for his kind collegiality in providing an interpretation of the Maya iconography in Hernández's *Libertad*, identifying these elements as most resembling the sculptural reliefs of Yaxchilan, particularly those in lintels 13 and 14, while noting the recurrence in various lintels of elements reproduced by the Chicana artist. All details regarding Maya iconography here are indebted to his expertise.

6. Assertions regarding the artist's methodology, intentions, and biography are from my interview of the artist in 2009.

7. See Hernández's own writing about this piece in *Born of Resistance* (Hernández 2015), where she explains that in her image, the hand holding the torch aloft was, originally, unintentionally reversed. Nonetheless, on discovering this, she chose to keep the image as is.

8. Consider Audre Lorde's *Sister Outsider* (1984a, 1984b) and Alma M. García's *Chicana Feminist Thought: The Basic Historical Writings*, collecting essays from the 1960s and 1970s on "double" or "triple oppression."

9. For further discussion of the history of Chicana feminist and queer thought and art articulating the theory of the simultaneity of oppression, see my previous publications *Chicana Art: The Politics of Spiritual and Aesthetic Altarities* (2007a) and "*El desorden*, Nationalism, and Chicana/o Aesthetics" (1999).

10. On this point, see Tomás Almaguer, *Racial Fault Lines: The Historical Origins of White Supremacy in California* (1994), and Michael Omi and Howard Winant, *Racial Formation in the United States: From the 1960s to the 1990s* (1994).

11. On the "berdache" and other "two-spirited" figures across North America, see Will Roscoe's *Changing Ones: Third and Fourth Genders in Native North America* (2000). For an overview on gender and sexual role complexity and the pitfalls of colonizing mistranslation and omission, and of ahistorical projection of current queer studies concepts in the study of the "Aztecs," see Pete Sigal's "Queer Nahuatl: Sahagún's Faggots and Sodomites, Lesbians and Hermaphrodites" (2007) and his books (2000, 2011) listed in the references.

6 'Ginas in the Atelier

1. Diane Gamboa's *Altered States* was produced in this workshop, as were pieces corresponding to ongoing projects by Laura Alvarez's *Double Agent Sirvienta* and

Yolanda López's *Women's Work Is Never Done* series. Alvarez's print was titled *The Double Agent Sirvienta: Blow Up the Hard Drive* and López's was *Jaguar Woman Warrior: Woman's Work Is Never Done*. I wrote about these works or pieces in these series, as well as about other works by Cervántez, in *Chicana Art: The Politics of Spiritual and Aesthetic Altarities* (2007a). The other prints produced in the Maestras Atelier were Rose Portillo's *Sor Juana Rebelling Once Again*, Pat Gomez's *The Trappings of Sor Juana*, Margaret Guzman's *Velo* (*Veil*), Noni Olabisi's *King James Version*, and Barbara Carrasco's *Dolores*.

2. Favianna Rodriguez, "The Pussy Power Imaginary," 2015, accessed June 20, 2018, http://favianna.tumblr.com/post/104806868870/the-pussy-power-imaginary-my -newest-project.

3. "National Endowment for the Arts Appropriations History," National Endowment for the Arts, accessed June 20, 2018, https://www.arts.gov/open-government /national-endowment-arts-appropriations-history.

4. "Porn Sites Get More Visitors Each Month Than Netflix, Amazon, and Twitter Combined," *Huffington Post*, May 3, 2013, http://www.huffingtonpost.com/2013/05 /03/internet-porn-stats_n_3187682.html.

5. See Eve Ensler's *The Vagina Monologues* (1991); 2008 version for the V-Day Campaigns available at http://web.mit.edu/dvp/Public/TVMScript2008.pdf.

6. See "Statistics," Rape, Abuse and Incest National Network (RAINN), accessed June 20, 2018, https://www.rainn.org/statistics/victims-sexual-violence.

7. Ejaz Khan, "Top 10 Countries with Maximum Rape Crimes," Wonderslist, accessed June 20, 2018, http://www.wonderslist.com/top-10-countries-with-maximum -rape-crimes/.

8. "Bruce Jenner: The Interview," *20/20*, April 24, 2015, http://abcnews.go.com /2020/fullpage/bruce-jenner-the-interview-30471558. There is controversy over Jenner's white privilege and failure to grasp the fate of transgender poor and people of color, unlike that of white celebrities such as herself. Susan Stryker and Paisley Currah explain in their introduction to the "Decolonizing the Transgender Imagination" issue of *TSQ: Transgender Studies Quarterly* (2014, 303): "We understand gender not just as a binary system of masculine/feminine codes or representations but also as a biopolitical apparatus that operates on all bodies to produce unequally distributed life chances; gender privileges not just men over women but also the legibly or functionally gendered over those who become inhuman waste through their incoherent, messy, resistant, or ambiguous relationship to biopolitical utility." The editors of the special issue point out, "Decolonizing transgender studies also needs to incorporate a transnational scope and methodology. By 'transnational,' we do not only mean work that focuses on regions outside Europe and North America

but work that addresses the asymmetries of globalization and that interrogates the six-hundred-year history of European colonial expansion. This work must contend with how social understandings of gender and sexuality are very different outside a global North framework. Thus categories of gender non-conforming practices or embodiments need to be understood in their own geographic and cultural specificity and not simply as a local instance of a falsely universalized 'transgender'" (Aizura et al. 2014, 314). See also Morgan Robyn Collado, *Make Love to Rage: Selected Poems* (2014); binaohan, *decolonizing trans/gender 101* (2014); and Nia King, *Queer and Trans Artists of Color: Stories of Some of Our Lives* (2014).

7 The Poetry of Embodiment

Linda Arreola's *Vaguely Chicana* art exhibition opened at Tropico de Nopal Gallery Art-Space, Los Angeles, in April 2008. This essay originally appeared in the exhibition catalog, published by Tropico de Nopal, that accompanied the exhibition, and I have chosen to reproduce it as it appeared there.

8 Art and Museums

1. See the work of Jean Pierre Larochette and Yael Lurie in chapter 18 and the work of Consuelo Jimenez Underwood in chapter 19.

2. There are countless studies of the art of this period. See, among others, Robert Short, *Dada and Surrealism* (1980); Whitney Chadwick, *Women Artists and the Surrealist Movement* (1991); and Whitney Chadwick, ed., *Mirror Images: Women, Surrealism, and Self-Representation* (1998).

3. See, for example, Carol Duncan, *Civilizing Rituals: Inside Public Art Museums* (1995).

4. See also Howard Thurman (1900–1981), *Jesus and the Disinherited* ([1949] 1976).

5. See also Edward J. McCaughan, *Art and Social Movements: Cultural Politics in Mexico and Aztlán* (2012). On Native American art, see W. Jackson Rushing III, ed., *Native American Art in the Twentieth Century* (1999).

6. See chapter 17 for a fuller discussion of racialization and visibility with respect to the Los Angeles art gallery Tropico de Nopal's Calavera Fashion Shows and "walking altars."

7. On racialization and visual culture, also see Nicole R. Fleetwood, *Troubling Vision: Performance, Visuality, Blackness* (2011), and Jennifer González, *Subject to Display: Reframing Race in Contemporary Installation Art* (2008).

8. On the Mujeres Muralistas see chapter 2 of María Ochoa's *Creative Collectives: Chicana Painters Working in Community* (2003), 33–58.

9. On feminist art historical critiques and studies, see Guerrilla Girls, *The Guerrilla Girls' Bedside Companion to the History of Western Art* (1998); Jo Anna Isaak, *Feminism and Contemporary Art: The Revolutionary Power of Women's Laughter* (1996); Nan Bauer Maglin and Donna Perry, eds., *"Bad Girls" / "Good Girls": Women, Sex, and Power in the Nineties* (1996); Emma Amos, "Changing the Subject" (1996); and Linda Nochlin, "Why Have There Been No Great Women Artists?," bell hooks, "An Aesthetic of Blackness: Strange and Oppositional," and Michele Wallace, "Variations on Negation and the Heresy of Black Feminist Creativity," all in *Women, Creativity, and the Arts: Critical Autobiographical Perspectives*, ed. Diane Apostolos-Cappodonna and Lucinda Ebersole (1995).

10. For a detailed, fine discussion of Amos's work, see Lisa Farrington, *Creating Their Own Image: The History of African-American Women Artists* (2004). See also Amos's (1996) own statement about these two pieces in "Changing the Subject."

11. For indigenous feminist perspectives, see Theresa Harlan's "Guest Curator Essay: To Watch, To Remember, and To Survive" and "Artist Essay: Frozen in the White Light" by Jolene Rickard in the exhibition catalog, *Watchful Eyes: Native American Women Artists* (1994), 7–14 and 15–19, respectively.

12. See more of the artist's work and essays on it in Santa Barraza, *Santa Barraza: Artist of the Borderlands*, ed. María Herrera-Sobek (2000).

13. Alongside Farrington's already cited book, see also Lisa Gail Collins, *The Art of History: African American Women Artists Engage the Past* (2002), and the Robert Farris Thompson classic, *Flash of the Spirit: African and Afro-American Art and Philosophy* (1984).

14. Mendieta's notes on this appear in Bonnie Clearwater, ed., *Ana Mendieta: A Book of Works* (1993), 41.

15. On Mendieta's work, see Jane Blocker, *Where Is Ana Mendieta? Identity, Performativity, and Exile* (1999), and Olga Viso, *Ana Mendieta: Earth Body* (2004).

16. There is a very rich bibliography on these questions, including Carol Duncan, *Civilizing Rituals* (1995); Sally Price, *Primitive Art in Civilized Places*, 2nd ed. (2001); the anthologies edited by Ivan Karp et al., *Museum Frictions: Public Cultures / Global Transformations* (2006), and Ivan Karp, Christine Mullen Kreamer, and Steven D. Lavine, *Museums and Communities: The Politics of Public Culture* (1992); Karen Mary Davalos, *Exhibiting Mestizaje: Mexican (American) Museums in the Diaspora* (2001); and artwork that meditates these questions, including the work of Fred Wilson and James Luna, discussed carefully in J. González, *Subject to Display* (2008).

17. See Harry Gamboa Jr.'s account in *Urban Exile: Collected Writings of Harry Gamboa, Jr.*, ed. Chon A. Noriega (1998), 79. For a detailed review of the events and analysis, also see Amelia Jones, "Traitor Prophets" (2011, 127–29). Jones wonders why Patssi Valdez did not sign her name with the other three artists. Valdez spoke at the Department of English, University of California, March 6, 2014, as a visiting Regents' Lecturer. In her talk, "Asco and Beyond," she explained that the well-known 1972 photograph of her in front of LACMA, above Herrón, Gamboa, and "Gronkie's" signatures, was taken the following day because her own name had not been included. The photo can be accessed through the internet by searching "Asco, Spray Paint LACMA (East Bridge)."

18. See Coco Fusco's account in "The Other History of Intercultural Performance" (1995).

9 Alex Donis's *My Cathedral*

The earlier version of the essay to which I refer, "On the Altars of Alterity: Celia Herrera Rodriguez's Altar and Performance Art and Alex Donis's 'My Cathedral,'" was presented at the American Studies Association, Seattle, Washington, November 19, 1998. The community meeting I refer to occurred on Sunday, September 21, 1997. I spoke to the artist about his work by telephone on December 3, 1997, and corresponded with him during that time. I presented an essay fully focused on Donis's work by the same title as the present essay at the National Association of Chicana and Chicano Studies Joto Caucus Conference on Spirituality and Sexuality at California State University, Los Angeles, October 11, 2008; and on October 12, 2008, I met again with him, accompanied by Luis León. I recorded in my journal that day: "Since I remember his discussing it with me 10½ years ago, I asked him about his relation to Buddhism. He said that he began practicing Vipassana meditation in 1996 and that was an accident. He stepped in for a friend that was supposed to accompany another mutual friend on a one-week meditation retreat and that the images that arose for him during meditation were of all these figures sitting in meditation together: Gandhi, Chavez, MLK, Jr., Kennedy, etc. And he asked himself why it couldn't be this way for them in reality. Later in the studio he decided to take it further by eroticizing them in pairs. In subsequent shows he went further, for example, superimposing masturbating figures onto images of holy figures, on the image of Juan Diego's open *tilma*, spilling with flowers. . . . He also talked about public art that he did, big flowers made from recycled materials left in various parts of the city as kind of actions. In Australia he was invited to do something at the same time the Biennial was going on there. That work caused a controversy: an aboriginal and white men's heads in a poster of them kissing. All 2,000 posters were distributed (sold?) and privately he'd been told, for example, that it was too much and couldn't be shown . . . but could I please have a poster? The poster circulated throughout Australia." Donis also gave León and myself copies of an exhibition catalog featuring gangsters and cops dancing, and in some images, erotically. As I wrote in my journal, "He was also asked to do a show at the Watts Tower Museum . . . but the museum cancelled the show before it opened and after the catalog was printed. . . . The show featured gangsters and cops dancing, in some images, erotically. Alex was advised that different gangs did not care for what they were hearing about the show or wouldn't like it." This was *War*, an exhibition at Watts Tower Arts Center, Los Angeles, September 16–November 4, 2001. Jaime Villaneda's essay in this small catalog briefly referred to *My Cathedral*: "The cosmopolitan universality of the installation speaks of the family of man, a theme Donis learned from his extensive travels" ("War and Peace," n.p.).

1. I attended. The event was reported on by Zachary Coile, "Mission Art Exhibit Stirs Strong Reactions: 200 at Forum Discuss Controversial Portraits of Same-Sex Kissing after Gallery Is Vandalized" (2007).

2. Coco Fusco's two-page exhibition essay, "Cathedral Carnivalesque," was no longer available when I saw the show, and I only became aware of it many years after and was finally able to obtain it from the gallery in 2015. Fusco states that Hitler is holding a Holocaust survivor, and that Queen Elizabeth is with Rigoberta Menchú. "By creating a 'fictitious outing' of these figures," she writes, "Donis actually succeeds in forcing us as spectators to 'out' ourselves. There is perhaps no better way to make a viewer more embarrassingly aware of the voyeuristic pleasure of looking than to surround him/her with kissing couples. It is virtually impossible to look at them without some sense of guilty pleasure derived from getting a glimpse of the forbidden." She reads Donis as a postmodern artist reaching beyond binaries, "call[ing] upon his viewers to contemplate a universe beyond the paradigms that have trapped Latino theoretical and cultural production in the binarist and spacio-centric logic of the border for far too long"(Fusco 1997, 2).

3. On pre-invasion and colonial-era sexual practices that complicate our idea of "gender" and sexual social identities, see Will Roscoe, *Changing Ones: Third and Fourth Genders in Native North America* (2000); Pete Sigal, *From Moon Goddesses to Virgins: The Colonization of Yucatecan Maya Sexual Desire* (2000); Pete Sigal, *The Flower and the Scorpion: Sexuality and Ritual in Early Nahua* Culture (2011). See also the work of philosopher Pedro J. DiPietro (2015, 2016) with respect to Andean pre-Columbian sexualities and worldviews and vestiges of these in contemporary Argentine queer communities.

4. When I refer to psychological costs, I am drawing on the writings not only of Sigmund Freud and Carl G. Jung on emotional repression and the unconscious but especially of more contemporary writers such as James Hillman, Robert A. Johnson, Alice Miller, Clarissa Pinkola Estés, Judith Herman, and Darian Leader, who have written extensively and relevantly on the topic.

5. On the erotic in theology, see Marcella Althaus-Reid, *The Queer God* (2003).

10 *Con o sin permiso*

My thanks to Tey Marianna Nunn for her contribution to developing the concept of *malcriadas*, or badgirls, in relation to Chicana artists in conjunction with my cocurator, Delilah Montoya. And thanks to C. Ondine Chavoya for his work in linking the malcriada to the hocicona in his essay "*Malcriada* Delilah Montoya Photographer" (2006), which inspired our exhibition title. My thanks also to John P. Strohmeier, coauthor of *Divine Harmony: The Life and Teachings of Pythagoras* (1999) and editor of numerous volumes on Gandhi, whose work contributes directly to this essay as well. I have decided not to expand the essay, originally published as one of the two cocurators' exhibition essays (and constrained by space limits of the brief catalog), but rather I reproduce it with only the necessary edits. The exhibition was held at 516 ARTS Gallery, Albuquerque, New Mexico. It included work in multiple media, including film of performance art, some of which is visible online. See *Chicana Badgirls: Las Hocicionas*, exhibition catalog, January 17–March 21, 2009, http://www.516arts.org/images/stories/PDF5/Chicana _badgirls_catalog.pdf.

11 *Maestrapeace*

My gratitude goes in particular to two members of the *Maestrapeace* collective, Juana Alicia and Susan Kelk Cervantes, for allowing me to interview them on April 13, 2004, and July 20, 2004, respectively. Juana Alicia and Meera Desai were also kind enough to carefully read and respond to earlier drafts of this essay. Other information on the mural was gathered from *fourStories; The Women's Building 2001 & 2002 Bi-Annual Report*; a two-page guide to the murals provided by the Women's Building staff at the entryway of the building; "Maestrapeace: A Guide to the Mural on the San Francisco Women's Building," a booklet produced by Aracely Soriano and Sandra Sánchez (San Francisco: Mission Cultural Center, 1996); and the Maestrapeace Art Works website, http://www.maestrapeace.com. Originally published in *Chicana/Latina Studies: The Journal of Mujeres Activas en Letras y Cambio Social* 6, no. 2 (2007): 56–66, this is an essay that, although published elsewhere, is included here, with different citation and editing conventions.

1. The mural's name was decided on after it was completed. According to Guisela Latorre's "Gender, Muralism and the Politics of Identity," "It can even be argued that Rigoberta Menchú *herself* collaborated with the making of the *Maestrapeace*. When she was unable to attend the mural's first dedication, a second one was organized to accommodate her busy schedule. As a way to justify the second dedication, Menchú simply asked, 'Why shouldn't a *maestrapiece* such as this have two inaugurations?' (Italics mine.) Unbeknownst to her, Menchú had just provided the perfect title for the mural" (2004, 338). Latorre cites as her source Miranda Bergman, "Big Women" (1995, 44–45).

2. The collective design creation involved a few months, and then was subjected to about another month of approval with different committees, then another two months were spent persuading the landlord board that the mural could be removed if necessary without destroying the integrity of the historical building. More than eighty women, not all of them artists, were asked to help in different aspects of the preparation and painting of the mural (Susan Kelk Cervantes, interview, July 20, 1994). The painting took thirteen months to complete. The collaboration was an enriching and bonding experience for the artists, and since its completion they have been meeting every month in an ongoing circle of support, and together host a website and sell images related to the mural (Susan Kelk Cervantes and Juana Alicia interviews, 1994/2004; Maestrapeace Art Works website).

3. The mural is painted over an existing, vanilla-covered layer of paint that the mural design works with, rather than engulfs, with its own color scheme or design. Windows, for example, are not disguised through color or drawing as being part of the images surrounding them. Visually, the mural coexists with these, while the false columns on the second floor of the building, above the main entrance way, are redesigned as parts of torchlike flowering plants.

4. Those of the 1960s to the present — judging by the scant amount of attention they have received in established national publications and exhibitions.

5. On Mujeres Muralistas and the Co-Madres, all-women collectives of the Bay Area, see María Ochoa, *Creative Collectives: Chicana Painters Working in Community* (2003). On the indigenous aesthetic at work in the contributions to the *Maestrapeace* mural of Chicana artists Juana Alicia and Irene Pérez, see Latorre, "Gender, Muralism and the Politics of Identity" (2004).

6. Kelk Cervantes, interview, July 20, 1994.

7. Joan of Arc (1412–31) was a saint who led the French to victory against the English in the early fifteenth century. Sojourner Truth was an African American

abolitionist and feminist during the nineteenth century and, like Susan B. Anthony, a feminist foremother who argued for women's right to vote. Rosa Luxembourg was a nineteenth-century German Jewish socialist thinker who warned of the elitist tendencies she saw among the Russian Marxist leaders. Rosa Parks, a contemporary of Martin Luther King Jr., is said to have sparked the civil rights struggles by refusing to sit at the back of the bus in the racially segregated south of the 1950s. Lillian Ngoya was a leader in the anti-apartheid struggle of South Africa.

8. The primacy given Menchú in the mural reflects the predominating frequency with which she was mentioned as an admired female figure in the surveys taken by the Women's Building (Kelk Cervantes, interview, 2004).

12   Decolonizing Self-Portraits

1. Adriana Zavala writes that "in the early 1930s, complex symbolic arrangements of flora and fauna began to characterize Kahlo's work, as exemplified in *Portrait of Luther Burbank* (pl. 3) and numerous self-portraits, including *Self-Portrait with Thorn Necklace and Hummingbird* (pl. 7)." See Zavala et al., *Frida Kahlo's Garden* (2015).

2. Julia Bryan-Wilson notes in her curatorial essay "Against the Body: Interpreting Ana Mendieta": "While Mendieta's practice has largely been understood as solitary, the foundational inter-relationality proposed by pieces such as these serves as a counter-argument to Donald Kuspit's assertion that her work is pathologically self-absorbed, masturbatory, and narcissistic. Mendieta's work proposes not a 'narcissistic' attention to her own body, as Kuspit would have it, but rather a more ambivalently dialogical relationship to bodies (including those off-scene) as they form, deform and influence each other" (2013, 29).

3. According to Margarita Nieto in "Across the Street: Self-Help Graphics and Chicano Art in Los Angeles," "Cervantez's *Untitled* (1983) reveals a decorative quasi-p & d style (with strong references to Mexican popular art) that launched her work on a long trajectory into self-absorption and the self-portrait" (1995, 32, 34).

4. In "Frida Kahlo: The Self as End" (1998), Salomon Grimberg proffers a remarkably castigating and judgmental reduction of Kahlo's self-portraiture as exercises in "self-absorption." Helga Prignitz-Poda, who in her book *Frida Kahlo: The Painter and Her Work* (2010) describes Frida's beauty as "exotic," adds to the "analysis" of pathological narcissism the conjecture that this involved "a certain expertise in witchcraft and sorcery" (41) and that "the mirrored reflection was only one of several techniques of magic Frida used in her desire to imaginarily tie people to herself" (41). She further explains, "The interpretation of Kahlo's work inevitably leads

one to the subject of evil. Whatever its form, it lurks in almost all of her paintings, be it in the guise of Judas, a monkey, or a poisonous plant" (46). Kahlo's sexuality is viewed as part of her pathology and she is described as "an extremely sensuous and erotic woman" (59). Prignitz-Poda does usefully cite the influence of Walt Whitman regarding nature in Kahlo's work, such that "her reflection, to her, was not a simple means of identification, like a passport photograph, but rather was invariably integral to the universe and, at the same time, an expression of her very essence" (55). However, in descriptions of *Self-Portrait with Thorn Necklace and Hummingbird*, Prignitz-Poda declares, following earlier ruminations on medieval symbolism, that "the monkey fumbling with Frida's prickly necklace is familiar to us from several of her paintings; it represents lasciviousness and 'suffocating love'" (158). The best that can be said about this sort of writing is that it amply illustrates the necessity of studying more than European history and art history when interpreting culturally hybrid artwork such as Kahlo's and of projecting colonial notions of sexuality, morality, and mental health on the Mexican bisexual artist; the worst is that it borders on Eurocentric racist demonization of Kahlo as a Third World woman. Kahlo's love of her animals is amply recorded by her niece, Isolda Kahlo (2004), among others, and in numerous photographs. In Mesoamerican indigenous cultures, including the Aztec/Mexica, the monkey signifies creativity, among other things, but not evil. Felines, dogs, and birds also hold non-European significance (Barrios [1999] 2009).

5. Kahlo's father's ancestry is German Lutheran (Franger and Huhle 2005), according to Varady (2008), who reviews discussion regarding Kahlo's Jewishness.

6. Isolda Kahlo, who grew up in Kahlo's and Rivera's extended household, writes in *Frida íntima* that at the age of seventy-five, she felt compelled to set the record straight about her aunt's character, life, and death. She considers most of what she has read on her aunt to be "*refritos de refritos de refritos*," rehashings of rehashed rehashes (2004, 15). Throughout the book, which also records the views of some of Kahlo's and Rivera's ex-students, Kahlo is described as authentic, courageous, intellectually and politically astute, direct, and strong in her views. Isolda Kahlo also writes that Frida was not manipulative, false, needy, or weak but was loving, inspiring, animating, generous, and widely loved. Even Kahlo's psychological examinations of 1949 and 1950, assessed by James B. Harris, PsyD, conclude after confirming what has now been generalized as the psychological and physical suffering she suffered, managed, and characteristically strove to overcome: "In a very clear sense, Kahlo was heroic" (Grimberg 2008a, 143).

7. See the excellent, creative documentary using Mendieta's own photographs and film footage documenting her *Silhueta* series and other work: Kate Horsfield and Nereida García-Ferraz, dirs., *Ana Mendieta: Fuego de Tierra* (VHS, 1987; DVD, 2010).

8. Telephone conversations with Yreina D. Cervántez, 2007 (cited in Pérez 2007a and revisited October 19, 2015).

9. According to her daughter's biography, Brenner dedicated her life to the defense of Mexican culture. Brenner authored *Idols behind Altars: Modern Mexican Art and Its Cultural Roots* ([1929] 2002). David Glusker, Anita Brenner's husband, was one of Kahlo's lifelong physicians.

10. See Rick A. López, *Crafting Mexico: Intellectuals, Artisans, and the State after the Revolution* (2010), for an excellent study of the contradictions of celebration of indigenous beauty and popular art and crafts, in particular chapters 1 and 2.

11. This letter is also striking for Kahlo's repetition of her own sense of self-worth at such a young age in such a conservative culture, in spite of Gómez-Arias's accusations. Rather than appearing a weak person whose sense of self depends on the approval of others, Kahlo asserts, in the face of gossip and the betrayal of intimacies by Gómez-Arias: "I love myself the way I am" and "the fact is that no one wants to be my friend because I have such a bad reputation, which is something I can't help. I'll just have to be a friend to those who love me as I am."

12. Frida Kahlo wrote about her motives for painting in 1945 in a brief statement requested for a group show, "Declaration Solicited by the Instituto Nacional de Bellas Artes" (Kahlo [2003] 2006, 315–16): "I really don't know if my paintings are surrealist or not, but I do know they are the frankest expression of myself, without ever taking into account the judgements or prejudices of anyone else. I have painted little, without the slightest desire for glory or ambition, in the hope, first of all, of giving myself pleasure."

13. On Kahlo's work as a search for self-knowledge, see Gannit Ankori, *Imaging Her Selves: Frida Kahlo's Poetics of Identity and Fragmentation*: "Kahlo's art is dominated by her systematic and conscious search for Self. . . . My argument is that Kahlo consciously investigated the possible definitions of the personal and generic Self through her art. Rather than present a fixed identity (the mythic / false identity that hides the real / true Self), she deliberately and systematically explored the numerous facets that composed her 'fractured' Self, or what may be viewed as her many Selves. In this sense, Kahlo's art is not only biographical or psychological. It is also decidedly philosophical" (2002, 7). Ankori's views are partly based on studies of the artist's work and her library.

13 Undead Darwinism

1. See Serge Gruzinski, *La guerra de las imágenes: De Cristóbal Colón a Blade Runner (1492–2019)* ([1990] 1994, 20–39), for a discussion of how the initially unfamiliar religious object and its function understood as a "zemi" was eventually translated

into the idea of the demonic and superstitious fetish, as part of the colonizing war on the indigenous imaginary.

2. For further discussion of the complex critique elaborated within early "second-wave" feminism of WOC, see Chela Sandoval, *Methodology of the Oppressed* (2000), and my essay "Enrique Dussel's *Etica de la liberación*, U.S. Women of Color Decolonizing Practices, and Coalitionary Politics amidst Difference" (2010). For a compilation of some early Chicana feminist writings, including those of Nieto Gómez and Martínez, see Alma García, *Chicana Feminist Thought* (1997). See Maylei Blackwell, *¡Chicana Power! Contested Histories of Feminism in the Chicano Movement* (2011), on the important work of Chicana feminists at CSU Northridge, *Las Hijas de Cuahtémoc*, including Anna Nieto Gómez. Elizabeth "Betita" Martinez, writing as Elizabeth Sutherland, and Frances M. Beal appear in Morgan, *Sisterhood Is Powerful: An Anthology of Writing from the Women's Liberation Movement* (1970). The Combahee River Collective's statement (1977) appeared in Moraga and Anzaldúa (1981), Hull et al. (1982), and Smith (1983). See Carol Lee Sanchez's "Sex, Class and Race Intersections: Visions of Women of Color" (1983).

Frances Beal, Audre Lorde, Anna Nieto Gómez, Elizabeth "Betita" Martínez, Marta Cotera, the Combahee River Collective, and Carol Lee Sanchez articulated "double," "triple," "multiple," and "simultaneous" oppressions.

14   The Paintings of Liliana Wilson

This chapter was originally published in *Ofrenda: Liliana Wilson's Art of Dissidence and Dreams*, ed. Cantú (Pérez 2015b), 83–86, and appears here with only slight edits. Warm thanks to Pedro DiPietro and Randy Conner for their thoughtful reading of this essay.

1. See, for example, *Girl and Red Fish* (1995), *Luciano* (1997), *Boy and Cage* (1997), *El día en que le hicieron pedazos la corona* (*The Day They Broke His Crown*) (1998), *La concha* (2002), *Vuelcos* (*Shifts*) (2000), *Invisible Lover* (2000), *Memories of Chile* (2001), *Bearing Witness* (2002), *El calvario* (2002), *Hombre y hoja* (2002), *Pedazos* (*Fragments*) (2002), *El prisionero* (2004), and *Memorias de su tierra* (2004). Liliana Wilson's work can be seen in Norma Cantú, ed., *Ofrenda: Liliana Wilson's Art of Dissidence and Dreams* (2015).

2. According to Audre Lorde in "Uses of the Erotic," "There are many kinds of power, used and unused, acknowledged or otherwise. The erotic as a resource within each of us that lies in a deeply female and spiritual plane, firmly rooted in the power of our unexpressed or unrecognized feeling. In order to perpetuate itself, every oppression must corrupt or distort those various sources of power within the culture

of the oppressed that can provide energy for change. For women, this has meant a suppression of the erotic as a considered source of power and information within our lives" (1984b, 53).

3. For the fragmentation that results from negatively gendered, racialized, homophobic, and classist cultural norms, see Anzaldúa, *Borderlands* (1987).

15 The Work of Gloria Anzaldúa

This essay was originally presented as the keynote lecture at the second meeting of the Society for the Study of Gloria Anzaldúa, November 4, 2010, and published in *El Mundo Zurdo 2: Selected Works from the 2010 Meeting of the Society for the Study of Gloria Anzaldúa*, ed. Sonia Saldívar-Hull, Norma Alarcón, and Rita E. Urquijo-Ruiz (San Francisco: Aunt Lute Books, 2012), 13–27. I have made some corrections, additions, and deletions to the original. To make this essay version more readable, I have cut the opening paragraph, which read: "I want to offer this *platica y homenaje* in honor of the visionary Gloria Anzaldúa and her courageous life's work. I would like to begin by thanking the two Normas, Dr. Norma Cantú, this newbie organization's founder, and Dr. Norma Alarcón, for thinking of me when considering the special themes of this conference, performance and art." I have, however, added some notes with additional information about references made in the essay.

1. "Negotiating New American Philosophies: Anzaldúa's *Borderlands / La Frontera*," paper presented at Philosophy, Interpretation, Culture, Mind annual conference, Binghamton University, Binghamton, New York, April 1993.

2. For Anzaldúa's own analysis of "dependent" academic critics of this aspect of her work, see *Interviews*, 18–19.

3. On the role of Mohandas K. Gandhi's role in SNCC (the Student Non-violent Coordinating Committee) and its effect on the black civil rights movements, including the one led by Martin Luther King Jr., see Hogan 2007.

4. "Everything is spiritual. . . . Nothing is alien, nothing is strange. Spirit exists in everything; therefore God, the divine, is in everything. . . . Everything is my relative. I'm related to everything" (interview with Weigland, in *Interviews*, 100).

5. On consciousness, see *Interviews*, 20; her 1982 interview with L. Smucker; and the preface interview with AnaLouise Keating.

6. Anzaldúa put it this way in the 1983 interview with Weiland: "We have to recognize the total self, rather than just one part and start to be true to that total self, that presence, that soul" (*Interviews*, 103).

7. *Cutting Through Spiritual Materialism* ([1973] 2002).

8. On what she imagined the future understanding of her work would be, see *Interviews*, 18–19.

9. This was during Lipsitz's keynote at the Multiethnic Alliances Conference: A Conversation for the 21st Century, University of California, Santa Barbara, May 12–13, 2006.

16   Daughters Shaking Earth

This piece was originally written as the closing remarks for the "Daughters of the Shaking Earth: Bay Area Latina Artists Symposium," organized by Yvonne Yarbro-Bejarano, at the Galería de la Raza, San Francisco, May 12, 2012. I do not italicize Spanish in this bilingual writing.

17   Fashioning Decolonial Optics

I would like to thank Marialice Jacob and Reyes Rodriguez for inviting me to see some of the preparation and staging of the Calavera Fashion Show in 2008, and for providing me with documents at that time. For speaking extensively with me about the Calavera Fashion Shows, I would like to thank Reyes Rodriguez, Marialice Jacob, Yreina D. Cervántez, and Rigo Maldonado. The gallery was in transition during the time of my research and writing, and many materials were no longer on the website or accessible. I thank Rodriguez for providing some documentary photos, videos, and an art video of the Calavera Fashion Show through Vimeo, Jacob for accessing and sending Calavera Fashion Show programs to me, and Maldonado for sharing his PowerPoint presentation on Days of the Dead and JPEGs of his walking altars. Thanks to Aida Hurtado and Norma Cantú for thoughtful suggestions. A note on the usage "Latina/o": the Los Angeles and San Francisco art communities, like the neighborhood communities they arise from, have historically been predominantly Mexican American or "Chicana/o," but they have also included Central Americans, Puerto Ricans, Cubans, and populations of other Latin American artists, including those from the Southern Cone.

1. Reyes Rodriguez initiated a new version of the Calavera Fashion Shows on the streets of East Los Angeles in 2014 that I will not address here.

2. See my chapter "Body, Dress" in *Chicana Art* (2007a) for more about paper fashions and Diane Gamboa's paper fashion work.

3. Detailed information regarding the gallery, the Calavera Fashion Show, and the walking altars is drawn from telephone interviews I had with artist, gallery cofounder, and originator of the Calavera Fashion Show idea, Reyes Rodriguez,

on July 9 and 12, 2013, and with artist and cofounder Marialice Jacob on December 13, 2014. My usage of "Mesoamerican" follows that of the late Guillermo Bonfil Batalla, who notes that over millennia the different peoples of the vast region of "middle" America have created a common, core culture theologically and philosophically, which includes the "Aztecs" or Mexica, the Maya, and numerous other peoples with their own local and specific cultural variations. See Guillermo Bonfil Batalla, *México Profundo: Reclaiming a Civilization*, trans. Philip A. Dennis (1996), originally published in Spanish in 1987. I am indebted to the artist Celia Herrera Rodríguez, a colleague and friend, for first bringing this work to my attention. For more continental generalizations about common and core traditional indigenous beliefs, see *Native Science: Natural Laws of Interdependence* (2000), by Tewa education and science scholar Gregory Cajete.

4. See, for example, Consuelo Flores's *Pictures of Juarez* (Calavera Fashion Show [CFS] 2008) and José Lozano's *Las Meseras de Juarez* (CFS 2008). On the undocumented, see Rosanna Ahrens, *El Camino Norte: Dedicated to the Mexican Immigrant* (CFS 2006). On the U.S.-Iraq war, see Consuelo Flores, *Sacrificed Truth* (CFS 2006). On the homeless, see Edith Abeyta, *Street Wear* (CFS 2008). On powerful female figures included, see Araceli Silva, *Recuerdos-Reminders — Honoring Mama Lola and All That Is Sacred* (CFS 2005); Victoria Delgadillo *Ay Mami! Honoring Celia Cruz* (CFS 2005); Maria Elena Castro and Sara Arias, *Azucar! Para Celia Cruz* (CFS 2006); Carolyn Castaño, *Homenaje a Sor Juana Inés de la Cruz* (CFS 2006); Aida Landeros, *Farewell to Selena* (CFS 2006); Cici Segura Gonzalez, *Circus Poetry: Homenaje to Maria Izquierdo, a Mexican Artist* (CFS 2006); Lara Medina, *Fashion Homenaje a Nahui Ollin: A Woman of Eternal Cosmic Movement* (CFS 2008); Sybil Venegas, *Fashion Homenaje a Rosa Covarrubias* (CFS 2008); Miguel J. Barragan, *Baile Sorpresa . . . A Tribute to Selena* (CFS 2010); Joe Bravo, *La Reina de las Gitanas*, in honor of Carmen Amaya (CFS 2010); Guadalupe Rodriguez and Sandy Rodriguez, *Ofrenda to Gloria Anzaldúa* (CFS 2010). Other well-known artists who were memorialized were J. G. Posada, Pablo Picasso, Frida Kahlo and Diego Rivera, David Alfaro Siqueiros, Keith Haring, Jean-Michel Basquiat, and Andy Warhol.

5. West African traditional healers Sobunfu Somé and Malidoma Patrice Somé (also a PhD) have written about the human importance of grief rituals and have spent a great deal of time teaching people in the United States how to create grieving rituals. See Malidoma Patrice Somé, *Ritual, Power, Healing and Community* (1997). In personal communications years ago, they expressed the need for our tears as the canoes that enable the spirits of our dead to travel to appropriate realms. When our dead are not sufficiently grieved, they explained, they are trapped here, in the realm

of the living, inadvertently causing havoc. In a book distinguishing mourning from melancholia, *The New Black: Mourning, Melancholia, and Depression*, psychoanalyst Darian Leader writes, "The public display of grief allows each individual to access their own losses. . . . Public mourning is there in order to allow private mourning to express itself" (2009, 76). Furthermore, "This is a basic function of public mourning rituals. The public facilitates the private" (77). I have found this book particularly useful for understanding the idea of melancholia as a kind of psychological and social death: "This is exactly the melancholic problem: the symbolic Other is not there to situate him, and so all he is left with is his own image unanchored and unchained, left at the mercy of not the symbolic but the very real Other. With no stable anchoring point, no fixity in the way he situates himself in relation to the other, how can any ideal point be established from which the person can see themselves as lovable? And so, perhaps, comes the certainty of being worthless, unwanted or condemned. And, perhaps, the very identification with the dead which we have seen to be at the heart of melancholia" (186). Also extremely useful in understanding death and psychological experiences of loss for indigenous and other non-Western traditions is the work of Latina Jungian psychologist Clarissa Pinkola Estés, *Women Who Run with the Wolves: Myths and Stories of the Wild Woman Archetype* (1996). On the relationship between melancholia and racialization, see Anne Cheng, *The Melancholy of Race: Psychoanalysis, Assimilation and Hidden Grief* (2001), and Antonio Viego, *Dead Subjects: Toward a Politics of Latino Loss* (2007). Nicole M. Guidotti-Hernández's *Unspeakable Violence: Remapping U.S. and Mexican National Imaginaries* (2011) is particularly useful for thinking about the repression of the violence of U.S.-Mexico borderlands histories of racialization.

6. On the importance of acknowledging trauma, violence, and loss, as well as death, see the work of Judith Herman, *Trauma and Recovery: The Aftermath of Violence; From Domestic Abuse to Political Terror* (1992), and the previously cited works by Clarissa Pinkola Estés (1992) and Darian Leader (2009).

7. On the uses by dominant elites of discourses of indigeneity and *mestizaje*, including the image of "the Indian," see Rebecca Earle, *The Return of the Native* (2007).

8. Reclamation of culturally indigenous practices such as Days of the Dead celebrations are misread as "nostalgic" because ostensibly they express the wish for an impossible return to a decisively broken cultural wholeness; as falsely indigenous because supposedly Hispanic mestiza/os are not allowed to recognize the indigeneity of our living cultures nor to lay claim to our ancestry, unlike non-Hispanic U.S. and Canadian mixed-bloods; as spiritually naive in that indigenous religions are supposedly a throwback to a primitive era in the history of religions; and as intellec-

tually inferior because we are to believe that the highly educated and most intelligent people have evolved into atheism.

9. The language of "deracination" is highly problematic, given that "race" is a pseudo-scientific concept created by imperialist science and rationalized by imperialist and Eurocentric philosophy, social sciences, and humanities to justify Eurocentric colonial invasion, occupation, cultural oppression, and Native American and African enslaved extreme exploitation and consequent death. See Enrique Dussel's "Europe, Modernity, Eurocentrism" (2000) and *Etica de la liberacíon en la edad de la globalización y exclusión* (2009) and Nelson Maldonado-Torres's *Against War: Views from the Underside of Modernity* (2008), whose book partly focuses on Dussel's work (2000, 2009), and Walter D. Mignolo's *The Darker Side of Western Modernity: Global Futures, Decolonial Options* (2011), for further elaboration of the construction of Eurocentric knowledges and decolonizing critique of same.

10. For statistics on the global economics of extreme wealth and poverty of these times, see David C. Korten's *Agenda for a New Economy: From Phantom Wealth to Real Wealth* (2010).

11. There is a large body of work in psychology on the healing role of the arts in their various forms. To quote again from Darian Leader's *The New Black*: "The arts exist to allow us to access grief, and they do this by showing publicly how creation can emerge from the turbulence of a human life. . . . We are encouraged so often to 'get over' a loss, yet bereaved people and those who have experienced tragic losses know full well that it is less a question of getting over a loss and on with life, than finding a way to make that loss a part of one's life. Life with loss is what matters, and writers and artists show us the many different ways in which this can be done" (2009, 87, 99). Note also that Clarissa Pinkola Estés's phenomenally successful *Women Who Run with the Wolves* (1992) is structured as storytelling. Indeed, this Jungian psychologist, whose practice includes trauma, privileges the retelling of ancient and cross-cultural wisdom tales as medicinal in the rethinking of them for the conditions of our times.

12. Telephone interview with Reyes Rodriguez, July 12, 2013. This tendency was also reported in Tere Romo's account of Days of the Dead at the Galería de la Raza in San Francisco and by Sybil Venegas with respect to Self Help Graphics, located in Los Angeles and responsible for both art and cultural centers ceasing to organize Days of the Dead processions. See their essays in the exhibition catalog edited by curator Tere Romo, *Chicanos en Mictlán: Día de los Muertos en California* (2000). For Disney/Pixar's community-thwarted attempt to trademark the words *Día de los Muertos*, see "Pixar's 'Day' Is Dead," *Disney Examiner*, May 28, 2013, http://disneyexaminer.com/2013/05/28/pixars-day-is-dead-dia-de-los-muertos-title

-controversy/: "It doesn't come as a surprise that both Mexicans and even other peoples of different cultures didn't take the action so nicely citing that Dia de los Muertos was a part of one's culture, not something that should be a money-maker. Long story short, Disney eventually took back their application [for U.S. trademark of 'Día de los Muertos']," which the article explains Disney/Pixar foresaw as words in the title of one of their films in production at that time (*Coco*, released in November 2017, without the words in its title). See also Chappell Ellison, "Digging into Disney's 'Day of the Dead' Problem," *Cartoon Brew*, May 18, 2013, http://www.cartoonbrew.com/disney/digging-into-disneys-day-of-the-dead-problem-82956.html. Learning from this fiasco, the *Coco* team at Pixar assembled a team of Chicana/o writers, museum directors, and scholars, which included myself, to advise throughout development. Leadership of Pixar's creative team also included Chicana/os, including the film's cowriter, Adrian Molina, who was promoted to codirector in 2016.

13. Among these friends and artists, and alongside Cervántez, Rodriguez mentioned Diane Gamboa and Consuelo Norte as especially influential in the development of the Calavera Fashion Show and walking altar concepts.

14. The late anthropologist Guillermo Bonfil Batalla ([1987] 1996) has written incisively about this point, arguing that twenty-five centuries of indigenous cultural knowledges do not and did not disappear over the past five hundred years. He further argues that even popular, rural, nonindigenous culture is saturated with the core beliefs and practices of a pan-Mesoamerican culture that developed over millennia and that unifies countless indigenous peoples who are otherwise different in distinct, locally specific ways.

15. On the development of Days of the Dead in California, see the essays in the exhibition catalog *Chicanos en Mictlán* (Romo 2000; Venegas 2000). See also Regina Marchi's *Day of the Dead in the USA: The Migration and Transformation of a Cultural Phenomenon* (2009) and Lara Medina's "Communing with the Dead: Spiritual and Cultural Healing in Chicana/o Communities" (2004). For Days of the Dead in museums, see Karen Mary Davalos's *Exhibiting Mestizaje: Mexican (American) Museums in the Diaspora* (2001).

16. I owe the last point to Gamboa herself, who in conversation throughout the years has remarked on the function of the uncurated or uncommissioned paper fashions, sometimes worn by herself and sometimes by others.

17. It has become customary to limit Asco, the Los Angeles conceptual and performance art group, to the four founding members: Harry Gamboa Jr., Glugio "Gronk" Nicandro, Pattsi Valdez, and Willie Herrón. However, Asco artwork and performance involved collaboration with other artists, including regular collabo-

ration with Gamboa's younger sibling, Diane Gamboa, as well as other artists, as pointed out to me on several occasions by Gamboa herself. Documenting Asco's history from this perspective of fluid "membership" or collaborations remains an ongoing task.

18. Telephone interview with Rodriguez, July 12, 2013. Gamboa was very active in the early years of the gallery's history, curating an *Ofrendas* altar installation exhibition, creating puppets for the first Calavera Fashion Show in 2003, and showing her own work in her *Bruhaha* exhibition.

19. The four-minute clip by Reyes Rodriguez was available at Tropico de Nopal's website, from which I downloaded it and the 2008 Calavera Fashion Show video, which includes footage from the end of the 2006 Calavera Fashion Show. Reyes Rodriguez and Tropico Productions, "Calavera Fashion Show 2005," video, 5:49 mins., downloaded from Tropico de Nopal Gallery–Art Space, July 3, 2013; Reyes Rodriguez and Tropico Productions, "Calavera Fashio [*sic*] Show and Walking Altars 2008," video, 1:06:17, downloaded from Tropico de Nopal Gallery–Art Space, July 3, 2013; Tropico de Nopal and Reyes Rodriguez, "2006 Calavera Fashion Show: Tropico de Nopal Gallery Art-Space [*sic*]," *YouTube*, video, 8:57 mins., posted September 21, 2012, http://www.youtube.com/watch?v=xbmqBzXoAaA. The gallery has uploaded some Calavera Fashion Show videos on Vimeo, and YouTube has shorts of particular pieces uploaded by audience members and artists from the 2009 shows. Tropico also had a Facebook page with images and announcements.

20. See the following essays in the exhibition catalog *Chicanos en Mictlán* (2000): Tere Romo's "Curatorial Perspective" and her "A Spirituality of Resistance"; Tomás Benítez's "Sister Karen Boccalero Remembered," and Sybil Venegas's "The Day of the Dead in Aztlán."

21. Romo also emphasizes the influence of pre-Columbian art and of Posada's satiric broadside calavera (skull) imagery circulated by Manuel Hernández among fellow artists that would go on to cofound the Galería de la Raza (e.g., René Yáñez, Ralph Maradiaga, Rolando Castellón, Francisco Camplis, Rupert García, and Peter Rodriguez).

22. For a fine feminist analysis of the unruly, gender-bending, and defiant aesthetic of pachuca and pachuco youth, see Catherine Ramírez's *The Woman in the Zoot Suit: Gender, Nationalism, and the Cultural Politics of Memory* (2009).

23. Disney/Pixar's bid was shut down successfully by the Chicana/o-Latina/o community's protest. See note 12.

24. The "Artist Dedication" appearing on the program of the 2008 Calavera Fashion Show reads: "To my mother, Juanita T. Flores, a pachuca from East Los Angeles

who married and had her first child at the age of 15. At 52, the pachuca became a teacher. This is a celebration of her courage and fierce determination." The "model" is credited as Monet Soto. The music is a recording by Cuarteto Don Ramon Sr. and Don Tosti's Pachuco Boogie Boys.

25. See artist, professor, and Santería priestess Marta Moreno Vega's *The Altar of My Soul: The Living Traditions of Santería* (2000).

26. The Calavera Fashion Show has invited local radio personality Rick Nunhes and the political satire cartoonist, author, and founding, one-time member of Chicano Secret Service Lalo Alcaraz to serve as master of ceremonies. Fellow visual artist and DJ Jose Ruiz has coordinated the music. According to Rodriguez, about 95 percent of the music for particular walking altars was selected by the artists. Telephone interview with Rodriguez, July 12, 2013.

27. Telephone interview with Rodriguez, July 12, 2013.

28. Telephone interview with Rodriguez, July 12, 2013; telephone interview with Rigo Maldonado, August 25, 2014; telephone interview with Yreina D. Cervántez, August 29, 2014.

29. Poli Marichal, email to author, November 24, 2014. Marichal's translation: "The walking altar of 2008 is the one I dedicated to my father, the Canary Islands artist Carlos Marichal. My parents lived a great love that my mother, Flavia Lugo, has maintained alive through the years. I wanted to honor him with this walking altar. In it, my mother goes to visit my father's tomb and he appears to her. She is frightened, but then when she realizes it is him, she touches his face and then embraces him. Together in that embrace, the two lovers dance and then they create a heart with the halves that each of them has in their hands when they unite them."

30. Telephone interview with Maldonado, August 25, 2014.

31. Tropico de Nopal website, archives, Calavera Fashion Show 2004.

32. I want to thank David Walker for a question about the relationship of the Evergreen Cemetery procession and U.S. Days of the Dead parades to religious processions in Mexico and Theresa Delgadillo for asking about the humor in walking altars, both of which helped to expand the essay.

33. I have made reference to other works that focus on the effects of loss, trauma, violence, and death. Here I will add the work of nonviolence scholar Rachel M. MacNair, who, drawing on extensive research on the psychology of violence, notes in *The Psychology of Peace: An Introduction*, "The third mechanism of moral disengagement, discounting the effects, is similar to the concept of distancing. To continue violence one can create mental distance from the reality of what is happening — isolation from the horror, a mental barrier" (2003, 3–4).

18 Larochette and Lurie's *Water Songs*

This text was written for Jean-Pierre Larochette and Yael Lurie's self-published book *Water Songs Tapestries: Notes on Designing, Weaving and Collaborative Work* (Berkeley, CA: Genesis Press, 2008). Note that *The Ancestor's Garment* was published in their book as a single panel, titled *Seven Generations*.

19 Prayers for the Planet

I want to thank the artist, who provided slides, PowerPoints, brief informal reflections on her rebozos, sketches, and materials from her other exhibitions. In addition, I was able to visit her at her studio many times over the years to see the works of the exhibition-in-progress and to discuss them with her. The *Welcome to Flower-Landia* exhibition was discussed with the artist extensively, as was this essay, on August 18–19, 2013. This essay was written for the exhibition catalog to be published on demand by the Triton Museum, in the future. Countless texts have gone into my understanding of traditional indigenous cultures' understanding of the desirability of a non-human-centered balance between all life-forms on the planet, including Domingo Martínez Parédez's works of the 1950s–1970s, five of which are now translated into English by Ysidro Ramon Macias and collected in *The Domingo Martinez Paredez Mayan Reader* (Macias 2017), and Gregory Cajete's *Native Science: Natural Laws of Interdependence* (2000).

1. Bird migration routes and natural water use and circulation have also been disrupted, and farms bisected and properties seized. Indeed, Homeland Security's border wall program has been implemented through national forest and wildlife refuges and private property otherwise normally protected by law. However, in 2005, Congress granted the Homeland Security manager unprecedented power to waive any existing law that stood in the way of the border wall's construction (REAL ID Act, section 102). To date, dozens of environmental laws protecting national parks, endangered animals, and water have been "waived." On March 1, 2018, the Mongabay Series: Global Environmental Impacts of U.S. Policy reported in "Judge OKs Waiving Environmental Laws to Build U.S.-Mexico Border Wall": "On Tuesday [February 27, 2018], a federal judge in California ruled that the U.S. Department of Homeland Security did not abuse its authority in waiving dozens of environmental laws to build sections of wall along the border between the U.S. and Mexico. The ruling frees the department to waive laws for future border wall construction projects. . . . In August and September the department waived more than 30 laws, including key environmental laws, to expedite construction of three border wall projects in California. The projects include the construction of eight wall prototypes, now completed, and

the replacement of two sections of existing border fencing. . . . Conservationists have issued dire warnings about the potential impact of a wall traversing the entire border. Numerous species would be negatively affected, including bison, pronghorn, bighorn sheep, bears, foxes, salamanders, and even certain bird species, they say. 'President Trump insists on constructing a wall along the entire border: if he achieves making this a reality this barrier will rewrite the biological history of North America. A history that for millennia allowed animals to travel along the grasslands and forests from Mexico to Canada,' Rurik List, an ecologist at Universidad Autónoma Metropolitana-Lerma in Mexico, wrote in an issue of *Jornada Ecologica* this summer. 'The future of the bison and many other species that the two countries share is at stake at the border'" (Mongabay Series 2018).

International law with Mexico has also been ignored with respect to shared water rights and responsibilities of the Rio Grande. Numerous studies report that due to various factors, the economies of both nations being major ones, migration had dropped before the Secure Fence Act of 2006, as it has continued to do, and that the border wall has not been notably efficient in deterring undocumented migration. What has occurred, however, is an increase in border deaths. In *The Guardian* (US edition) article "US-Mexico Border Migrants Deaths Rose in 2017 Even as Crossing Fell, UN Says," it was reported that "last year 412 migrant deaths were recorded on either side of the border, up from 398 a year earlier, with 16 recorded so far in 2018" (February 6, 2018, https://www.theguardian.com/us-news/2018/feb/06/us-mexico -border-migrant-deaths-rose-2017). In February 2017 the cost of President Trump's border wall, estimated by him to be $12 billion, and by a Senate Democratic Report to be $70 billion, was estimated by Homeland Security to be $21.6 billion. See Vanda Felbab-Brown, "The Wall: The Real Costs of a Barrier between the United States and Mexico," Brookings Institution, August 2017, https://www.brookings.edu/essay /the-wall-the-real-costs-of-a-barrier-between-the-united-states-and-mexico/.

2. Consuelo Jimenez Underwood, 1995–96 PowerPoint presentation, notes to slide 26.

3. *Rebozos de la Frontera: Día/Noche* is in the collection of the Mexican Museum, San Francisco.

4. Consuelo Jimenez Underwood, "Political Threads: A Personal History," Textile Arts Council lecture, De Young Museum, April 20, 2013, recorded by the author.

5. *Tortillas, Chiles, and Other Border Things*, MACLA (Movimiento de Arte y Cultura Latina), San Jose, California, 2006, and *Tortilla Meets Tortilla Wall*, performance at the U.S.-Mexico Border, 2005, in the collection of the National Museum of Mexican Art, Chicago, Illinois.

6. This was part of an exhibition I cocurated with Delilah Montoya, *Chicana Bad-girls: Las Hociconas*, January 17–March 21, 2009, at the 516 Art Gallery in Albuquerque, New Mexico (see chapter 10).

7. See Stacy B. Schaefer, *To Think with a Good Heart: Wixárika Women, Weavers, and Shamans* (2002), and *The Heart of the World: Elder Brother's Warning* (1990), a BBC documentary directed by Alan Ereira at the invitation of the self-isolated indigenous Kogi people of Colombia.

20 "UndocuNation," Creativity, Integrity

I want to thank Marco Antonio Flores, one of the key organizers of the "Undocu-Nation" symposium (University of California, Berkeley, February 15, 2014), a daylong event bringing together scholars, activists, and artists to address immigration justice, where the original version of this essay was presented. See Pérez 2013 for a related online article with an image of Cervántez's *La ruta turquisa*, referred to in this essay.

1. At the time of the presentation of this essay, Escudero and Flores were students at UC Berkeley, where they led research, events, and, in Flores's case, publications around undocumented youth and the diversity among these.

2. See the advertisement for *Undocumented Borderlands*, Conley Art Gallery, CSU Fresno, YouTube, September 2011, https://www.youtube.com/watch?v=l2XCKa3lYKY; and the PBS *Craft in America* episode featuring her work, *Threads* (2012), http://www.craftinamerica.org/episodes/threads/.

3. See Carlos Barrios, "What the Mayan Elders are Saying about 2012," Activist Post, January 3, 2012, https://www.activistpost.com/2012/01/what-mayan-elders-are-saying-about-2012.html.

4. Phone conversation with Diane Gamboa, January 2009.

21 Writing with Crooked Lines

This essay was originally published in *Fleshing the Spirit: Spirituality and Activism in Chicana, Latina, and Indigenous Women's Lives*, edited by Elisa Facio and Irene Lara (Tucson: University of Arizona Press, 2014), 23–33. Only minimal editorial changes have been made, including the addition of some bibliographic information.

1. As Masanobu Fukuoka states in *The One Straw Revolution: An Introduction to Farming*, "Nature is in constant transition, changing from moment to moment. People cannot grasp nature's true appearance. The face of nature is unknowable. Trying to capture the unknowable in theories and formalized doctrines is like trying to catch the wind in a butterfly net" ([1978] 2009, 145).

2. As discussed by Robert A. Johnson in *Owning Your Own Shadow: Understanding the Dark Side of the Psyche*, "We are all born whole but somehow the culture demands that we live out only part of our nature and refuse other parts of our inheritance. We divide the self into an ego and a shadow because our culture insists that we behave in a particular manner.... But the refused and unacceptable characteristics do not go away; they only collect in the dark corners of our personality" (1971, 4). For the importance of integrating the wild or natural under patriarchy, particularly for women and the feminized, see Clarissa Pinkola Estés, *Women Who Run with the Wolves* (1992).

3. For elaboration, see Gregory Cajete's *Native Science*: "All of nature, not only humans, has rights. This is the essential 'cosmological clash' between the foundations of Native culture and those of modern society.... The cosmology that has shaped the evolution of the West with its focus on dominion over nature, the hierarchy of life, and a transcendent male God, has also shaped modern people's perception of the 'real world.'... an essentially dysfunctional cosmology, a cosmology that can no longer sustain us at any level" (2000, 53).

4. See Chogyam Trungpa's *Shambhala*: "If we try to solve society's problems without overcoming the confusion and aggression in our own state of mind, then our efforts will only contribute to the basic problems, instead of solving them.... The warrior's journey is based on discovering what is intrinsically good about human existence and how to share that basic nature of goodness with others. There is a natural order and harmony to this world, which we can discover" (2009, 126).

5. See the work of Michael N. Nagler (2001), Gandhi scholar and cofounder of Peace and Conflict Studies at the University of California, Berkeley.

6. By "s/Spirit(s)" I mean to indicate that different cultures and historical eras define "spirit," "spirituality," and related concepts differently and that therefore these are not universally synonymous or translatable concepts. Thus, for example, in some cultures one might speak of spirits rather than spirit, or of both a creator Spirit and manifestations of this as "spirits," and so on. All of this is quite apart from what indeed might be universal across cultures and times, and apart from specific discussions of how s/Spirit(s) is or are understood in different cultural traditions.

7. On harmonization of the mind-body-spirit, see Estela Román, *Nuestra medicina*: "El ser humano, ya separado y dividido de sí mismo, se ha vuelto incapaz de entender los mensajes de la Tierra y ahora es más factible de ser manipulable, de ahí que las visiones que se le presenten como mensajes se vuelvan solo una historia creada. La oscuridad, se vuelve, cada vez más la condición cotidiana del ser humano" (The human being, already separated and divided from self, has been incapable of understanding the messages of the Earth and is now more vulnerable to being manipu-

lated, and because of this the visions that present themselves as messages are taken only to be created fiction. Darkness becomes, increasingly, the everyday condition of the human being) (2012, 40; translation mine). As Lorie Eve Dechar explains in *Five Spirits: Alchemical Acupuncture for Psychological and Spiritual Healing*: "From a Taoist alchemical perspective, the body/mind split is a pathological state because there is blockage when the qi cannot transform freely from yin form to yang formlessness, from yang formlessness to yin form. An excess accumulates on one side, bringing deficiency and exhaustion on the other. . . . Traditional Chinese medicine regards these splits and blockages as the cause of all disease and pain" (2006, 18).

8. See Masaru Emoto's *Hidden Messages in Water* (2005) for the harmonizing, beneficial effects of loving thoughts and the destructive effects of negative thoughts on the molecular structure formation of water crystals. With respect to the science of the body's fields of energy and interaction with those outside itself, and the centrality of the heart, see Joseph Chilton Pearce, *The Biology of Transcendence* (2002).

9. These warnings date in the Americas to the warnings of Native American elders during the European invasions of the continent. For a more recent message from the Kogi indigenous people of Colombia, see the documentary *The Heart of the World* by Alan Ereira (1992). Authorized Mayan elders traveled throughout the world to dispel the 2012 doomsday scenarios of unauthorized writers and filmmakers and to emphasize humanity's power and responsibility to transform the dangerous ecological and social disharmonies of the planet. In the San Francisco Bay Area, that message was conveyed by don Miguel Angel Chiquín in April 2011. He spoke publicly at several locations, including the Ethnic Studies Library, University of California, Berkeley, April 7, 2011. Carlos Barrios ([1999] 2009) also serves this function.

10. "Interpellation" (Althusser [1971] 2001) refers to the shaping of the subjectivity of individuals through the circulation of dominant cultural ideology to reflect the interests of the economically, politically, and socially powerful.

11. The Greek etymological root of the word *psyche* is "soul," as psychologists like Carl Jung and Jungian psychologists like James Hillman, Robert A. Johnson, and Clarissa Pinkola Estés have emphasized. By *psychic*, I refer to the psychologically conscious and unconscious, to the intuitive and "paranormal" potentialities of the body, but also more broadly to the mind as a multidimensional, organwide system of awareness, as discussed in work such as Pearce, *The Biology of Transcendence* (2002).

12. As Jean Baudrillard iterates in "Simulacra and Simulations," "Simulation is . . . the generation by models of a real without origin or reality: a hyperreal. The territory no longer precedes the map, nor survives it. Henceforth, it is the map that precedes the territory — precession of simulacra — it is the map that engenders the territory. . . .

It is the real, and not the map, whose vestiges subsist here and there, in the deserts which are no longer those of the Empire, but our own. The desert of the real itself" (1998, 166–84).

13. That patriarchal, heteronormative, and racist scientists have constructed narratives that serve their own ideological interests as to what is "natural" does not mean we cannot know something of what in fact is natural. The ancient, unbroken sciences of India, China, and the Maya, Nahua, and other Native American peoples, for example, are the basis of their philosophical and spiritual beliefs.

14. For more in this regard, see Trungpa, *Shambhala* ([1984] 2009); Hanh, *Being Peace* ([1987] 2005) and *Together We Are One* (2010); Nagler, *Is There No Other Way?* (2001); Mani, *SacredSecular* (2009).

15. Mindful of dominant culture's ethos of rationalized appropriation of the land, beliefs, and even bodies of the colonized and enslaved in the Americas, I have asked Mexica and Maya spiritual elders if I, and if we Chicana/os and Latina/os, have a right to "know," participate, and reclaim indigenous ways of being, and I have been told both that we do and that Maya spirituality is for humanity, not just the Maya. Furthermore, my experience with all people of wisdom is that our intention in humbly and sincerely seeking guidance for the greater good, rather than for personal aggrandizement or enrichment, is the heart of any deeply meaningful and nourishing act of cultural exchange and of imparting/receiving of knowledge. Knowledge is not to be tricked out of people, obtained falsely, or otherwise ill gotten.

16. See Anzaldúa's (1990) introduction to *Making Face, Making Soul*. Drawing on the codices, Miguel León-Portilla (1992) wrote about this concept in many of his works on Aztec philosophy and literature. The title of this section makes reference to the anthology edited by Anzaldúa in 1990, and, more to the point, her reclamation of the Nahua concept of personal, social, and cosmic integrity: the alignment of the inner or unseen soul self with the outer and social self or "face." The concept of nonviolent, spiritually and mentally disciplined conduct akin to the discipline of a warrior comes from Trungpa, *Shambhala* ([1984] 2009).

17. On the crucial, spearheading role of Lawson and this civil rights organization, see Wesley Hogan, *Many Minds, One Heart* (2007).

18. Regarding "diversity in unity," see Nagler, *Is There No Other Way?* (2001); Hanh, *Being Peace* ([1987] 2005) and *Together We Are One* (2010).

19. Performance as repetition and therefore coproduction of socially prescribed roles and disidentification in cross-dressing and other queer practices as only partial and subversive identification with these are theorized by Judith Butler, *Bodies That Matter* (1993), and José Esteban Muñoz, *Disidentifications* (1999).

20. The concept of *In Lak'ech* was circulated in Chicana/o literature and culture by playwright Luis Valdez (1990) in his 1971 essay, "Pensamiento Serpentino." Valdez took many concepts, including that of the title of his theological-philosophical poem and the ars poetica of his theater, from Domingo Martínez Parédez's *Un continente y una cultura* (1960), which he cites. I follow Valdez's widespread spelling.

Martínez Parédez traces the linguistic and theological-philosophical unity of Mesoamerican and Southern indigenous cultures, characterized by *pensamiento serpentino*, serpentine thought. In *Hunab Ku: Síntesis del Pensamiento Filosófico Maya*, Martínez Parédez (1973, 40) writes of the cosmic rather than tribal or nationalist concept of Hunab Ku, an absolute being who represented cosmic dynamism and unity in plurality. Mayan elder don Miguel Angel Chiquín confirmed the meaning of the concept of *In Lak'ech* and of Maya theo-philosophy as "cosmic," that is, as belonging to all of humanity, in a conversation with me in April 2011. He further confirmed that Maya thought has been safeguarded through the centuries orally by generations of Maya elders. Five of Martínez Parédez's books are now translated (Macias 2017).

21. Consider Fukuoka's *The One-Straw Revolution*: "Culture is usually thought of as something created, maintained, and developed by humanity's efforts alone. But culture always originates in the partnership of man and nature. When the union of human society and nature is realized, culture takes shape of itself. Culture has always been closely connected with daily life, and so has been passed on to future generations, and has been preserved up to present times. . . . Something born from human pride and the quest for pleasure cannot be considered true culture. True culture is born within nature, and is simple, humble, and pure. Lacking true culture, humanity will perish. . . . When people rejected natural food and took up refined food instead, society set out on a path toward its own destruction. This is because such food is not the product of true culture. Food is life, and life must not step away from nature" ([1978] 2009, 138).

REFERENCES

Agamben, Giorgio. (1995) 1998. *Homo Sacer: Sovereign Power and Bare Life*. Translated by Daniel Heller-Roazen. Stanford, CA: Stanford University Press.

Agamben, Giorgio. 2009. *What Is an Apparatus? and Other Essays*. Translated by David Kishik and Stefan Pedatella. Stanford, CA: Stanford University Press.

Ahmed, Sara. 2010. *The Promise of Happiness*. Durham, NC: Duke University Press.

Aizura, Aren Z., Trystan Cotton, Carsten Balzer/Carla LaGata, Marcia Ochoa, and Salvador Vidal-Ortiz. 2014. "Introduction." In "Decolonizing the Transgender Imaginary," special issue, *TSQ: Transgender Studies Quarterly* 1, no. 3 (August): 308–19.

Alarcón, Norma. 1989. "Traddutora, Traditora: A Paradigmatic Figure of Chicana Feminism." *Cultural Critique*, no. 13 (autumn): 57–87.

Alexander, M. Jacqui. 2006. *Pedagogies of Crossing: Meditations on Feminism, Sexual Politics, Memory, and the Sacred*. Durham, NC: Duke University Press.

Allen, Paula Gunn. 1992. *The Sacred Hoop: Recovering the Feminine in American Traditions*. Boston: Beacon.

Almaguer, Tomás. 1994. *Racial Fault Lines: The Historical Origins of White Supremacy in California*. Berkeley: University of California Press.

Althaus-Reid, Marcella. 2003. *The Queer God*. London: Routledge.

Althusser, Louis. (1971) 2001. "Ideology and Ideological State Apparatuses (Notes toward an Investigation)." In *Lenin and Philosophy and Other Essays*, 85–126. New York: Monthly Review Press.

Amos, Emma. 1996. "Changing the Subject." In *"Bad Girls" / "Good Girls": Women, Sex, and Power in the Nineties*, edited by Nan Bauer Maglin and Donna Perry, 281–84. New Brunswick, NJ: Rutgers University Press.

Ankori, Gannit E. 2002. *Imaging Her Selves: Frida Kahlo's Poetics of Identity and Fragmentation*. Westport, CT: Greenwood.

Ankori, Gannit. 2013. *Frida Kahlo*. London: Reaktion Books.

Anzaldúa, Gloria E. 1987. *Borderlands / La Frontera: The New Mestiza*. San Francisco: Spinsters / Aunt Lute Books.

Anzaldúa, Gloria E., ed. 1990. *Making Face, Making Soul / Haciendo Caras: Creative and Critical Perspectives by Feminists of Color*. San Francisco: Aunt Lute Books.

Anzaldúa, Gloria E. 2000. *Interviews/Entrevistas: Gloria E. Anzaldúa*. Edited by AnaLouise Keating. New York: Routledge.

Anzaldúa, Gloria E. 2002a. Foreword to the Second Edition, 1983. In *This Bridge Called My Back: Writings by Radical Women of Color*, edited by Cherríe Moraga and Gloria E. Anzaldúa, 351–52. Berkeley, CA: Third Woman Press.

Anzaldúa, Gloria E. 2002b. "now let us shift . . . the path of conocimiento . . . inner work, public acts." In *This Bridge We Call Home: Radical Visions of Transformation*, 540–78. New York: Routledge.

Anzaldúa, Gloria E. 2009. *The Gloria Anzaldúa Reader*. Edited by AnaLouise Keating. Durham, NC: Duke University Press.

Anzaldúa, Gloria E. 2015. *Light in the Dark / Luz en lo Oscuro: Rewriting, Identity, Spirituality, Reality*. Edited by AnaLouise Keating. Durham, NC: Duke University Press.

Anzaldúa, Gloria E. and AnaLouise Keating, eds. 2002. *The Bridge We Call Home: Radical Visions for Transformation*. London: Routledge.

Apostolos-Cappodonna, Diane, and Lucinda Ebersole, eds. 1995. *Women, Creativity, and the Arts: Critical Autobiographical Perspectives*. New York: Continuum.

Avila, Elena. 1999. *Woman Who Glows in the Dark: A Curandera Reveals Traditional Aztec Secrets of Physical and Spiritual Health*. New York: J. P. Tarcher/Putnam.

Badiou, Alain, with Nicolas Truong. (2009) 2012. *In Praise of Love*. New York: New Press.

Barraza, Santa C. 2000. *Santa Barraza, Artist of the Borderlands*. Edited by María Herrera-Sobek. College Station: Texas A&M University Press.

Barrios, Carlos. (1999) 2009. *The Book of Destiny: Unlocking the Secrets of the Ancient Mayans and the Prophecy of 2012*. Translated by Lisa Carter. New York: HarperCollins.

Barthes, Roland. 2010. *A Lover's Discourse: Fragments*. New York: Hill & Wang.

Baudrillard, Jean. 1998. "Simulacra and Simulations." In *Selected Writings*, edited by Mark Poster, 166–84. Stanford, CA: Stanford University Press.

Baugh, Scott L., and Victor A. Sorell, eds. 2015. *Born of Resistance: Cara a Cara Encounters with Chicana/o Visual Culture*. Tucson: University of Arizona Press.

Beal, Frances. (1969) 1970. "Double Jeopardy: To Be Black and Female." Revised version in *Sisterhood Is Powerful: An Anthology of Writings from the Women's Liberation Movement*, edited by Robin Morgan, 340–53. New York: Random House.

Benítez, Tomás. 2000. "Sister Karen Boccalero Remembered." In *Chicanos en Mict-lán: Día de los Muertos en California*, exhibition catalog, curated by Tere Romo, 12–18. San Francisco: Mexican Museum.

Bennett, Jane. 2010. *Vibrant Matter: A Political Ecology of Things*. Durham, NC: Duke University Press.

Bennett, Tony. 1995. *The Birth of the Museum: History, Theory, Politics*. London: Routledge.

Berger, Martin A. 2005. *Sight Unseen: Whiteness and American Visual Culture*. Berkeley: University of California Press.

Bergman, Miranda. 1995. "Big Women: Monumental Mural on San Francisco's Women's Building." *Public Art Review* 6 (spring/summer): 44–45.

Berry, Ray. 2000. *The Spiritual Athlete: A Primer for the Inner Life*. Olema, CA: Joshua Press.

binaohan, b. 2014. *decolonizing trans/gender 101*. Toronto: Biyuti.

Blackwell, Maylei. 2011. *¡Chicana Power! Contested Histories of Feminism in the Chicano Movement*. Austin: University of Texas Press.

Blocker, Jane. 1999. *Where Is Ana Mendieta? Identity, Performativity, and Exile*. Durham, NC: Duke University Press.

Boggs, Grace Lee. 2011. *The Next American Revolution: Sustainable Activism for the Twenty-First Century*. With Scott Karashige. Berkeley: University of California Press.

Bonfil Batalla, Guillermo. (1987) 1996. *México Profundo: Reclaiming a Civilization*. Translated by Philip A. Dennis. Austin: University of Texas Press.

Bourdieu, Pierre. (1979) 1998. *Distinction: A Social Critique of the Judgment of Taste*. Translated by Richard Nice. Cambridge, MA: Harvard University Press.

Brant, Beth, ed. 1983. "A Gathering of Spirit." North American Indian Women's Issue, *Sinister Wisdom*, no. 22/23.

Brenner, Anita. (1929) 2002. *Idols behind Altars: Modern Mexican Art and Its Cultural Roots*. Mineola, NY: Dover.

Brown, Norman O. 1966. *Love's Body*. Berkeley: University of California Press.

Bryan-Wilson, Julia. 2013. "Against the Body: Interpreting Ana Mendieta." In *Traces: Ana Mendieta*, edited by Stephanie Rosenthal, 26–37. London: Hayward.

Burger, Peter. 1984. *Theory of the Avante-Garde*. Minneapolis: University of Minnesota Press.

Burroughs, Gaylnn, and Debra S. Katz. 2015. "Won't Back Down: Student Activists and Survivors Are Using the Legal System to Fight Sexual Assault and Harassment on College Campuses." *Ms. Magazine*, summer, 24–29.

Butler, Judith. 1990. *Gender Trouble: Feminism and the Subversion of Gender*. New York: Routledge.

Butler, Judith. 1993. *Bodies That Matter: On the Discursive Limits of Gender.* New York: Routledge.

Cajete, Gregory. 2000. *Native Science: Natural Laws of Interdependence.* Santa Fe, NM: Clear Light.

Campbell, Joseph. 1990. *The Hero's Journey: Joseph Campbell on His Life and Works.* Edited by Phil Cousineau. San Francisco: Harper & Row.

Cantú, Norma, ed. 2015. *Ofrenda: Liliana Wilson's Art of Dissidence and Dreams.* College Station: Texas A&M University Press.

Carstensen, Jeanne. 1997. "Profile: Alex Donis. A Kiss Is Not a Kiss." October 31. http://www.sfgate.com/eguide/profile/donis~profile.shtml.

Caso, Alfonso. 1958. *The Aztecs: People of the Sun.* Illustrated by Miguel Covarrubias. Translated by Lowell Dunham. Norman: University of Oklahoma Press.

Cazadyn, Eric. 2012. *The Already Dead: The New Time of Politics, Culture, and Illness.* Durham, NC: Duke University Press.

Chadwick, Whitney. 1991. *Women Artists and the Surrealist Movement.* Boston: Little, Brown.

Chadwick, Whitney, ed. 1998. *Mirror Images: Women, Surrealism, and Self-Representation.* Cambridge, MA: MIT Press.

Chavoya, Ondine. 2006. "*Malcriada* Delilah Montoya Photographer." In *Women Boxers: The New Warriors,* 90–93. Houston: Arte Público.

Chavoya, C. Ondine, and Rita Gonzalez. 2011. *Asco: Elite of the Obscure. A Retrospective, 1972–1987.* Los Angeles: Williams College Museum of Art / Los Angeles County Museum of Art / Hatje Cantz Verlag.

Cheng, Anne. 2001. *The Melancholy of Race: Psychoanalysis, Assimilation and Hidden Grief.* New York: Oxford University Press.

Chicago, Judy. 1979. *The Dinner Party: A Symbol of Our Heritage.* New York: Anchor Books.

Cisneros, Luisa. 1997. "bésame, bésame mucho . . . A Comment." *San Francisco Frontlines,* September 25.

Cisneros, Sandra. (1994) 1995. *Loose Woman: Poems.* New York: Vintage Contemporaries.

Clearwater, Bonnie, ed. 1993. *Ana Mendieta: A Book of Works.* Miami Beach: Grassfield Press.

Cobián, Dora Luz. 1999. *Génesis y evolución de la figura femenina en el Popol Vuh.* Mexico City: Plaza y Valdés Editores.

Coffey, Mary K. 2012. *How a Revolutionary Art Became Official Culture: Murals, Museums, and the Mexican State.* Durham, NC: Duke University Press.

Coile, Zachary. 2007. "Mission Art Exhibit Stirs Strong Reactions: 200 at Forum Discuss Controversial Portraits of Same-Sex Kissing after Gallery Is Vandalized." *San Francisco Examiner*, October 7.

Collado, Morgan Robyn. 2014. *Make Love to Rage: Selected Poems.* Toronto: Biyuti.

Collins, Lisa Gail. 2002. *The Art of History: African American Women Artists Engage the Past.* New Brunswick, NJ: Rutgers University Press.

Combahee River Collective. (1977) 1983. "A Black Feminist Statement." In *This Bridge Called My Back: Writings by Radical Women of Color*, 2nd ed., edited by Cherríe Moraga and Gloria Anzaldúa, 210–18. New York: Kitchen Table: Women of Color Press.

Cordova, Viola F. 2007. *How It Is: The Native American Philosophy of V. F. Cordova.* Edited by Kathleen Dean Moore, Kurt Peters, Ted Jojola, and Amber Lacy. Tucson: University of Arizona Press.

Coronel Rivera, Juan Rafael. 2015. "A Nahuatl Garden of Delights." In *Frida Kahlo's Garden*, edited by Adriana Zavala, Mia D'Avanza, and Joanna L. Groarke, 49–55. New York: New York Botanical Garden/Delmonico Books/Prestel.

Cotera, Marta. (1977) 1997a. "Among the Feminists: Racist Classist Issues — 1976." In *Chicana Feminist Thought: The Basic Historical Writings*, edited by Alma García, 213–20. New York: Routledge.

Cotera, Marta. (1977) 1997b. "Femenism: The Chicano and Anglo Versions. A Historical Analysis." In *Chicana Feminist Thought: The Basic Historical Writings*, edited by Alma García, 223–31. New York: Routledge.

Cotera, Marta. (1977) 1997c. "Feminism as We See It." In *Chicana Feminist Thought: The Basic Historical Writings*, edited by Alma García, 202–4. New York: Routledge.

Cotera, Marta. (1977) 1997d. "Our Feminist Heritage." In *Chicana Feminist Thought: The Basic Historical Writings*, edited by Alma García, 41–44. New York: Routledge.

Covarrubias, Miguel. 1947. *Mexico South: The Isthmus of Tehuantepec.* New York: Alfred A. Knopf.

Crenshaw, Kimberlé. 1991. "Mapping the Margins: Intersectionality, Identity Politics, and Violence against Women of Color." *Stanford Law Review* 43, no. 6 (July): 1241–99.

Davalos, Karen Mary. 2001. *Exhibiting Mestizaje: Mexican (American) Museums in the Diaspora.* Albuquerque: University of New Mexico Press.

De Certeau, Michel. (1984) 1988. *The Practice of Everyday Life.* Translated by Steven Rendall. Berkeley: University of California Press.

Dechar, Lorie Eve. 2006. *Five Spirits: Alchemical Acupuncture for Psychological and Spiritual Healing.* New York: Lantern Books.

De la Torre, Miguel A. 2004. *Santería: The Beliefs and Rituals of a Growing Religion in America*. Grand Rapids, MI: William B. Eerdmans.

Del Castillo, Adelaida R. (1974) 1997a. "Malintzín Tenepal: A Preliminary Look into a New Perspective." In *Chicana Feminist Thought: The Basic Historical Writings*, edited by Alma García, 122–26. New York: Routledge.

Del Castillo, Adelaida R. (1974) 1997b. "La Visión Chicana." In *Chicana Feminist Thought: The Basic Historical Writings*, edited by Alma García, 44–48. New York: Routledge.

Deleuze, Gilles, and Félix Guattari. (1972) 1983. *Anti-Oedipus: Capitalism and Schizophrenia*. Translated by Robert Hurley, Mark Seem, and Helen R. Lane. Preface by Michel Foucault. Minneapolis: University of Minnesota Press.

Delgado, Ray. 1997. "Mission Art Show Depicting Gay Kisses Hit by Vandals." *San Francisco Examiner*, September 18.

Derrida, Jacques. (1993) 1995. *On the Name*. Edited by Thomas Dutoit. Translated by David Wood, John P. Leavey Jr., and Ian McLeod. Stanford, CA: Stanford University Press.

DiPietro, Pedro J. 2015. "Decolonizing Travesti Space in Buenos Aires: Race, Sexuality, and Sideways Relationality." In *Gender, Place, and Culture: A Journal of Feminist Geography*, 1–17. http://dx.doi.org/ 10.1080/0966369X.2015.1058756.

DiPietro, Pedro J. 2016. "Of Huachaferia, Asi, and M' e Mati: Decolonizing Transing Methodologies." In *TSQ: Transgender Studies Quarterly* 2, no. 4: 67–76. DOI 10.1215/23289252-3334211.

Du Bois, W. E. B. (1903) 1994. *The Souls of Black Folks*. New York: Dover.

Duncan, Carol. 1995. *Civilizing Rituals: Inside Public Art Museums*. New York: Routledge.

Dussel, Enrique. 2000. "Europe, Modernity, and Eurocentrism." *Nepantla: Views from the South* 1, no. 3: 465–78.

Dussel, Enrique. 2009. *Etica de la liberación en la edad de la globalización y de la exclusión*. Madrid: Editorial Trotta.

Earle, Rebecca. 2007. *The Return of the Native: Indians and Myth-Making in Spanish America, 1810–1930*. Durham, NC: Duke University Press.

Emoto, Masaru. 2005. *Hidden Messages in Water*. New York: Atria Books.

Ensler, Eve. 1991. *The Vagina Monologues*. New York: Villard.

Ereira, Alan. 1990. *The Heart of the World: Elder Brother's Warning*. London: British Broadcasting Corporation. Film. VHS, 88 mins.

Eribon, Didier. 1991. *Michel Foucault*. Translated by Betsey Wing. Cambridge, MA: Harvard University Press.

Estés, Clarissa Pinkola. 1992. *Women Who Run with the Wolves: Myths and Stories of the Wild Woman Archetype*. New York: Ballantine Books.

Ewen, Elizabeth, and Stuart Ewen. 2006. *Typecasting: On the Arts and Sciences of Human Inequality; A History of Dominant Ideas.* New York: Seven Stories.

Facio, Elisa, and Irene Lara. 2014. *Fleshing the Spirit: Spirituality and Activism in Chicana, Latina, and Indigenous Women's Lives.* Tucson: University of Arizona Press.

Fanon, Frantz. (1952) 2008. *Black Skin, White Masks.* New York: Grove Press.

Faris, Wendy B. 2000. "Primitivist Construction of Identity in the Work of Frida Kahlo." In *Primitivism and Identity in Latin America: Essays on Art, Literature, and Culture,* edited by Erik Camayd-Freixas and José Eduardo González, 221–40. Tucson: University of Arizona Press.

Farrington, Lisa. 2004. *Creating Their Own Image: The History of African-American Women Artists.* New York: Oxford University Press.

Fernandes, Leela. 2003. *Transforming Feminist Practice: Non-Violence, Social Justice, and the Possibilities of a Spiritualized Feminism.* San Francisco: Aunt Lute Books.

Fernández-Sacco, Ellen. 2002. "Framing 'the Indian': The Visual Culture of Conquest in the Museums of Pierre Eugene Du Simitiere and Charles Wilson Peale, 1779–96." *Social Identities: Journal for the Study of Race, Nation and Culture* 8, no. 2: 571–618.

Ferry, Luc. 2013. *On Love: A Philosophy for the Twenty-First Century.* Cambridge, UK: Polity.

Fleetwood, Nicole R. 2011. *Troubling Vision: Performance, Visuality, Blackness.* Chicago: University of Chicago Press.

Franger, Gaby, and Rainer Huhle. 2005. *Fridas Vater: Der Fotograf Guillermo Kahlo, Von Pforzheim bis Mexiko.* Munich: Schirmer u. Mosel.

Fukuoka, Masanobu. (1978) 2009. *The One-Straw Revolution: An Introduction to Natural Farming.* New York: New York Review Books.

Fusco, Coco. 1995. "The Other History of Intercultural Performance." In *English Is Broken Here: Notes on Cultural Fusion in the Americas,* 37–63. New York: New Press.

Fusco, Coco. 1997. "Cathedral Carnivalesque." In *My Cathedral,* exhibition catalog, 2 pp. San Francisco: Galería de la Raza.

Galton, Francis. 1978. *Hereditary Genius. An Inquiry into Its Laws and Consequences.* New York: St. Martin's Press.

Gamboa, Harry, Jr. 1998. *Urban Exile: Collected Writings of Harry Gamboa, Jr.* Edited by Chon A. Noriega. Minneapolis: University of Minnesota Press.

Gandhi, Mohandas K. 1956. *The Gandhi Reader: A Sourcebook of His Life and Writings.* Complete and Unabridged. Edited by Homer A. Jack. New York: Grove Press.

Gandhi, Mohandas K. 2004. *Mohandas Gandhi: Essential Writings.* Selected with an introduction by John Dear. Maryknoll, NY: Orbis Books.

Garber, Marjorie. 1997. *Vested Interests: Cross-Dressing and Cultural Anxiety.* New York: Routledge.

García, Alma, ed. 1997. *Chicana Feminist Thought: The Basic Historical Writings*. New York: Routledge.

Garcíagodoy, Juanita. 1998. *Digging the Days of the Dead: A Reading of Mexico's Día de los Muertos*. Boulder: University Press of Colorado.

Gardner, Howard. 2006. *Multiple Intelligences: New Horizons in Theory and Practice*. New York: Basic Books.

Gardner, Howard. (1983) 2011. *Frames of Mind: The Theory of Multiple Intelligences*. New York: Basic Books.

Gates, Henry Louis, Jr. 1988. *The Signifying Monkey: A Theory of African American Literary Criticism*. New York: Oxford University Press.

Gay, Peter, ed. 1989. *The Freud Reader*. New York: W. W. Norton.

Glusker, Susannah Joel. 1998. *Anita Brenner: A Mind of Her Own*. Austin: University of Texas Press.

Goldberg, RosieLee. 2011. *Performance Art: From Futurism to the Present*. 3rd ed. World of Art. New York: Thames & Hudson.

Gonzales, Patrisia. 2012. *Red Medicine: Traditional Indigenous Rites of Birthing and Healing*. Tucson: University of Arizona Press.

González, Jennifer. 2008. *Subject to Display: Reframing Race in Contemporary Installation Art*. Cambridge, MA: MIT Press.

Gonzalez, Rita, Howard N. Fox, and Chon A. Noriega. 2008. *Phantom Sightings: Art after the Chicano Movement*. Los Angeles: University of California Press and Los Angeles County Museum of Art.

González-Wippler, Migene. 1999. *Santería: La religión*. St. Paul, MN: Llewellyn Español.

Grimberg, Salomon. 1998. "Frida Kahlo: The Self as End." In *Mirror Images: Women, Surrealism, and Self-Representation*, edited by Whitney Chadwick, 82–104. Cambridge, MA: MIT Press.

Grimberg, Salomon. 2008a. *Frida Kahlo: Song of Herself*. New York: Merrell.

Grimberg, Salomon. 2008b. *Frida Kahlo: The Still Lives*. New York: Merrell.

Gruzinski, Serge. (1989) 1994. *La guerra de las imágenes: De Cristóbal Colón a Blade Runner (1492–2019)*. Mexico City: Fondo de Cultura Económica.

Guerrilla Girls. 1998. *The Guerrilla Girls' Bedside Companion to the History of Western Art*. New York: Penguin Books.

Guidotti-Hernández, Nicole M. 2011. *Unspeakable Violence: Remapping U.S. and Mexican National Imaginaries*. Durham, NC: Duke University Press.

Hall, James. 2014. *The Portrait: A Cultural History*. London: Thames & Hudson.

Hanh, Thich Nhat. (1987) 1998. *Interbeing: Fourteen Guidelines for Engaged Buddhism*. 3rd ed. Berkeley, CA: Parallax.

Hanh, Thich Nhat. (1987) 2005. *Being Peace*. Berkeley, CA: Parallax Press.

Hanh, Thich Nhat. 2006. *Understanding Our Mind*. Berkeley, CA: Parallax Press.

Hanh, Thich Nhat. 2007. *Teachings on Love*. Berkeley, CA: Parallax Press.

Hanh, Thich Nhat. 2010. *Together We Are One: Honoring Our Diversity, Celebrating Our Connection*. Berkeley, CA: Parallax Press.

Harlan, Theresa, guest curator. 1994. *Watchful Eyes: Native American Women Artists*. Phoenix, AZ: Heard Museum.

Harvey, David. 1991. *The Condition of Post-Modernity: An Enquiry into the Origins of Cultural Change*. City: Wiley-Blackwell.

Herman, Judith. 1992. *Trauma and Recovery: The Aftermath of Violence; From Domestic Abuse to Political Terror*. New York: Basic Books.

Hernández, Ester. 2015. "(Re)Forming America's *Libertad*." In *Born of Resistance: Cara a Cara Encounters with Chicana/o Visual Culture*, edited by Scott L. Baugh and Victor A. Sorell, 37–40. Tucson: University of Arizona Press.

Herrera, Hayden. 1983. *The Biography of Frida Kahlo*. New York: Harper & Row.

Herrera, Hayden. 2002. *Frida: A Biography of Frida Kahlo*. New York: Harper Perennial.

Hewlett, Sylvia Ann, Laura Sherbin, and Karen Sumberg. 2009. "How Gen Y and Boomers Will Reshape Your Agenda." *Harvard Business Review* (July–August): 71–76.

Hillman, James. (1975) 1976. *Re-Visioning Psychology*. New York: Harper Perennial.

Hogan, Wesley C. 2007. *Many Minds, One Heart: SNCC's Dream for a New America*. Chapel Hill: University of North Carolina Press.

Hopcke, Robert H. 1989. *Jung, Jungians, and Homosexuality*. Boston: Shambhala.

Horsfield, Kate, and Nereyda García-Ferraz, dirs. 2010. *Ana Mendieta: Tierra de Fuego*. VHS, 1987. DVD, 49 mins.

Hull, Gloria T., Patricia Bell Scott, and Barbara Smith. 1982. *All the Women Are White, All the Blacks Are Men, but Some of Us Are Brave*. Black Women's Studies. New York: Feminist Press, City University of New York.

Irigaray, Luce. (1974) 1985. *Speculum of the Other Woman*. Translated by Gillian C. Gill. Ithaca, NY: Cornell University Press.

Isaak, Jo Anna. 1996. *Feminism and Contemporary Art: The Revolutionary Power of Women's Laughter*. New York: Routledge.

Isasi-Díaz, Ada María. 1996. *Mujerista Theology: A Theology for the Twenty-First Century*. Maryknoll, NY: Orbis Books.

Jimenez Underwood, Consuelo. 2013. "Political Threads: A Personal History." Textile Arts Council lecture, De Young Museum, April 20. Recorded with permission by Laura E. Pérez.

Johnson, Robert A. 1971. *Owning Your Own Shadow: Understanding the Dark Side of the Psyche*. New York: HarperOne.

Johnston, Adrian. 2013. "Jacques Lacan." *Stanford Encyclopedia of Philosophy*. April 2. https://plato.stanford.edu/entries/lacan/.

Jones, Amelia. 2011. "Traitor Prophets: Asco's Art as Politics of the In-Between." In *Asco: Elite of the Obscure. A Retrospective, 1972–1987*, edited by C. Ondine Chavoy and Rita Gonzalez, 107–41. Los Angeles: Williams College of Art and Los Angeles County Museum of Art.

Jung, Carl G. (1945) 1953. *Psychological Reflections. Selections*. Edited by Jolande Jacobi. New York: Bollingen Foundation.

Jung, Carl G. (1933) 1965. *Modern Man in Search of a Soul*. Translated by W. S. Dell and Cary F. Baynes. New York: Harcourt, Brace & World.

Jung, Carl G. (1961) 1989. *Memories, Dreams, and Reflections*. Rev. ed. Recorded and edited by Aniela Jaffé. Translated by Richard and Clara Winston. New York: Random House.

Jung, Carl G. 1990. *The Undiscovered Self with Symbols* and *The Interpretation of Dreams*. Rev. ed. Translated by R. F. C. Hull. New Brunswick, NJ: Princeton University Press.

Jung, Carl G. 2009. *The Red Book: Liber Novus*. Edited by Sonu Shamdasani. New York: W. W. Norton.

Jung, Carl G. 2012. *The Red Book: Liber Novus; A Reader's Edition*. Edited and with an introduction by Sonu Shamdasani. New York: W. W. Norton.

Kahlo, Frida. 1995. *The Diary of Frida Kahlo: An Intimate Self-Portrait*. Mexico City: Banco de México as Trustee for the Diego Rivera and Frida Kahlo Museums.

Kahlo, Frida. (2003) 2006. *Frida by Frida: Selection of Letters and Texts*. 2nd ed. Foreword and notes by Raquel Tibol. Translated by Gregory Dechant. Mexico City: Editorial RM.

Kahlo, Isolda P. 2004. *Frida íntima*. Bogotá, Colombia: Ediciones Dipon; Buenos Aires, Argentina: Ediciones Gato Azul.

Karp, Ivan, Corrine A. Kratz, Lynn Szwaja, and Tomás Ybarra-Frausto, eds. 2006. *Museum Frictions: Public Cultures / Global Transformations*. Durham, NC: Duke University Press.

Karp, Ivan, Christine Mullen Kreamer, and Steven D. Lavine. 1992. *Museums and Communities: The Politics of Public Culture*. Washington, DC: Smithsonian Institution Press.

Karp, Ivan, and Steven D. Lavine, eds. 1991. *Exhibiting Cultures: The Poetics and Politics of Museum Display*. Washington, DC: Smithsonian Institution Press.

Katzew, Ilona. 2005. *Casta Painting: Images of Race in Eighteenth-Century Mexico*. New Haven, CT: Yale University Press.

Keating, AnaLouise. 2012. *Transformation Now: Towards a Post-Oppositional Politics of Change*. Urbana: University of Illinois Press.

King, Martin Luther, Jr. (1963) 1981. *Strength to Love*. Philadelphia: Fortress.

King, Nia. 2014. *Queer and Trans Artists of Color.* Interviews by Nia King, coedited by Jessica Glennon-Zukoff and Terra Mikalson. San Bernardino, CA: Self-published.

King, Richard. 1972. *The Party of Eros: Radial Social Thought and the Realm of Freedom.* Chapel Hill: University of North Carolina Press.

Kishik, David. 2012. *The Power of Life: Agamben and the Coming Politics.* Stanford, CA: Stanford University Press.

Knafo, Danielle. 2009. *In Her Own Image: Women's Self-Representation in Twentieth-Century Art.* Madison, NJ: Fairleigh Dickinson University Press.

Korten, David C. 2010. *Agenda for a New Economy: From Phantom Wealth to Real Wealth.* San Francisco: Berrett-Koehler.

Kristeva, Julia. 1984. *Revolution in Poetic Language.* New York: Columbia University Press.

Kulkarni, Claudette. 1997. *Lesbians and Lesbianisms: A Post-Jungian Perspective.* New York: Routledge.

Laird, Cynthia. 1997. "Vandals Lash Out at Same-Sex Kissing Latino Icons: Artist to Attend Community Forum Sunday." *Bay Area Reporter*, September 18, 1, 5, 19 (pagination unclear).

Larochette, Jean Pierre, and Yael Lurie. 2008. *Water Songs Tapestries: Notes on Designing, Weaving and Collaborative Work.* Berkeley, CA: Genesis Press.

Latorre, Guisela. 2004. "Gender, Muralism and the Politics of Identity: Chicana Muralism and Indigenist Aesthetics." In *Disciplines on the Line: Feminist Research on Spanish, Latin American, and U.S. Latina Women*, edited by Anne J. Cruz, Rosilie Hernández-Pecoraro, and Joyce Tolliver, 321–56. Newark, DE: Juan de la Cuesta.

Latorre, Guisela. 2008. *Walls of Empowerment: Chicana/o Indigenist Murals of California.* Austin: University of Texas Press.

Leader, Darian. 2009. *The New Black: Mourning, Melancholia, and Depression.* Minneapolis: Graywolf.

León, Luis. 2014. *The Political Spirituality of Cesar Chavez: Crossing Religious Borders.* Berkeley: University of California Press.

León-Portilla, Miguel, ed. 1980. *Native Mesoamerican Spirituality: Ancient Myths, Discourses, Stories, Doctrines, Hymns, Poems from the Aztec, Yucatec, Quiche-Maya and Other Sacred Traditions.* Translated by Miguel León-Portilla, J. O. Arthur Anderson, Charles E. Dibble, and Munro S. Edmonson. Ramsey, NJ: Paulist Press.

León-Portilla, Miguel. (1961) 1988. *Los antiguos mexicanos a través de sus crónicas y cantares.* 4th ed. Mexico City: Fondo de Cultura Ecónomica.

León-Portilla, Miguel. (1963) 1990. *Aztec Thought and Culture: A Study of the Ancient Nahuatl Mind.* Translated by Jack Emory Davis. Norman: University of Oklahoma Press.

León-Portilla, Miguel. 1992. *The Aztec Image of Self and Society: An Introduction to Nahua Culture.* Salt Lake City: University of Utah Press.

Lindsay, Arturo. 1996. *Santería Aesthetics in Contemporary Latin American Art.* Washington, DC: Smithsonian Institution Press.

López, Rick A. 2010. *Crafting Mexico: Intellectuals, Artisans, and the State after the Revolution.* Durham, NC: Duke University Press.

Lorde, Audre. 1984a. "The Master's Tools Will Never Dismantle the Master's House." In *Sister Outsider: Essays and Speeches*, 110–13. Berkeley, CA: Crossing Press.

Lorde, Audre. 1984b. "Uses of the Erotic: The Erotic as Power." In *Sister Outsider: Essays and Speeches*, 53–59. Berkeley, CA: Crossing Press.

Lugones, María. 2003. *Pilgrimages/Peregrinajes: Theorizing Coalition against Multiple Oppressions.* Lanham, MD: Rowman & Littlefield.

Lugones, María. 2007. "Heterosexism and the Colonial/Modern Gender System." *Hypatia* 22, no. 1: 186–209.

Lugones, María. 2010. "Toward a Decolonial Feminism." *Hypatia* 25, no. 4: 742–59.

Macias, Ysidro Ramon, ed. and trans. 2017. *The Domingo Martinez Paredez Mayan Reader.* Self-published, on demand.

MacNair, Rachel M. 2003. *The Psychology of Peace: An Introduction.* Westport, CT: Praeger.

Maffie, James. 2014. *Aztec Philosophy: Understanding a World in Motion.* Boulder: University of Colorado Press.

Maglin, Nan Bauer, and Donna Perry, eds. 1996. *"Bad Girls" / "Good Girls": Women, Sex, and Power in the Nineties.* New Brunswick, NJ: Rutgers University Press.

Maldonado-Torres, Nelson. 2008. *Against War: Views from the Underside of Modernity.* Durham, NC: Duke University Press.

Mani, Lata. 2009. *SacredSecular: Contemplative Cultural Critique.* New York: Routledge.

Marchi, Regina. 2009. *Day of the Dead in the USA: The Migration and Transformation of a Cultural Phenomenon.* New Brunswick, NJ: Rutgers University Press.

Marcos, Sylvia. 2006. *Taken from the Lips: Gender and Eros in Mesoamerican Religions.* Leiden: Brill Academic.

Martínez, Elizabeth. (1972) 1997a. "La Chicana." In *Chicana Feminist Thought: The Basic Historical Writings*, edited by Alma García, 32–34. New York: Routledge.

Martínez, Elizabeth. (1971) 1997b. "Viva La Chicana and All Brave Women of La Causa." In *Chicana Feminist Thought: The Basic Historical Writings*, edited by Alma García, 80–81. New York: Routledge.

Martínez, Elizabeth. 1998. *De Colores Means All of Us: Latina Views for a Multi-Colored Century.* Cambridge, MA: South End.

Martínez Parédez, Domingo. 1960. *Un continente y una cultura: Unidad filológica de la América prehispánica.* Mexico City: Editorial "Poesía de América."

Martínez Parédez, Domingo. (1953) 1973. *Hunab Ku: Síntesis del pensamiento filosófico maya*. Expanded 2nd ed. Mexico City: Editorial Orion.

McCaughan, Edward J. 2012. *Art and Social Movements. Cultural Politics in Mexico and Aztlán*. Durham, NC: Duke University Press.

Medina, Lara. 2004. "Communing with the Dead: Spiritual and Cultural Healing in Chicano/a Communities." In *Religion and Healing in America*, edited by Linda L. Barnes and Susan Starr Sered, 205–15. New York: Oxford University Press.

Medina, Lara. 2005. *Las Hermanas: Chicana/Latina Religious-Political Activism in the U.S. Catholic Church*. Philadelphia: Temple University Press.

Mignolo, Walter D. 2011. *The Darker Side of Western Modernity: Global Futures, Decolonial Options*. Durham, NC: Duke University Press.

Miller, Mary, and Karl Taube. 1993. *An Illustrated Dictionary of the Gods and Symbols of Ancient Mexico and the Maya*. London: Thames and Hudson.

Milos, Lisa. 1997. "Seeing the Elephant." *New Mission News*, October, 7.

Mongabay Series: Global Environmental Impacts of U.S. Policy. 2018. "Judge OKs Waiving Environmental Laws to Build U.S.-Mexico Borderwall." March 1. https://news.mongabay.com/2018/03/judge-oks-waiving-environmental-laws-to-build-u-s-mexico-border-wall/.

Moraga, Cherríe, and Gloria Anzaldúa, eds. 1981. *This Bridge Called My Back: Writings by Radical Women of Color*. Watertown, MA: Persephone.

Morgan, Robin, ed. 1970. *Sisterhood Is Powerful: An Anthology of Writings from the Women's Liberation Movement*. New York: Random House.

Mosquera, Gerardo, ed. 1996. *Beyond the Fantastic: Contemporary Art Criticism from Latin America*. Cambridge, MA: MIT Press.

Muñoz, José Esteban. 1999. *Disidentifications: Queers of Color and the Performance of Politics*. Minneapolis: University of Minnesota Press.

Muscio, Inga. 1998. *Cunt: A Declaration of Independence*. Emeryville, CA: Seal.

Nagler, Michael. 2001. *Is There No Other Way? The Search for a Nonviolent Future*. Berkeley, CA: Berkeley Hills Books.

Naranjo, Claudio. 1994. *Character and Neurosis: An Integrative View*. Nevada City, CA: Gateways/IDHHB.

Naranjo, Claudio. 2010. *Healing Civilization*. Nevada City, CA: Gateways Books and Tapes.

Navarro, Jenell. 2017. "The Promise of the Jaguar: Indigeneity in Contemporary Chican@ Graphic Art." In *ChicanX and Native American Indigeneities*, edited by Gerardo Aldana, Salvador Guerena, and Felicia Lopez. Special issue, *rEvista: A Multimedia, Multi-genre e-Journal for Social Justice*. *California Ethnic and Multicultural Archive (CEMA) Anthology*, University of California Digital Library, Santa Barbara, vol. 5, no. 2: 23–40.

Nieto, Margarita. 1995. "Across the Street: Self-Help Graphics and Chicano Art in Los Angeles." In *Across the Street: Self-Help Graphics and Chicano Art in Los Angeles*, by Bolton Colburn, 21–38. Laguna Beach, CA: Laguna Art Museum.

Nieto-Gómez, Anna. (1975) 1997a. "La Chicana — Legacy of Suffering and Self Denial." In *Chicana Feminist Thought: The Basic Historical Writings*, edited by Alma García, 48–50. New York: Routledge.

Nieto-Gómez, Anna. (1976) 1997b. "Chicana Feminism." In *Chicana Feminist Thought: The Basic Historical Writings*, edited by Alma García, 52–57. New York: Routledge.

Nieto-Gómez, Anna. (1974) 1997c. "La Femenista." In *Chicana Feminist Thought: The Basic Historical Writings*, edited by Alma García, 86–92. New York: Routledge.

Nieto-Gómez, Anna. (1976) 1997d. "Sexism in the Movimiento." In *Chicana Feminist Thought: The Basic Historical Writings*, edited by Alma García, 97–100. New York: Routledge.

Ochoa, María. 2003. *Creative Collectives: Chicana Painters Working in Community*. Albuquerque: University of New Mexico.

Omi, Michael, and Howard Winant. 1994. *Racial Formation in the United States: From the 1960s to the 1990s*. New York: Routledge.

Ortega, Mariana. 2006. "Being Lovingly, Knowingly Ignorant: White Feminism and Women of Color." *Hypatia* 21, no. 3: 56–74.

Ortega, Mariana. 2016. *In-Between: Latina Feminist Phenomenology, Multiplicity, and the Self*. Albany: State University of New York Press.

Pearce, Joseph Chilton. 2002. *The Biology of Transcendence: A Blueprint of the Human Spirit*. Rochester, NY: Park Street Press.

Pérez, Laura E. 1993. "Negotiating New American Philosophies: Anzaldúa's *Borderlands / La Frontera*." Paper presented at Philosophy, Interpretation, Culture, Mind annual conference, Binghamton University, Binghamton, New York, April.

Pérez, Laura E. 1998a. "On the Altars of Alterity: Celia Herrera Rodriguez's Altar and Performance Art and Alex Donis's 'My Cathedral.'" Conference presentation, American Studies Association, Seattle, WA, November 19.

Pérez, Laura E. 1998b. "Spirit Glyphs: Reimagining Art and Artist in the Work of Chicana *Tlamatinime*." *Modern Fiction Studies* 44, no. 1: 36–76.

Pérez, Laura E. 1999. "*El desorden*, Nationalism, and Chicana/o Aesthetics." In *Between Women and Nation: Nationalisms, Transnational Feminisms, and the State*, edited by Caren Kaplan, Minoo Moallem, and Norma Alarcón, 19–46. Durham, NC: Duke University Press.

Pérez, Laura E. 2003. "Long Nguyen: Flesh of the Inscrutable." In *Fresh Talk, Daring Gazes: Conversations on Asian American Art*, edited by Elaine Kim, Margo Machida, and Sharon Mizota, 127–28. Berkeley: University of California Press.

Pérez, Laura E. 2006. "Decolonizing Spiritualities: Spiritualities That Are Decolonizing and the Work of Decolonizing Our Understanding of These." In *Latin@s in the World-System: Decolonization Struggles in the 21st Century U.S. Empire*, edited by Ramón Grosfoguel, Nelson Maldonado-Torres, and José David Saldívar, 157–62. Boulder, CO: Paradigm.

Pérez, Laura E. 2007a. *Chicana Art: The Politics of Spiritual and Aesthetic Altarities.* Durham, NC: Duke University Press.

Pérez, Laura E. 2007b. "*Maestrapeace*: Picturing the Power of Women's Histories of Creativity." *Chicana/Latina Studies: The Journal of Mujeres Activas en Letras y Cambio Social* 6, no. 2: 56–66.

Pérez, Laura E. 2008a. "The Poetry of Embodiment: Series and Variation in Linda Arreola's *Vaguely Chicana*." In *Vaguely Chicana*, exhibition catalog, 3–4. Los Angeles: Tropico de Nopal Gallery Art-Space.

Pérez, Laura E. 2008b. "Thea/o Erotics in Alex Donis's 'My Cathedral' Installation." The@-Erotics: Decolonizing Sex and Spirituality in the Latin@americas panel, National Association of Chicana and Chicano Studies Joto Conference, California State University, Los Angeles. March 22.

Pérez, Laura E. 2010. "Enrique Dussel's *Etica de la liberación*, U.S. Women of Color Decolonizing Practices, and Coalitional Politics amidst Difference." *Qui Parle: Critical Humanities and Social Sciences* 18, no. 2: 121–46.

Pérez, Laura E. 2012. "The Performance of Spirituality and Visionary Politics in the Work of Gloria Anzaldúa." In *El Mundo Zurdo 2: Selected Works from the 2010 Meeting of the Society for the Study of Gloria Anzaldúa*, edited by Sonia Saldívar-Hull, Norma Alarcón, and Rita Urquijo-Ruiz, 13–28. San Francisco: Aunt Lute Books.

Pérez, Laura E. 2013. "Rethinking Immigration with Art." *Tikkun* 28, no. 3: 38–40.

Pérez, Laura E. 2015a. "Freedom and Gender in Ester Hernández's *Libertad/Liberty*." In *Born of Resistance: Cara a Cara Encounters with Chicana/o Visual Culture*, edited by Scott L. Baugh and Victor A. Sorell, 41–46. Tucson: University of Arizona Press.

Pérez, Laura E. 2015b. "The Inviolate Erotic in the Paintings of Liliana Wilson." In *Ofrenda: Liliana Wilson's Art of Dissidence and Dreams*, edited by Norma E. Cantú, 83–86. College Station: Texas A&M University Press.

Pérez, Laura E. Forthcoming. "Fashioning Decolonial Optics: Days of the Dead 'Walking Altars' and 'Calavera Fashion Shows' in Chicana/o-Latina/o L.A." In *meXicana Fashions*, edited by Aída Hurtado and Norma Cantú.

Pérez, Laura E., and Delilah Montoya, cocurators. 2009. *Chicana Badgirls: Las hociconas.* http://www.516arts.org/images/stories/PDFs/chicana_badgirls_catalog.pdf.

Plato. 1982. *Timaeus.* Translated by Benajamin Jowett. In *The Collected Dialogues of Plato: Including the Letters*, edited by Edith Hamilton and Huntington Cairns, 1151–1211. Bollingen Series. Princeton, NJ: Princeton University Press.

Pollock, Griselda. 1996. *Generations and Geographies in the Visual Arts: Feminist Readings.* New York: Routledge.

Portillo, Lourdes, and Susana Muñoz's, dirs. 1988. *La Ofrenda: The Days of the Dead.* Los Angeles: Xochitl Productions. VHS, 55 min.

Price, Sally. (1989) 2001. *Primitive Art in Civilized Places.* 2nd ed. Chicago: University of Chicago Press.

Prignitz-Poda, Helga. 2010. *Frida Kahlo: The Painter and Her Work.* Munich: Schirmer/Mosel.

Puar, Jasbir. 2007. *Terrorist Assemblages: Homonationalism in Queer Times.* Durham, NC: Duke University Press.

Puga, María Luisa. 1977. *Las posibilidades del odio.* Mexico City: Siglo Veintiuno.

Quijano, Aníbal. 2000a. "Colonialidad del poder y clasificación social." *Journal of World-Systems Research* 6, no. 2: 242–386.

Quijano, Aníbal. 2000b. "Coloniality of Power, Eurocentrism, and Latin America." *Nepantla: Views from the South* 1, no. 3: 533–80.

Ramírez, Catherine. 2009. *The Woman in the Zoot Suit: Gender, Nationalism, and the Cultural Politics of Memory.* Durham, NC: Duke University Press.

Richard, Nelly. 1996. "Postmodern Decentredness and Cultural Periphery: The Disalignments and Realignments of Power." In *Beyond the Fantastic: Contemporary Art Criticism from Latin America*, edited by Gerardo Mosquera, 260–69. Cambridge, MA: MIT Press.

Román, Estela. 2012. *Nuestra medicina: De los remedios para el aire y los remedios para el alma.* Bloomington, IN: Palibrio.

Romo, Tere. 2000a. "Curatorial Perspective." In *Chicanos en Mictlán: Día de los Muertos in California*, exhibition catalog, 6–8. San Francisco: Mexican Museum.

Romo, Tere. 2000b. "A Spirituality of Resistance: Día de los Muertos and the Galería de la Raza." In *Chicanos en Mictlán: Día de los Muertos in California*, exhibition catalog, 30–41. San Francisco: Mexican Museum.

Roscoe, Will. 2000. *Changing Ones: Third and Fourth Genders in Native North America.* New York: Palgrave Macmillan.

Rushing, W. Jackson, III, ed. 1999. *Native American Art in the Twentieth Century: Makers, Meanings, Histories.* New York: Routledge.

Sanchez, Carol Lee. 1983. "Sex, Class and Race Intersections: Visions of Women of Color." In "A Gathering of Spirit," edited by Beth Brant. North American Indian Women's Special Issue, *Sinister Wisdom* 22/23:150–54.

Sandoval, Chela. 2000. *Methodology of the Oppressed.* Minneapolis: University of Minnesota Press.

Schaefer, Stacy B. 2002. *To Think with a Good Heart: Wixárika Women, Weavers, and Shamans.* Salt Lake City: University of Utah Press.

Scheid, John, and Jesper Svenbro. 2001. *The Craft of Zeus: Myths of Weaving and Fabric*. Cambridge, MA: Harvard University Press.

Schneeman, Carolee. 2002. *Imagining her Erotics: Essays, Interviews, Projects*. Cambridge, MA: MIT Press.

Schneider, Norbert. 1994. *The Art of the Portrait. Masterpieces of European Portrait-Painting 1420–1670*. Cologne, Germany: Benedikt Taschen Verlag.

Short, Robert. 1980. *Dada and Surrealism*. Secausus, NJ: Chartwell Books.

Sigal, Pete. 2000. *From Moon Goddesses to Virgins: The Colonization of Male Yucatecan Maya Sexual Desire*. Austin: University of Texas Press.

Sigal, Pete. 2007. "Queer Nahuatl: Sahagún's Faggots and Sodomites, Lesbians and Hermaphrodites." *Ethnohistory* 54, no. 1: 9–34.

Sigal, Pete. 2011. *The Flower and the Scorpion: Sexuality and Ritual in Early Nahua Culture*. Durham, NC: Duke University Press.

Smith, Barbara, ed. 1983. *Home Girls: A Black Feminist Anthology*. New Brunswick, NJ: Rutgers University Press.

Smith, Linda Tuhiwai. 2002. *Decolonizing Methodologies: Research and Indigenous Peoples*. London: Zed Books.

Somé, Malidoma Patrice. 1997. *Ritual, Power, Healing and Community*. New York: Penguin Books.

Soriano, Aracely, and Sandra Sánchez. 1996. "Maestrapeace: A Guide to the Mural on the San Francisco Women's Building." Mission Cultural Center, San Francisco.

Sosa Riddell, Adaljiza. (1974) 1997. "Chicanas and El Movimiento." In *Chicana Feminist Thought: The Basic Historical Writings*, edited by Alma García, 92–94. New York: Routledge.

Stein, Murray, ed. 1995. *Jung on Evil. Encountering Jung*. Princeton, NJ: Princeton University Press.

Strohmeier, John, and Peter Westbrook. 1999. *Divine Harmony: The Life and Teachings of Pythagoras*. Berkeley, CA: Berkeley Hills Books.

Stryker, Susan, and Paisley Currah. 2014. "General Editors' Introduction." In "Decolonizing the Transgender Imaginary," special issue, *TSQ: Transgender Studies Quarterly* 1, no. 3 (August): 303–7.

Thiong'o, Ngugi Wa. 1986. *Decolonising the Mind: The Politics of Language in African Literature*. Portsmouth, NH: Heinemann.

Thompson, Robert Farris. 1984. *Flash of the Spirit: African and Afro-American Art and Philosophy*. New York: Vintage.

Thurman, Howard. (1949) 1996. *Jesus and the Disinherited*. Boston: Beacon Press.

Torres, Eliseo "Cheo." 2005. *Curandero: A Life in Mexican Folk Healing*. With Timothy L. Sawyer Jr. Albuquerque: University of New Mexico Press.

Trinh T. Minh-ha. (1989) 2009. *Woman Native, Other: Writing Postcoloniality and Feminism*. Bloomington: Indiana University Press.

Trujillo, Carla. 1991. *Chicana Lesbians: The Girls Our Mothers Warned Us About*. Berkeley, CA: Third Woman Press.

Trungpa, Chogyam. (1973) 2002. *Cutting Through Spiritual Materialism*. Rev. ed. Boston: Shambhala.

Trungpa, Chogyam. (1984) 2009. *Shambhala: The Sacred Path of the Warrior*. Boston: Shambhala.

Turok, Marta. 2007. "Frida's Attire: Eclectic and Ethnic." In *Self-Portrait in a Velvet Dress: Frida's Wardrobe; Fashion from the Museo Frida Kahlo*, edited by Denise Rosenzweig and Magdalena Rosenzweig, 51–173. San Francisco: Chronicle Books.

Tzu, Lao. 1992. *Tao Te Ching*. Translated by Stephen Mitchell. New York: Harper Perennial.

Valdez, Luis. 1990. *Early Works: Actos, Bernabé and Pensamiento Serpentino*. Houston: Arte Público.

Varady, Aharon N. 2008. "On Frida's Jewish Identity." *Aharon's Omphalos. Spinning Navel Lint into Fine Art*. Posted May 22. https://aharon.varady.net/omphalos /2008/05/on-frida-kahlos-jewish-identity.

Vasconcelos, José. (1925) 1997. *The Cosmic Race/La raza cósmica: A Bilingual Edition*. Translated by Didier T. Jaén. Baltimore: Johns Hopkins University Press.

Vega, Marta Moreno. 2000. *The Altar of My Soul: The Living Traditions of Santería*. New York: Ballantine Books.

Venegas, Sybil. 2000. "The Day of the Dead in Aztlán: Chicano Variations on the Theme of Life, Death, and Self-Preservation." In *Chicanos en Mictlán: Día de los Muertos en California*, exhibition catalog, curated by Tere Romo, 42–54. San Francisco: Mexican Museum.

Vidal, Mirta. (1971) 1997. "New Voice of La Raza: Chicanas Speak Out." In *Chicana Feminist Thought: The Basic Historical Writings*, edited by Alma García, 21–24. New York: Routledge.

Viego, Antonio. 2007. *Dead Subjects: Toward a Politics of Latino Loss*. Durham, NC: Duke University Press.

Viso, Olga. 2004. *Ana Mendieta: Earth Body*. Ostfildern-Ruit, Germany: Hatje Cantz.

Viso, Olga. 2008. *Unseen Mendieta: The Unpublished Works of Ana Mendieta*. Munich: Prestel.

Young, Bette Roth. 1995. *Emma Lazarus in Her World: Life and Letters*. Philadelphia: Jewish Publication Society.

Zavala, Adriana. 2015. "Frida Kahlo: Art, Garden, Life." In *Frida Kahlo's Garden*, edited by Adriana Zavala, Mia D'Avanza, and Joanna L. Groarke, 15–39. New York: New York Botanical Garden / Delmonico Books / Prestel.

INDEX

Brenner, Anita, 100, 104, 228n9

bridges and borderlands, 137

Buddha, 204

Buddhist, xvi, 14, 141, 205, 206

Buffalo Shroud-Almost 1,000 Left (Jimenez Underwood), 181, 183

Burton, Tim, 163

Butler, Judith, 3, 243n19

Calaveras, 161–63, 236n21

Callas (Maldonado), 168–69

Campbell, Joseph, 195

Carillo, Graciela, 62

Carrington, Leonora, 60, 128. *See also individual works*

Carter, Jimmy (U.S. president), 50

casta, 75

Castaño, Carolyn, 166

Castro, Maria Elena, 166

Catrina, 171

catwalk, 163

Cervántez, Yreina D., 41, 65, 92–94, 99, 101–11, 135, 160, 162, 165, 198. *See also individual works*

character, 93, 101; death of, 166; flaws, 47

Character and Neurosis. An Integrative View (Naranjo), 13

Chavez, Cesar, 222

Chavez, Cruz, and Warhol (Maldonado), 169

Chicago, Judy, 43, 90

Chicana Art: The Politics of Spiritual and Aesthetic Altarities (Pérez), 117, 135

Chicana feminists, 39, 42, 46, 101; feminist and queer thought and, 218n9

Chicana/Latina women, 78

Chicana/o Nation, 193

Chiquín, Don Miguel Angel, 124, 193, 242n9, 244n20

Chiquin Yak, Don Miguel, 193

Chogyam Trungpa, 16, 141, 207

choreography of discourses, 165

Christianity, 29, 75; mystical, 213n1

Christian mystics, 205

Cisne (Wilson), 132

Cisneros, Sandra, 44, 135. *See also individual works*

civil rights movement, 36, 61, 67, 84, 199, 226n7; black, 116; racial, gender, and sexual, 35

Clearwater, Bonnie, 108

coalitionary, art and activist project, 84

coalitions, 6, 9, 89; across policed differences, 4; U.S. women of color and, 122

Coatlicue, 182, 216n4; Coatlicue State, 20, 137

coexistence, 7, 9–15, 200, 202, 208; of different forms of knowing, xx; of the living and the dead, 157, 160, 165; of so-called feminine and masculine attributes, 127; of spiritual and physical being, 93

Coffey, Mary K., 98, 105

Coile, 72

Colombian Kogi, 190

colonial, 20, 75, 81, 114–15, 117, 123–24, 158, 172; adventures, 4; eras, 49; glyphs, 101; invasions, 55; notions of sexuality, 227n4; representing the mindset, 182; thought, 142

colonialism, 116, 137, 196–97; violence of, 171

colonization, xvii, 4, 6, 60, 63, 67, 78, 107, 114, 199; of the Americas, 37–38, 201; different kinds, 5; globally visible struggles against, 123

Combahee River Collective, 14, 117, 121, 229n2

commemoration, 157

community, 2, 8, 30, 37, 67, 71, 76, 83–84, 119, 159, 161, 189, 208; activists, 86; art, 157, 162; of Aztlán, 20; Chicana/o, 166; as communion, 100; Eros ideologies and, 10; Latina/o, 72–73, 75; planetary, 107

conformation: multicultural, 205

Conley Art Gallery at California State University, 186

conocimiento, 202; of *la facultad*, 16

conocimiento y desconocimiento, 137, 143

consciousness, 12, 128, 138, 142, 196, 205; decolonized, 204; different forms of, 202; differential, 20; fleshless, 111; fluid property of, 22; new forms of, 30, 33; shift of, 207; social, 85; split, 130

Corazón de roca con sangre (Mendieta), 64

Cotera, Marta, 121

Cox, Laverne, 49

Coyolxauhqui, 88–89, 206

craft, 58, 159, 180; "mere," 89; modern human, 189

craft-work, 202

creativity as a methodology, 194

creativity, xx, 3, 22, 47, 87, 89, 136, 161, 193–94, 203, 205; critical mind and, 2; male, 43; natural, xxi; people of color critique and, 45; power of female, 83; the vagina and, 44; women's, 84

Kahlo, Frida, 30, 43–44, 60, 70–71, 164, 169; art-
    work, 97; tribute to, 101. *See also individual
    works*
Kahlo, Isolda, 97, 104, 227n4
Kandinsky, Wassily, 54
Karp, Ivan, 68
Keating, AnaLouise, 14, 138
Kelk Cervantes, Susan, 82, 84, 225n2
khora, 18, 21–22, 203, 216n2
King, Martin Luther, Jr., 61, 71, 73, 139, 141, 213n2
Kishik, David, 122
Knafo, Danielle, 96–97
knowledge, 2, 38, 59, 86, 97, 105, 134, 139, 208;
    through and from the body, 9; cultural,
    180; elders and, 197; the erotic and, 204;
    global body, 123; imperialist, 11; indigenous
    worldviews and, 118; integrated knowing,
    2; patriarchy and, 51; production of, 4; as a
    quest, 130; Santeria and, 100; spiritual and
    scientific, 172; Statue of Liberty and, 35; va-
    gina and, 44; Women of Color and, 117, 122
knowledges, 3, 196; ancestral, 200; Eurocentric,
    234n9; European, xvii; human, 190; mind-
    body-spirit, 13
Kollwitz, Käthe, 101
Korten, David, 158
Kurosawa, Akira, 141. *See also individual works*

La bella durmiente (Wilson), 132.
laboratories: creating new forms, xv; visions for
    the future, 194
La caída de un ángel (Wilson), 129, 130
Lacan, Jacques, 30
LACMA (Los Angeles County Museum of Art),
    68, 118
La diosa del amor (Wilson), 127, 132
La Divina . . . A Tribute to Gia (Maldonado), 168
La espera (Wilson), 127, 132
*La guerra de las imágenes: De Cristóbal Colón a
    "Blade Runner" (1502–2019)* (Gruzinski), 114
Lamba, Jacqueline, 99
*La muerte de los niños de la calle / The Death of
    Homeless Children* (Marichal), 167
Land Grabs (Jimenez Underwood), 198
Lange, Dorothea, 61
language: assemblage and disassemblage, 116;
    conocimiento and, 139; dominant, 14; Euro-
    pean philosophers and, 122; as expression, 196;
    foreign, 58–59; male creativity, 43; pulsating,

175; revolutionary, 2; spectral or the fantastic,
    128; visual, 31, 85, 104; Westernized, 30
La ofrenda: The Days of the Dead (Portillo and
    Muñoz), 163
Larochette, Jean Pierre, 58, 175
Las 4 Xewam (i.e., "flowers" in Yaqui) (Jimenez
    Underwood), 182
Las amantes (Wilson), 127, 131–32
Las posibilidades del odio (Hatred's Possibilities)
    (Puga), 140
Latinoamérica (Mujeres Muralistas), 62
Latour, Bruno, 120
La vida es una ilusión (Cervántez), 102
Lawson, James M., 207
Lebrón, Lolita, 87
León-Portilla, Miguel, 30, 100, 243n16
Les fetiches (Mailou), 60
Liberation of Aunt Jemima, The (Saar), 63
Libertad/Liberty (Esther Hernández), 35–36,
    38–29
life and death: continuum of, 172; dance of, 165;
    Mesoamerican duality, 102, 157
life art, 195
life force: ashé, 100, 108, 203; binding, 185; ener-
    getic, 188; erotic and, 128; interdependence
    and, 10; matter and, 15; sacred, 65, 104
liminal threshold, 163
Lindsay, Arthur, 28, 114
Lipsitz, George, 146
Lissitzky, Lazar Markovich, 53–54
Little Deer, The (Kahlo), 93
Littleton, Yvonne, 82, 84
living death, 137
living dioramas, 67
Loose Woman (Cisneros), 44
López, Yolanda, 71, 135
Lorde, Audre, 16, 87, 121; erotic and, 128, 204,
    213n1; master's tools and, 14, 122; spirit of, xviii
los maestros maya, 146
love, 51, 76, 139, 146, 208; capacity to, 132;
    decolonizing practice, 3; for future genera-
    tions, 86; healing, 141; for indigenous people
    of Mexico, 100; juices, 72; lack of sufficient,
    13; life energy of, 127; logic of, 61; physics of,
    22; politics of, 14, 73; politically significant
    practice and, xviii; queerness and, 21; of
    self, 204; sexual, 128; social body and, 10;
    source of all life, 203; spiritual and, 11, 75, 80;
    uncolonized, 20; warrior of, 153

274

thropomorphization of the, 94; benevolent,
90; care for, xviii; environmental pollution
of the, 15; five hundred years of inhumanity
against, 137; how to survive on, 122; intellectual superiority over, 142; life on this, 122–23,
150; planetary ecosystem, 204; planetary
habitat, 203; thinking about life on the, 9;
weaving this, 149

Plato, 18, 53

poetic: arts language and, 136; body, 9; hybrid
theorizations, xx; nonverbal arts, 196; the
poetic, 2, 53–54

poetics: experimental, 134; of transformation, 18

poetry, 135, 194; Aztec, 102; and form, 53–54;
obeys natural, not social, 54; Rumi, 205

politics of hope, 22

Pollock, Jackson, 30

poor, the, 4, 15, 47, 62, 79, 81

Popul Vuh, 96

Portillo, Lourdes, 163

Portrait of Diego Rivera (Kahlo), 98, 100

Portrait of Ilya Ehrenberg (Rivera), 59

Portrait of Mariana Morillo Safa (Kahlo), 110

postcolonialism, 115; postcolonial feminists, 116;
postcolonial theory, 135

postfeminism/postfeminist, 48, 115, 123, 158

postidentitarian, 115, 120, 123

postidentity, 102

postimperial, 115

postindustrialism, 4, 115

postmodern, 114; aesthetic, 38; Chicana/o cutting edge, 120; "phantom capital" globalization, 158; postmodernism, 115; postmodern-
like conditions, 20; sensibilities, 118; versus
the modern, 117; white feminism, 116

postnationalist, 115

postrace/postracial, 115, 158

poststructuralism, 115; atheism and, 142; French
thinkers and, 14; poststructuralist denials
of spiritual essence, 107; poststructuralist
philosophy, 30; poststructuralist projects, 29;
poststructuralist theory, 118, 135; theoretical
naïveté of pre-European influence, 117; and
white feminism, 116

power, xx, 4, 46, 53, 124, 140–41, 191, 207; of
art, 45; of art making, 7, 100; critiquing, 14;
dominant cultural worldviews and dynamics,
115; of the Earth, 187; enduring of a natural
world, 107; exercising personal, xv; of female

creativity, 83; globally unequal relations, 188;
harnessing of, 190; human gone awry, 202;
images of, 36; implicit relations, 63; individual pursuit of wealth and, 189; inviolate of
the erotic, 128; life-giving, 87; material and
political, 79; patriarchal, 43; prevailing relations, 122; racist regimes of, 142; "real" forms
of, 203; resides within us, 4, 193; returns to
us, 204; right use of, 141, 143; sacred and life
force, 104; seizing our own, 4, 208; social
or visionary, 138; struggles, 15; to be as one
wishes, 194; uncovering spiritual, 139; understanding of, xviii; unjust, 2, 9; of walls as a
medium, 84; wielders, 62; words of, 137

prayer, 137; awareness, 186; intention, 190–91,
204; ties, 187

pre-Columbian: America, 84, 101; art, 36, 95,
100; female social life, 37; indigenous philosophies, 31; non-Christian notions of deity,
80; past, 98; symbols and identifications, 119

presence: awakening feminine, 146; of the dead,
157, 163; differently materialized, 108; joyful,
177; of powerful legacies, 86; socially liminal,
158; of undocumented youth, 193; of a vision
serpent, 37

Price, Sally, 65–66

Prigntiz-Poda, Helga, 95

primitive religiosities, 142

Proposition 188, 198

psyche, xvii, xx, 4, 12–13, 202; colonial and
neocolonial, 4; healthy human, xix; human,
9; integrated, 51, 204; Jung and, 37; power
within, 140; as product of human imagination, 37; "real," 14–15, 38; soul and, 5, 194;
split within, 11

psychic: forces, 12; fragmentation, 127, 136;
intra-, 159; la facultad, 16, 134; landscape,
203; members, 206; perception, 128; power,
138–39

psychological-spiritual boundaries, 206

psychologies, post-Jungian, 13

psychology, xvii, 3, 139, 195; analytic, 12; for
women, 13; Jungian, 51; patriarchal field of, 96

Puar, Jasbir, 116, 121

Puga, Maria Luisa, 115

Pussy Power Imaginary Project, 41–42, 46–47, 50

Pussy Riot, 50; *Pussy Riot: A Punk Prayer*
(Lerner and Podorovkin), 50

Pythagoras, 53, 79, 205